DIAGNOSIS AND TREATMENT PLANNING IN COUNSELING

DIAGNOSIS AND TREATMENT PLANNING IN COUNSELING

Linda Seligman, Ph.D., LPC

Associate Professor of Counseling and Development
George Mason University
Fairfax, Virginia

Counselor & Psychologist in Private Practice
Alexandria, Virginia
Laurel, Maryland

HUMAN SCIENCES PRESS, INC.
72 FIFTH AVENUE
NEW YORK, N.Y. 10011

Copyright © 1986 by Human Sciences Press, Inc.
72 Fifth Avenue, New York, New York 10011

Printed in the United States of America
987654321

Library of Congress Cataloging-in-Publication Data

Seligman, Linda.
Diagnosis and treatment planning in counseling.
Bibliography: p.
Includes index.
1. Counseling. 2. Mental health planning.
3. Mental illness—Diagnosis. I. Title. [DNLM:
1. Counseling—methods. 2. Patient Care Planning.
WM 55 S465d]
BF637.C6S44   1985   616.89   85-19728
ISBN 0-89885-259-5
ISBN 0-89885-262-5 (pbk.)

CONTENTS

FOREWORD

In June, 1983, the *Personnel and Guidance Journal* published an article I wrote to introduce counselors to the process of diagnosis (Seligman, 1983). I received many requests for reprints of that article as well as several invitations to conduct workshops throughout the country on diagnosis and treatment planning. I also received some negative reactions; some felt that counselors should not engage in diagnosis and treatment planning and saw no need for counselors to study differential therapeutics.

By 1985, the new and rapidly growing specialization of mental health counseling was more firmly established, meriting its inclusion in the *Occupational Outlook Handbook*. Many factors, discussed in chapter 1 of this book, were leading counselors in all areas of specialization to seek information on diagnosis and treatment planning in order to help their clients more effectively and to demonstrate their own credibility and accountability.

To date, however, little of value to counselors has been written on diagnosis and treatment planning. There are several reasons for this. The third edition of the *Diagnostic and Statistical Manual of Mental Disorders* was published in 1980, necessitating a reconceptualization of the field of diagnosis and treatment planning. Most of the relevant literature written since that time has adopted the medical model and has been written by psychiatrists, alone or in collaboration with psychologists. Also, the literature on differential therapeutics (which technique is best to treat which client) is still sparse and must be interpreted with a large measure of clinical judgment.

This book, designed for counselors and other nonmedical mental health professionals, seeks to integrate and provide an overview of what is known about diagnosis and treatment planning. This book assumes that readers have some knowledge of theories and techniques of individual, group, and family counseling. It should enable counselors to expand on this body of knowledge so they can more effectively help their clients.

Linda Seligman, Ph.D.

ACKNOWLEDGEMENTS

I would like to express my appreciation to some of the people who contributed to the writing of this book.
Thank You,

—Howard Fields, for your editing as well as your support and encouragement.

—Bettie MacLennan, for your friendship and understanding, even when I was busy and harried.

—My parents, Irving and Florence Goldberg, and my sisters, Gerri Cotton and Terri Karol.

—Leslie Weinstock, for your encouragement and your contribution to the manuscript.

—My colleagues and the staff at George Mason University, especially Jack Levy, Judy Dickman, Avelina Jansen, Lisa Porter, and Isabel Schulte.

All persons appearing in this book are presented as composite characters to protect their privacy.

ACKNOWLEDGMENTS

Chapter 1

THE CHANGING ROLE OF THE COUNSELOR

THE EVOLUTION OF THE COUNSELING PROFESSION

Trends over the past decade have greatly altered the role of the counselor. They include the decreased job market for school counselors, increased opportunities for counselors in mental health agencies and businesses, the advent of licensure and certification for counselors, and a growing emphasis on accountability for mental health professionals. Counselors today have a broadened and more responsible role. In mental health agencies, private practices, businesses, industries, and schools and colleges, they are part of a mental health team with responsibility for the diagnosis and treatment of their clients.

HISTORICAL OVERVIEW

At its inception in the early 1900s, the field of counseling was a relatively well-defined and circumscribed one. The primary task of the counselor was to help clients make occupational choices by seeking a good match between person and job. That view of counselors predominated for more than 30 years. The

National Vocational Guidance Association (NVGA), forerunner of the American Personnel and Guidance Association, was founded in 1913.

The role of the counselor changed and expanded through the 1940s and 1950s. World War II and the Korean War led to a need for counselors to facilitate the readjustment and rehabilitation of veterans. Counselors began to realize they could best meet the needs of these individuals by considering their emotional development as well as their physical concerns and occupational aspirations.

Carl Rogers contributed to the shift in the counselors' role with the 1942 publication of *Counseling and Psychotherapy*. Rogers' writing encouraged counselors to define their goals in terms of clients' needs and to adopt a broader and more flexible array of skills. During the 1950s, Erik H. Erikson *(Childhood and Society)*, Fritz Perls *(Gestalt Therapy)*, Leona Tyler *(The Work of the Counselor)*, Robert J. Havighurst *(Human Development and Education)*, and Albert Bandura *(Principles of Behavior Modification)* all published influential texts that focused counselors' attention on clients' developmental needs. Counselors began to attend to prevention and to the personal growth of their clients as well as to remediation of concerns. When the American Personnel and Guidance Association was founded in 1951, it reflected the growing and multifaceted role of counselors.

The 1960s formed a transitional period in which politicians as well as the general public recognized that large segments of the population were dissatisfied and had emotional and physical needs which were not being met. Race riots, campus unrest, increasing drug abuse, and antiwar demonstrations contributed to a growing national feeling of discontent. That feeling was especially strong among the poor and the underprivileged who had often been neglected by traditional helping agencies. Many programs were developed during the 1960s in response. Among them were the Peace Corps, VISTA, the War on Poverty, and Operation Headstart. In addition, strong special interest groups were formed to promote racial equality and women's rights.

Those movements had a strong effect on the role of the counselor. They brought increasing recognition to the importance of the community or environment in an individual's emotional development. Clients were less often thought of as "sick" or troubled and more often as unable to cope successfully with a stressful or destructive environment.

That recognition led to the realization that mental health professionals were reaching only a small fraction of people in need of help. The medical model, emphasizing one-to-one contact with troubled individuals who actively sought help, increasingly seemed outmoded and ineffective. Changes had to be effected in communities as well as in individuals before progress could be made in reducing the number of individuals with emotional difficulties.

In 1963, the Community Mental Health Centers Act was passed, which provided a great impetus to the redefinition of the field of counseling. That act mandated establishment of a nationwide network of community mental health centers (CMHCs) intended to be multifaceted and comprehensive agencies providing a broad range of readily accessible services. The goal of the centers was to minimize the eruption of emotional difficulties by enabling the community and its people to expand upon and share their abilities and strengths and to develop skills needed to cope with their weaknesses. Preventive approaches were emphasized as mental health workers became change agents in the community.

At the outset, CMHCs were controlled largely by the well-established helping professionals, the psychiatrists and doctoral level psychologists. In order to meet the unique needs of the CMHCs, however, community psychology, a new area of specialization, soon evolved. As defined by Zax and Specter (1974), "Community psychology is regarded as an approach to human behavior problems that emphasizes contributions made to their development by environmental forces as well as the potential contributions to be made toward their alleviation by the use of these forces" (p. 3). The growth in CMHCs as well as their community focus led to the hiring of masters-level helping professionals (counselors, psychologists, and social workers) and paraprofessionals to meet staffing needs and provide workers who might have common backgrounds with catchment area residents.

Counselor education programs, responding to growth in employment of school and mental health counselors, began to expand and diversify. In the early 1960s, the National Institutes for Mental Health provided funds for pilot training programs for mental health counselors (Magoon, Golann, & Freeman, 1969). NDEA Institutes for counselors also lent credibility and refinement of skills to the profession. Between 1964 and 1976, the number of counselor education programs increased by about 35 percent (Shertzer & Stone, 1980). Important ideas and writings by C. Gilbert Wrenn *(The Counselor in a Changing World)*, Albert Ellis *(Reason and Emotion in Psychotherapy)*, John Krumboltz *(behavioral counseling)*, Robert Carkhuff and C. B. Truax *(facilitative conditions)*, and Norman Kagan *(Interpersonal Process Recall)* further expanded the counselors' repertoire of skills and promoted diversification and a sense of growth in the profession.

The 1970s was a time of reorientation for the profession. Counseling was maturing and the influx of counselors into mental health facilities was continuing. However, the declining birthrate over the previous decade, coupled with nationwide financial constraints on state and local budgets, led to a decline in the employment of school counselors. In 1976, Jones found that the ratio of trained school counselors to available positions was 2.4 to 1, although counselor-student ratios had increased by 50 percent (Shertzer & Stone, 1980). At the same time, however, counselor education programs, many only recently initiated, were being forced to increase enrollments due to universities' financial concerns.

Clearly, then, the way to meet the needs of indivduals who wanted to counsel and of programs that needed to grow lies in a redefinition of the counselors' role and the expansion of the field of mental health counseling. This trend has been evident on many fronts over the past decade.

RECENT TRENDS AND CHANGES

In 1980, 552 counselor education programs could be identified in the United States and its territories (Wantz, Scherman, & Hollis, 1982). Between 1978 and 1980, nearly all of the programs expanded and added an average of 2.76 new courses, typically in areas such as (in order of frequency) family counseling, consultation, geriatric counseling, career and life planning, and women's studies. Specializations in mental health counseling were being offered under a variety of names: agency counseling, social agency, community agency, clinical counseling, human development, marriage and family counseling, corrections counseling, pastoral counseling, personal counseling, or rehabilitation counseling. Although most of the programs were housed in schools or colleges of education, the term "counselor" was no longer synonymous with "school counselor"; mental health counselors were being graduated in numbers equal to if not greater than school counselors (Wantz et al., 1982). Other changes in counselor preparation included a stronger emphasis on developmental rather than preventive or corrective counseling, an increase in field experience requirements, a focus on integrating and applying existing counseling modalities rather than searching for new approaches, and contact with a broad range of client groups (e.g., substance abusers, geriatric clients, families).

The changes were reflected in the counselors' primary professional organization, the American Personnel and Guidance Association (APGA). That organization has grown rapidly since its inception and had over 42,000 members in 1984. The American Mental Health Counselors Association (AMHCA), formed in 1976 as an independent professional organization for community mental health counselors and allied professionals, became the thirteenth division of APGA in 1978. AMHCA is now APGA's largest division with over 9,000 members. (American School Counselors Association is the second largest.) In 1984, after years of debate, APGA changed its name to the American Association for Counseling and Development (AACD), reflecting the altered and broadened role of the counselor of the 1980s.

Credentialing

When counselor equalled school counselor, credentialing counselors followed procedures established for credentialing teachers and attracted little attention or controversy. Counselors' coursework and experience were reviewed by state education agencies and, if qualified, the counselors were endorsed, certified, or licensed to serve as school counselors.

However, when counselors joined the staffs of mental health agencies, another sort of credential was needed to give counselors credibility and autonomy, to help the public identify qualified practitioners, and to enhance professional identity so counselors could achieve the status of the other nonmedical credentialed mental health practitioners (social workers and psychologists). Credentialing of counselors also facilitates efforts to obtain reimbursement for services from health insurance companies and to establish legislation to give counselors the right of privileged communication. Credentialing of counselors currently includes both licensure and certification methods. Licensure is a credential granted by a governmental agency, permitting those meeting specified competency standards to engage in an occupation; certification or registration is granted by an association or nongovernmental agency (Messina, 1979).

In 1972, in Weldon vs. the Board of Psychological Examiners, the Virginia Supreme Court found that "the profession of personnel and guidance counseling is a separate profession from psychology and should be so recognized" (Seiler & Messina, 1979, p. 4). This paved the way for Virginia to become, in 1976, the first state to license counselors. Between 1976 and 1984, nine other states have adopted credentialing procedures for mental health counseling (Alabama, Arkansas, Florida, Georgia, Idaho, North Carolina, Ohio, Tennessee, and Texas). Most of the remaining 40 have licensure laws pending or in preparation. Although licensure requirements vary from state to state, the Virginia model is typical. It requires 60 credits of relevant graduate coursework, including a masters degree in counseling or an allied profession; the equivalent of 2 years of full-time, post-masters supervised work experience; letters of recommendation; satisfactory performance on a written examination; a case study; and an interview. In states that have licensure laws for counselors, no unlicensed individuals can legally call themselves counselors or perform the work of counselors, except while under approved supervision or employed by certain types of agencies.

Several nationwide programs also are available to credential counselors. The National Board of Certified Counselors (NBCC) credentials generic or general counselors. Requirements include a masters degree in counseling, 2 years of professional experience in the field, and satisfactory performance on an examination. Some of the requirements can be waived, depending on the nature of the applicant's training and other credentials. NBCC-credentialed counselors are required to complete 100 hours of continuing education every 5 years in order to maintain certification. In 1984, there were more than 9000 NBCC certified counselors and a register of National Certified Counselors (NCCs) was being prepared.

Specialist certification is offered to counselors through the National Academy for Certified Clinical Mental Health Counselors (NACCMHC). Initiated by AMHCA and now an AACD-affiliated corporate body, NACCMHC goes beyond the generic certification of NBCC and credentials certified clinical mental health counselors (CCMHCs). As of 1984, NACCMHC had certified about 600 counselors in its 5 years of operation. NACCMHC distributes a register of CCMHCs to insurance companies, mental health centers, and other relevant organizations and has been negotiating with health insurance companies to obtain reliable reimbursement (third party payments) of CCMHCs for services provided to insured clients. Other credentialing bodies for counselors include the Commission of Rehabilitation Counselor Certification (CRCC) and the newer National Council for Credentialing of Career Counselors (NCCC), founded in 1983 by the National Vocational Guidance Association and slated to become a special committee of NBCC (Harold, 1984). The development of state and national credentialing bodies should promote the development of the counseling profession and enhance the quality and reputation of its members. It also furthers the establishment of counselors within mental health settings.

The credentialing procedure for counselor education programs as well as for counselors has been undergoing modification during the 1980s. For many years, most counselor education programs had been reviewed for approval by the National Council for the Accreditation of Teacher Education (NCATE). At the time when counselor preparation focused primarily on school counselors, the well-established NCATE was an appropriate evaluator for such programs. However, with the expansion of counselor education into mental health counseling, it was apparent there was a need for a credentialing body that was familiar with and had criteria for evaluating the increasing range of counseling specialities. In 1981, AACD led the development of the Council for Accreditation of Counseling and Related Educational Programs (CACREP) to perform that function. As of 1984, only a small fraction of the existing counselor education programs had been visited by CACREP. However, the advent of CACREP should establish more uniform and rigorous standards for counselor preparation and further enhance the reputation of counselors.

Health Care Programs

Changes in the way health care services, counseling among them, are being provided also is expected to have a significant impact upon counselors' role and image. There seems to be a growing nationwide acceptance of the idea that all individuals should be permitted ready access to treatment for physical and emotional problems. The value of a preventive approach to health maintenance also is being recognized. At the same time, the escalation of health care costs has led health insurance companies to seek more economical methods of meeting the health care needs of subscribers. New approaches have resulted from those potentially conflicting thrusts.

The most widespread of them are health maintenance organizations (HMOs). In 1979 (Davis), 7.4 million people were serviced by 203 HMOs, most of them emphasizing preventive approaches and treatment of the whole person. The number of HMOs has continued to grow. HMO subscribers pay a predetermined monthly or annual fee regardless of the frequency or nature of their health problems. Services are then provided by the HMOs at little or no additional cost.

A newer development is Preferred Provider Organizations (PPOs), groups of otherwise independent health care providers who offer reduced-rate services to insurance subscribers. In turn, the PPOs acquire an increased and more stable patient load and reliable payment (subscribers who use the PPOs recommended by their insurance company generally have their co-payment, the part of the cost paid by the patient, reduced or eliminated). Blue Cross/Blue Shield (BC/BS) has developed a similar organizational structure. Health service providers who agree to accept a fee established by BC/BS will be included on a special list made available to subscribers. Individuals obtaining services from co-operating service providers will have little or no co-payment.

Although Medicare and a substantial number of insurance companies are reimbursing clients for counseling fees, the status of counselors in PPOs and as professionals approved to receive third party payments remains unclear. It is anticipated that certified and licensed counselors will have greater opportunity for such recognition, but time and legislation are needed. In Florida, for example, "freedom of choice" legislation has been passed, requiring insurance companies to reimburse participants for services provided by any credentialed mental health professional chosen by the client (e.g., counselor, social worker, psychologist, psychiatrist).

Some insurance companies, in order to promote containment of health care costs, are proposing to reimburse health care providers based on the nature of the subscriber's illness rather than on the type or amount of treatment required. Counselors could benefit, since they typically charge less than psychiatrists or doctoral level psychologists. For example, counselors could provide more extensive treatment for a specified fee than psychiatrists. Counselors also could become important adjuncts in such a model, working with physicians to promote patients' mental health and adjustment, thereby reducing the amount of medical treatment they require.

Some BC/BS policies advise subscribers to obtain approval from the insurance carrier before being admitted for in-patient psychiatric services. Payment of medical costs is not guaranteed if approval is not obtained. That could increase the percentage of clients using out-patient services, potentially providing more opportunities for counselors.

The modifications in health care described here are relatively new and their implementation has just begun. It remains to be seen what their impact on counselors will be, but they will certainly have an impact on the counseling profession.

THE CHANGING ROLE OF THE COUNSELOR

In 1978, the American Mental Health Counselors Association defined the professional counselor as one who was involved in ". . .the process of assisting individuals or groups, through a helping relationship, to achieve optimal mental health through personal and social development and adjustment to prevent the debilitating effects of certain somatic, emotional, and intra- and/or interpersonal disorders" (p. 19). The mental health field of the '80s, then, is a broad and diverse one which calls for counselors who are flexible and knowledgeable generalists who can draw on a wide range of skills and approaches to meet the multifaceted needs of their clients. It calls for people who can discard the security and prestige of conducting individual counseling sessions in an office and who can become involved with and accepted by a community. It calls for people who can assess social as well as individual difficulties, define what triggers or exacerbates them, anticipate problems before they arise, and develop effective and innovative preventive approaches. At the same time, counselors also should be able to use traditional tools to ameliorate the concerns of a troubled client. Counselors need to have a high tolerance for ambiguity and change and a low need for power and immediate gratification; their rewards often come from developing the strengths of the community and the individual and fostering self-help and shared learning, rather than from displaying their own ability to heal others. Counselors need to be self-motivated, focusing on strengths rather than weakness or illness. They need to relate successfully to clients who may seem different from themselves and to learn to prize and foster the individuality of those clients. Counselors have to be able to deal with resistance by demonstrating quickly and effectively that they do have something to offer and are capable of meeting client needs. They have to be politically aware and assertive and assume the role of being their clients' advocate, often focusing on issues and groups rather than on individuals. Counselors will have to accept and establish a true partnership with their clients and their community. In order to accomplish this, there are several roles and skills which counselors generally need to develop.

Counselor Skills

A review of the literature on current course offerings in counselor education, as well as on the functions of the counselor, suggests that preparation of counselors should include the following areas of preparation (under each area are listed those competencies which the counselor should acquire as a result of that preparation):

Areas of preparation and competency of the counselor
A. Communication Skills

1. Possesses and can model good oral communication skills.
2. Can write clearly and correctly and can prepare well-written reports, letters, and other communications.
3. Can generally hear and respond appropriately to both overt and covert, verbal and nonverbal client messages.
4. Can teach communication skills to individuals or groups and promote improved interpersonal relations.
5. Can communicate to clients the nature of the counseling process and help them to understand both its value and its limitations.
6. Can effectively conduct an interview or discussion with people from various educational and socioeconomic backgrounds.

B. Human Growth and Development

1. Understands the processes and principles of human development and the typical concerns of various age groups.
2. Can discriminate between healthy and disturbed development, has knowledge of abnormal psychology and behavior, and can make diagnoses using standard diagnostic systems.
3. Can take a holistic view of clients.
4. Can enable others to gain insight into their own development.

5. Can use crisis counseling, brief psychotherapy, educational programs, and other appropriate techniques to promote positive human development.

C. Techniques and Theories of Counseling

1. Is familiar with and able to use a broad range of counseling techniques, especially the reality-oriented, brief, and action-based methods.
2. Is able to engage effectively in many levels of counseling (e.g., individual, family, group, organization, community).
3. Can assess clients' needs and can develop both preventive and remedial treatment plans which effectively meet those needs.
4. Can help clients to set viable long- and short-range goals.
5. Can promote client motivation and deal effectively with resistance.

D. Group Counseling

1. Possesses understanding of group development and dynamics.
2. Can help others to understand and modify group process.
3. Can work effectively with both small and large groups, homogeneous and heterogeneous groups.
4. Knows the strengths and limitations of group counseling and can determine when it is likely to be helpful to clients.

E. Career Counseling

1. Understands the lifelong process of career development and the broad scope of career counseling.
2. Is familiar with sources of career information and knows how to help clients acquire and use that information.
3. Is familiar with a broad range of inventories designed to assess interests, abilities, and values and can use those instruments effectively as a part of career counseling.

4. Can promote improved life/work planning via client self-exploration, values clarification, development of alternatives, decision-making, reality testing, pre-retirement planning, leisure counseling, and other appropriate techniques.
5. Can help clients develop the skills needed for effective job seeking (e.g., interview skills, resume writing).

F. Family (Couples) Counseling

1. Has understanding of patterns of family dynamics and of the family life cycle.
2. Is familiar with and able to use the major approaches to family and couples counseling.
3. Can use methods to promote positive parent/child interaction.
4. Can determine when family/couples counseling would be an effective treatment modality.

G. Consultation

1. Understands the roles and responsibilities of the consultant.
2. Can function independently and define own goals and those of clientele with little structure or supervision.
3. Understands organizational development.
4. Can attend to and balance organizational and individual needs.
5. Can promote problem-solving and conflict resolution.
6. Can promote communication and change in organizations in a way that fosters self-help and increased competence.

H. Training and Program Development

1. Can develop programs that reach large numbers of individuals and promote mastery and shared learning.
2. Is comfortable in a teaching role and can integrate teaching and counseling skills.

3. Can conduct in-service training programs.
4. Can supervise, train, and work effectively with indigenous and paraprofessional workers.
5. Possesses administrative skills.
6. Can coordinate and collaborate effectively with other human service workers.
7. Can plan and execute outreach programs and approaches to bring services to communities.

I. Social Systems and Community Organization

1. Understands and can use the principles of social systems analysis and community planning and organization.
2. Can understand issues as well as individual and community needs.
3. Can identify and work effectively with both community strengths and growth-inhibiting and stressful aspects of the community; can assess the need for community change.
4. Can take a multifaceted approach to helping others.
5. Can assume the roles of advocate, change agent, and political activist when appropriate.
6. Is familiar with and can make effective use of community and other resources via referral, linkage, and consultation in order to provide a comprehensive and continuous system of services.
7. Can facilitate the strengthening of socially devalued groups.
8. Can involve the community in program planning and develop and draw on community leadership.
9. Has knowledge of causes and dynamics of major social problems (e.g., substance abuse, child abuse, rape, delinquency), their legal ramifications, and ways to prevent and treat them.
10. Has a broad range of approaches to help others develop their life skills and their abilities to help themselves (e.g., parent effectiveness training, assertiveness training, sex education).

J. Special Populations

1. Is aware of and appreciates individual and cultural differences.
2. Can interact well with individuals of all ages and backgrounds, functioning at various intellectual and emotional levels, and can understand their points of view.
3. Can take account of the effect that a cultural and environmental background has had on an individual's development.
4. Can help clients and special populations to become aware of their needs and set their own priorities and goals and can accept the validity of their wants.
5. Can help clients develop and make use of appropriate support systems.

K. Research and Appraisal

1. Understands the principles of assessment and evaluation.
2. Is conversant with important research in the field of counseling.
3. Can understand, plan, and conduct research studies.
4. Appreciates the importance of evaluating the impact of one's efforts and the need for accountability.
5. Can develop and execute valid evaluation procedures.

L. Self-Growth and Awareness

1. Is aware of and can deal with own prejudices and stereotypes as well as those of clients.
2. Is flexible and able to cope with constant change.
3. Can function effectively as leader, team member, and autonomous helper.
4. Has good overall awareness of own strengths and weaknesses, likes and dislikes.
5. Is committed to lifelong learning and professional development.
6. Understands the ethical standards of counselors and behaves in a way that is consistent with those standards.

Certainly, not all counselors need to possess all of the above competencies. However, the growing emphasis on the generalist model of counseling and on the broad and diverse range of employment opportunities open to counselors suggest that the most effective and employable counselors will be those who have acquired a substantial number of these skills.

Perhaps some idea of the relative importance of the competencies can be gleaned from a study by Randolph (1979). From 117 community mental health center directors he obtained ratings on the requisite skills for masters-level helping professionals. The highly desirable competencies the directors listed included: good oral and written communication skills; knowledge of community resources; assessment skills; individual, group, and family counseling skills; consultation skills; crisis counseling; mastery of supportive-reflective techniques; diagnosis of learning difficulties; and ability to conduct intake interviews. Coursework they recommended included abnormal psychology, personality theory, learning theory, developmental psychology, social psychology, behavior modification, and child development. They emphasized the value of a practitioner rather than a research model of training and stressed the need for counselors to possess personal warmth.

In a more recent study, DeRidder, Stephens, English, and Watkins (1983) surveyed 345 administrators or directors of agencies providing mental health services. They were asked to indicate competencies that were most significant in enabling counselors to function effectively in their agencies. Although there were disparities, depending upon the nature of the agency, those surveyed viewed the following four areas of understanding as essential:

1. Learning and adjustment—understanding how clients develop and change
2. Counseling skills and techniques
3. Ethics of the counseling profession
4. Report writing

The role of new professional counselors often requires them to move away from the traditional client-centered model, emphasizing personal growth and a client-counselor partnership, and toward a more active and responsible model stressing prevention, community intervention, brief and directive approaches, and concrete evidence of change.

Counselor Roles and Options

The professional counselor of the 1980s has a wide range of roles and employment opportunities. The following are some of the counselors' roles: diagnostician and treatment planner, psychotherapist, teacher/trainer, community organizer, case manager, consultant, human relations specialist, workshop leader, grant writer, coordinator/program developer, agent of referral, researcher, evaluation specialist, report writer, and whatever else is needed to help clients in a professional way.

Correspondingly, counselors seeking to work in nonschool or mental health settings have an extensive and expanding array of employment options:

1. *Community mental health centers.* The movements of the 1950s and '60s to reduce the psychiatric inpatient population (deinstitutionalization) and increase readily available mental health services led to a rapid growth in community mental health centers (CMHCs) and a corresponding growth in employment of mental health counselors. Emphasizing preventive services and treating clients of all ages and economic circumstances, CMHCs and the mental health workers they employ typically offer 10 essential services: inpatient treatment, outpatient treatment, emergency service, partial hospitalization, consultation and education, diagnostic services, rehabilitation, pre- and after-care, training, and research and evaluation (Bloom, 1977).

2. *Marriage and family counseling agencies.* The past 20 years have witnessed the growth of the field of family counseling, partially because of a growing divorce rate. National attention has been paid to situations such as spouse and child abuse, blended and step-families, and single-parent families. Mental health agencies that specialize in family-related concerns are numerous. Some prefer their employees to have specialized training

(e.g., divorce mediation, brief family therapy), but others provide employment to entry-level counselors.

3. *Rehabilitation counseling agencies.*   Rehabilitation counselors may work with the physically disabled, the mentally retarded, substance (drug or alcohol) abusers, clients with a history of incarceration, or the emotionally disturbed. Typically, rehabilitation counselors have specialized training in the medical aspects of their clients' disorders. These counselors often have fairly large caseloads and focus on the adjustment and career-related needs of their clients, planning with the clients for appropriate training and employment.

4. *Career counseling or employment agencies.*   Increasing social acceptance of the lifelong nature of career development and increasing frequency of midlife career change have led to the growth of career counseling services aimed at an adult population. Such agencies may serve a general clientele or an identified group (e.g., displaced homemakers, reentry women, military retirees). These agencies typically offer a combination of services: counseling, assessment, information-giving, training in job-seeking skills, and placement. Employment agencies also hire career counselors, but their focus tends to be more on matching clients to job opportunities listed with the agencies than on providing a broad range of services.

5. *Employee assistance programs.*   One of the fastest growing areas of employment for counselors, employee assistance programs, are generally affiliated with or hired by businesses, industries, or governmental organizations to provide counseling to employees. Employers generally provide this service in order to maximize employee productivity, retain capable employees, and reduce absenteeism. Clients may be self-referred or supervisor-referred, although strict confidentiality is almost always guaranteed. Common concerns presented are substance abuse, family difficulties, and employee-supervisor conflict. Employee assistance counselors often take a preventive approach: helping supervisors to perform more effectively, presenting workshops

of general interest (e.g., stress management, assertiveness), handling personnel concerns, or planning human resource development programs.

6. *Hospitals.*   Because of their focus on developmental concerns rather than pathology, counselors have been less likely to be employed in inpatient or psychiatric hospital settings than have other helping professionals. Gradually, however, counselors are finding employment in working with a seriously disturbed or ill population. Often, in such settings, a team approach is used with counselors offering career or family counseling while psychotherapy and drug therapy are provided by psychiatrists. There also seems to be a place for counselors to play a rehabilitative role in working with hospitalized clients who must understand and cope with potentially life-threatening illnesses or surgery that has caused an alteration in appearance and functioning.

7. *Other medical services/settings.*   Counselors also have been working with medical personnel in outpatient settings in response to the growing awareness that attending to both physical and emotional concerns can facilitate decisions, adjustment, and recovery. Examples of such settings are centers to help clients with unplanned pregnancies, counseling with people suffering from cancer to help them control pain and reduce side-effects of their treatment, and genetic counseling facilities designed to provide information on genetically transmitted disorders to prospective parents, enabling them to make informed decisions.

8. *Residential facilities.*   Residential facilities such as group homes for troubled adolescents, apartments for mentally retarded adults, and halfway houses for substance abusers and those recently released from prison often employ counselors. In such settings, counselors tend to have small caseloads but work closely with their clients in flexible ways, perhaps teaching them to cook or helping them to locate housing. Work hours also tend to be flexible.

9. *Day treatment programs.*   Such programs are established for clients who are not currently capable of total independence

and who need a supervised and therapeutic daytime program. The programs are available for older people and for recently discharged psychiatric inpatients. These programs often are designed to simulate a community, and counselors may provide education, treatment, activities, and family counseling.

10. Corrections facilities.   Counselors interested in corrections may find employment in prisons or parole settings. Often, such mental health workers fill both counseling and authoritative roles, perhaps serving as parole officers.

11. Crisis-intervention settings.   Counselors engaged in crisis-intervention may focus on suicide-prevention, may accompany the police to deal with reports of domestic violence, may be intake workers in a hospital or CMHC, or may staff a hot line, offering counseling over the telephone to troubled clients. Such counseling tends to be short-term, perhaps only one contact, and typically calls for the counselor to be able to make decisions, intervene quickly, and to have knowledge of and make use of referral sources.

12. Specific focus agencies.   There are a broad range of mental health agencies which have specific foci. They can be categorized according to the age group served (e.g., children, people over sixty-five), the special population or problem addressed (e.g., recently bereaved clients, rape victims, Hispanics, Vietnam veterans), or the approach to treatment espoused (e.g., Rational Emotive Therapy, biofeedback, hypnosis). Counselors with special areas of interest or training may seek employment in such settings.

13. Consulting settings.   Counselors may be self-employed or employed by agencies to engage in the process of consulting. Typically, the counselor-consultant would be hired by several different agencies on a short-term, fee-for-service contract to provide expertise in a specified area. Consultants might conduct vocational testing for a rehabilitation firm, communications workshops for supervisors in a business, or stress management workshops for members of a professional association. While consulting may be an unpredictable and potentially stressful endeavor, many counselors enjoy part-time consulting in addition to full-time employment.

14. Private practice. The advent of licensure and certification for counselors has led counselors to enter private practice in increasing numbers. Weikel, Daniel, and Anderson (1981) surveyed a random sample of 1,000 AMHCA members and found that 37 percent of the 621 respondents maintained private practices while 45 percent planned to start a practice. Most (74.8 percent) had part-time private practices, often in addition to full-time employment. Seligman and Whiteley (1983) obtained similar findings in their study of counselors in private practice in Virginia. They found that 43 percent of those in practice had received third-party payments from insurance companies and that 26 different companies had reimbursed Virginia counselors. These figures are cited to demonstrate that private practice is a viable option for counselors, that they are generally recognized by health insurance companies, and that, as private practitioners, counselors must be prepared to assume full responsibility for the diagnosis and treatment planning of their clients.

THE MENTAL HEALTH TEAM

The increasing diversity of mental health professionals employed in CMHCs and other multiservice mental health centers has led to the evolution of the mental health team. This has also been referred to as a generic model of staffing. In such a model, a mental health team will be composed of two or more professionals from different areas of specialization. Such a team generally will include a psychiatrist and a psychologist, a counselor, or a social worker. Depending upon the nature of the treatment facility, the team might also include recreation therapists, psychiatric nurses, peer counselors, or other specialists. Members of a team will have some roles or duties they all perform such as individual counseling or psychotherapy and some that are assigned only to certain members of the group, based on their training or expertise. For example, the psychiatrist will determine whether clients need medication as part of their treatment, the social worker may specialize in family therapy, and the counselor may focus on clients with academic or career-related concerns. Generally, the team will meet as a unit to develop treatment plans for clients and evaluate them at regular intervals.

In some agencies, the treatment team is formed at the time of the intake interview; the counselor gathers developmental data from the client, the social worker interviews the client's family, the psychologist conducts an assessment through projective tests and other inventories, and the psychiatrist performs a medical examination. When the intake procedures have been completed, all four mental health workers meet to share their findings and develop a diagnosis and treatment plan.

In other settings, the team will develop on an "as needed" basis. For example, a counselor who conducts an intake interview of a confused client, age sixty-three, with a history of alcoholism may ask a psychiatrist to evaluate the client for the presence of an organic brain syndrome and may ask a psychologist to test the client to determine whether a schizophrenic process is present.

The mental health team approach offers many advantages. It allows mental health workers to become experts in some areas and draws on the expertise of others to supplement. The collaboration afforded by the team approach can yield considerable information and insights about clients and should promote sounder diagnoses and treatment plans. Also, it can contribute to cost containment and increased availability of services. There is currently a shortage of psychiatrists, typically the highest paid mental health professionals (Fields, 1984). A shortfall of 4,900 psychiatrists is expected by 1990. The team approach can circumvent this problem by using psychiatrists primarily in those areas where they have unique expertise (e.g., prescribing medication) and using more available and less expensive mental health workers to perform tasks in areas of shared expertise (e.g., individual psychotherapy).

The Mental Health Professionals

The diversity of helping professionals can be confusing to clients as well as to helping professionals themselves. However, it is important that counselors understand the differences and similarities among the various mental health professionals to know whom to consult when help is needed with a client and to facilitate productive communication and collaboration.

1. Psychiatrists.   Psychiatrists are unique among the mental health professionals in that they, alone, have a medical degree, an MD, and are qualified to assess physical condition, diagnose medical problems, and prescribe medication. They are typically the most educated of the mental health professionals, having 4 years of medical school and several years of residency beyond college. However, the training that psychiatrists receive in psychotherapy tends to vary; some concentrate on studying the biochemical treatment of mental illness and so may have relatively brief training and experience in psychotherapy, while others may have completed advanced training programs and additional residencies and so may have great expertise in psychotherapy. Counselors, then, may actually have more expertise in human development and psychotherapy than do some psychiatrists.

Although counselors, of course, cannot diagnose physical complaints or prescribe medication, they are often the first to hear of clients' medical complaints or of undesirable side effects or lack of effectiveness of prescribed medication. Consequently, it is important that counselors stay informed of their clients' medication and physical condition and refer the client to a psychiatrist when a medical evaluation seems warranted.

2. Psychologists—doctoral level.   Doctoral level psychologists can be categorized by their areas of specialization and their degrees. Most will have a PhD degree (Doctor of Philosophy), but some will have an EdD (Doctor of Education) and others will have a PsyD (Doctor of Psychology). The PsyD is a relatively new degree, generally granted by programs focused on preparing practitioners rather than researchers. Psychologists may specialize in such areas as clinical, counseling, developmental, experimental, or industrial psychology. Psychologists in mental health facilities are most likely to be clinical or counseling psychologists. Although there is considerable overlap between those two areas of specialization, clinical psychologists are typically more interested in abnormal behavior and severely disturbed clients, and counseling psychologists tend to be more interested in normal development and problems of adjustment.

Most practicing psychologists have completed 3 to 4 years of post-baccalaureate study, an internship, and a thesis or dissertation, and are licensed or certified by the states in which they practice. They are trained in psychotherapy and, among the mental health professionals, are particularly skilled in psychological testing, including the use of projective techniques (e.g., Rorschach Test, Thematic Apperception Test).

3. Psychologists—masters level.   Masters level psychologists typically receive specialized training in a particular area of psychology (e.g. testing, counseling, industrial, or school psychology). They are often employed as psychometricians or school psychologists where their primary function is assessment. Masters level psychologists generally cannot be licensed or certified to practice independently. Consequently, their role is somewhat circumscribed. Some psychologists are circumventing this by taking extra coursework and seeking credentialing as counselors.

4. Social workers.   Practicing social workers typically have the masters degree (MSW) and credentials from state (LSW) or national (ACSW) credentialing bodies. Requirements for credentialing of social workers are comparable to those for counselors: approximately 60 credits of coursework and 2 to 3 years of supervised experience. However, social workers have a longer history in the mental health field. Initially, they often worked with psychiatrists, seeing the families of troubled clients. Over the years, they have acquired considerable independence and credibility. Consequently, there seems to be more public awareness of the functions of social workers than there is of the newer field of mental health counseling. While there is considerable overlap between the interests and training of clinical or psychiatric social workers and mental health counselors, social workers tend to be better trained in dealing with severely disturbed clients and more knowledgeable of public policy. However, they generally do not have counselors' expertise in testing and in dealing with educational or career-related concerns.

5. *Paraprofessionals, peer counselors.* The education and training of such workers tends to vary widely; they may be 4-year college graduates with a major in psychology, graduates of 2-year colleges with degrees as mental health technicians, or have only an elementary school education. Typically, they are hired because they have personal knowledge and common experiences to offer to the clients; the paraprofessionals may be recovering alcoholics, former abused spouses, or have similar ethnic and language backgrounds to many of their clients. As members of a treatment team, paraprofessional counselors, who may be able to establish rapport rapidly with clients, can offer unique insights and information. Many are talented counselors and assume considerable responsibility.

6. *Psychiatric nurses.* Psychiatric nurses generally have a bachelors or masters degree in their field. They have training in counseling and human development as well as in medical diagnosis and treatment. They often are part of a treatment team in hospital settings and in settings involving clients with physical or medical concerns (e.g., detoxification programs, rehabilitation programs).

7. *Pastoral counselors.* Credentialed pastoral counselors generally have the same training and experience as other mental health counselors with additional or previous training in theology. The best-qualified pastoral counselors seem to be guided by and interested in spiritual principles but also follow accepted principles of effective counseling such as offering advice sparingly and attempting to maintain objectivity.

8. *Psychoanalyst.* This term refers to individuals who have received extensive specialized training in the field of psychoanalysis and who have generally undergone personal analysis. Nearly all are either psychiatrists or doctoral level psychologists. The term "psychoanalyst," however, does not indicate a degree received but, rather, the nature of an individual's training and practice (e.g., seeing clients five times a week for several years or more and using the ideas and techniques of Freud and his followers).

9. *Psychotherapist.* This is a relatively meaningless term describing anyone who engages in the practice of counseling or psychotherapy. It does not indicate anything about education, training, or techniques.

10. *Mental health counselors.* AMHCAs definition of mental health counselors provided earlier in this chapter offers a comprehensive description of such counselors. There is considerable overlap and commonality between counselors and other helping professionals. Counselors, however, are particularly well-trained to use a wide range of techniques and approaches to help clients with developmental, social, emotional, family, and career-related concerns; to conduct assessments, using interviews and standardized, objective tests; and to make use of community resources and support systems to help clients. There also are a few clear limits typically imposed upon counselors; they cannot evaluate physical concerns, prescribe medication, or use projective tests. Despite these few limitations, the roles and skills of mental health counselors are broad, enabling them to effectively treat a wide range of clients.

Projections of the Future

The role of the new mental health professional, the counselor, is still in flux and probably will continue that way for the foreseeable future. While it is impossible to predict with certainty what shape that role will take in the future, trends and patterns impinging on the mental health counselor can be identified and hypotheses can be advanced as to the nature of their impact:

1. Changes are anticipated in counselor education programs in terms of both the students and the curriculum. Proportionately fewer students interested in school or college counseling will be enrolled while the mental health component of many programs will expand (Rotter, 1979). The average age of students in such programs seems to be increasing with many of them being reentry or second-career students. Many school counselors are acquiring a second area of expertise by taking additional courses in mental health counseling and seeking licensure. Counselor education

programs are requiring more courses to enable students to meet state licensure requirements and function effectively in mental health settings. Some professionals believe that 60 semester hours should be the standard preparation for a master's degree in counseling (Forster, 1978). These changes will increase the number of qualified mental health counselors and should increase the visibility and credibility of the counseling profession.

2. Demographic and social trends will change and expand the composition of mental health counselors' clientele, requiring counselors to develop new skills. Examples of such trends are the growing number and percentage of people over sixty-five years of age in the population, the high divorce rate, the increasing number of mid-life career changers, and the growth in bilingual and foreign-born individuals in the United States.

3. Greater emphasis will be placed on developmental and preventive approaches to counseling (Whitely & Fretz, 1980). This should enhance the counselors' role in working in nonmedical settings and as consultants, trainers, and human resource managers.

4. Increasing numbers of states will pass licensure laws for counselors. That trend also should increase counselors' visibility and credibility and open up new opportunities (e.g., private practice).

5. Shortages of both psychiatrists (Fields, 1984) and psychologists (Turkington, 1983) are predicted with the gap being filled, at least in part, by mental health counselors. Cooperation among mental health professionals should increase and their distinctions decrease.

6. Federal funds, grants, and insurance reimbursements for mental health services all seem to be growing scarcer and more tightly controlled. In order to obtain a substantial share of those funds, counselors will have to demonstrate their effectiveness and accountability.

7. Acceptance of holistic health and the relationship of physical and emotional concerns seems to be increasing and should lead to a corresponding increase in the number and frequency of counselors working with physicians to ameliorate physical illness via stress management, mental imagery, and other approaches.

8. Improved computer technology and other research developments should bring counselors more efficient systems of record keeping, better time management, and new and more precise tests and inventories.

9. The rapid change in counselors' roles and the increasing demand on counselors to work with a wide range of client groups often may be stressful and lead to feelings of frustration, apathy, cynicism, and anger. These feelings seem to be engendered in some counselors by the gap that they perceive between their ideal of what a counselor should be able to accomplish and what they actually can do. Attention will need to be paid to the professional and emotional development of counselors via peer support groups, peer counseling (already initiated by AMHCA), continuing education programs for counselors, and the further development of support services provided by AACD and other professional associations for counselors.

Chapter 2

DIAGNOSTIC SYSTEMS AND THEIR USE*

WHY DIAGNOSE?

The changing role of the counselor, discussed in chapter 1, has required counselors to assume major responsibility for diagnosis and treatment planning. For some counselors, the process of attaching a diagnostic label to a client is uncomfortable; that process is antithetical to their view of the counselor as an individual who promotes positive growth and who does not emphasize past emotional difficulties.

However, there are several ways in which effective diagnosis can be beneficial to both clients and counselors. Accurately diagnosing a client's concerns can facilitate effective treatment planning; research indicates that clients with some diagnoses respond better to certain kinds of treatments than to others. Placing clients' concerns in a diagnostic context can help counselors anticipate the nature and progress of the counseling process. Since the same diagnostic framework is used by all helping profes-

---

*Portions of this chapter were previously published as An introduction to the new *DSM-III* (1983). *Personnel and Guidance Journal, 61,* 601-605. Copyright AACD. Reprinted with permission. No further reproduction authorized without permission of AACD.

sionals, an understanding of diagnostic terminology helps counselors to communicate more effectively and professionally with social workers, psychologists, psychiatrists, and other counselors. That understanding also should contribute to the effective functioning of a mental health treatment team since all members can have a common frame of reference. If a client relocates or is transferred from one counselor to another, the use of a shared diagnostic language can promote continuity of service. Diagnosis also has become a vehicle for human service agencies to classify the clients they serve in order to determine needed services, demonstrate accountability, and justify the agencies' roles in the community. Counselors in private practice or in fee-for-service agencies will have to provide diagnoses for clients with health insurance coverage. Since not all diagnostic categories are viewed as "illnesses," the nature of clients' diagnoses generally determines whether they will be reimbursed for counseling. Most health insurance companies, for example, will not provide third-party payments if a client is diagnosed as having an "Occupational Problem" or a "Parent-child Problem" since those are not viewed as mental illnesses. Counselors should be knowledgeable of diagnosis so they can consult with insurance companies and advise clients whether treatment for their concerns is likely to be paid for by their medical insurance.

OVERVIEW OF DIAGNOSTIC SYSTEMS

The Diagnostic Process

In order to make an accurate diagnosis, counselors must gather information on clients' presenting concerns, their backgrounds and history, and their present situations. Data gathered is then organized and analyzed by the counselors. Detailed information on the process of data-gathering and analysis is provided in chapters 3 and 4.

Although diagnostic systems seek to objectify the diagnostic process, it should be borne in mind that diagnoses can change over relatively brief intervals and that there is considerable room for error in the diagnostic process. Spitzer, Endicott, and Robins (1975) cite five causes of low reliability in the diagnosis of emotional disorders:

1. Subject variance—The client may exhibit different conditions at different times.
2. Occasion variance—Clients are at different stages of their conditions at different times.
3. Information variance—Diagnosticians have access to different sources and pieces of information about their clients.
4. Observation variance—Diagnosticians evaluating the same piece of information or behavior differ in what they notice and view as important.
5. Criterion variance—Diagnosticians may use different criteria for extrapolating a diagnosis from available data.

Research has shown that a high degree of agreement on diagnoses can be obtained from experienced clinicians (Blocher & Biggs, 1983; *Diagnostic and Statistical Manual of Mental Disorders,* 1980). Nevertheless, diagnosis is an imprecise science and counselors should treat it as such, seeking consultation on difficult diagnoses and labelling uncertain diagnoses as "provisional." The ambiguity in the diagnostic process can be uncomfortable but it also serves to remind counselors not to view their clients in terms of their labels or diagnoses.

Diagnostic Systems

There are two systems of diagnosis that are widely used in the United States, the third edition of the *Diagnostic and Statistical Manual of Mental Disorders (DSM-III)* (1980) and the *Manual of the International Statistical Classification of Diseases, Injuries, and Causes of Death,* volume 1 (1977), known as the *ICD-9.* The *ICD-9* was adopted by the nineteenth World Health Assembly and published by the World Health Organization for international use. Relevant parts of the *ICD-9* are available in the *DSM-III* (1980) and the similarities between the two systems are numerous.

Counselors familiar with the *DSM-III* will find they also have some understanding of the *ICD-9* and will be able to satisfy nearly all requests for diagnoses by using the *DSM-III* framework.

HISTORICAL DEVELOPMENT OF THE *DSM-III*

The first edition of the *DSM* appeared in 1952. It was developed primarily by and for psychiatrists and presented a psychobiological approach to emotional disorders. The long-lived *DSM-II* was published in 1958 and established a perspective on mental illness that emphasized the categories of neurosis, psychosis, and personality disorder. The *DSM-III,* a collaborative venture of the American Psychiatric Association and the American Psychological Association, was in preparation for several years and was field-tested by over 500 clinicians before it was finally published in 1980. The *DSM-III* seeks to provide a detailed description of all categories of mental illness. For each disorder, the description generally contains:

1. a list of the disorder's essential features and a clinical sketch.
2. a summary of characteristics usually associated with the disorder.
3. information on the typical onset and course of the disorder, the impairment caused, and potential complications.
4. information on known predisposing factors and frequency of occurrence of the disorder.
5. information on similar disorders, to facilitate differential diagnosis.
6. diagnostic criteria for the disorder.

The *DSM-III* covers a wide range of human concerns, including developmental, educational, and vocational areas. The *DSM-III* ". . .defines a mental disorder as a clinically significant behavioral or psychological syndrome or pattern that occurs in an individual and that is typically associated with a painful symptom (distress) or impairment in one or more important areas of functioning (disability)" (Blocher & Biggs, 1983, p. 191). The *DSM-III* is atheoretical and does not seek to elucidate the causes of mental disorders. Its primary functions are description and classification.

There are several important changes from the *DSM-II* to the *DSM-III* which have an impact on the concept of mental illness. In general, the *DSM-III* is more comprehensive and detailed and tends to use less highly charged language than the *DSM-II*. The term "neurosis" is no longer recommended for diagnostic use so that *DSM-II's* depressive neurosis has become *DSM-III's* dysthymic disorder. Homosexuality is no longer classified as an emotional illness although there is a diagnosis for homosexuals who are uncomfortable with their sexual orientation (ego-dystonic homosexuality). Schizophrenia has been defined more narrowly, thereby curtailing abuse of that diagnostic category, while the categories of mood disorder and adjustment disorder have been broadened to encompass a greater range of symptoms. Less use is made of the term "psychosis." The category labeled "psychosomatic disorders" has been redefined and renamed.

USING THE *DSM-III*

The *DSM-III* is a complex publication. To be able to use it with facility probably would require several months of frequent experience with it. However, the *DSM-III* is not meant to be memorized; rather, it should be used as a dictionary or reference book. In order to use a dictionary one must have some basic information such as knowledge of the alphabet, understanding of how a dictionary is organized, and some awareness of the symbols used. This chapter seeks to enable counselors to understand the structure and overall nature of the *DSM-III* so they can use it as a reference book. The chapter also will familiarize counselors with some of the available literature on the appropriate treatment of particular disorders. However, that body of literature is fairly limited. What is available was written primarily for psychiatrists and focuses mainly on the use of medication in the treatment of mental disorders. More comprehensive information on treatment planning is provided in chapters 5, 6, 7, and 8 of this book. However, in those chapters, too, the concepts presented are based on limited available research. Becoming skilled in diagnosis and treatment planning, then, will require study of the *DSM-III*, practice in its use, and application of available research as well as logic, intuition, and clinical skill in the development of viable treatment plans.

MULTIAXIAL DIAGNOSES

The Five Axes

Providing a full diagnostic picture of a client involves diagnosing that client according to five axes described in the *DSM-III* (1980). In practice, however, many clinicians use only Axes I and II.

Axis I includes clinical psychiatric syndromes and other conditions. It is on this axis that a client's presenting problem generally would appear. This is a broad category, encompassing most of the disorders listed in the *DSM-III* with the exception of personality disorders and specific developmental disorders such as a developmental language disorder. Those two categories are diagnosed on Axis II.

Axis II is distinguished from Axis I in that categories of disorder listed on Axis II generally are presumed to be long-standing and developmental. They often would not be viewed as mental illnesses by health insurance carriers and insurance often would not cover treatment for Axis II disorders. Only personality disorders and specific developmental disorders are coded on Axis II. All other disorders are included in Axis I.

Axis III includes physical disorders or conditions, either mentioned in a client's record or reported by the client. It should be borne in mind that Axis III diagnoses are not medical diagnoses but, rather, are reports of physical complaints described or experienced by clients. A listing of physical disorders on Axis III does not imply medical knowledge on the part of the helping professional.

Axis IV, severity of psychosocial stressor, is a way of objectively assessing the amount of pressure or disruption in a client's life. Disruption is rated on a 1 (none)–to–7 (catastrophic) scale that evaluates the degree to which the events in a client's life would be troubling to the average person. For example, change in work hours is viewed as an example of a mild stressor (3) while divorce is an example of an extreme stressor (6). This rating is not designed to reflect clients' subjective or individual reaction to events but, rather, to assess the magnitude of the events. This assessment would involve considering the amount of change produced in the client's life by the stressor, the degree to which the event is wanted, the amount of control that is had over the event, and the number of stressors anticipated or experienced in the past year. A comparison of Axis IV with Axis I provides information on the relationship between clients' life circumstances and their emotional difficulties.

Axis V, highest level of adaptive functioning, calls for the counselor to rate, on a 1 (superior)–to–7 (grossly impaired) scale, the highest level of a client's social relationships, leisure pursuits, and occupational performance in the past year, with the most weight being given to the first area (*DSM*, 1980). Ratings generally should not reflect the debilitation caused by the client's current concerns but, rather, should be a way to indicate the client's ego strength and coping abilities. Axes IV and V, both viewed in relation to Axis I, can facilitate treatment planning and provide information on prognosis by enabling the counselor to compare nature and level of disturbance with level of client resources.

Example

The following example illustrates a multiaxial diagnosis:
The client, a forty-seven-year-old woman, always has been very dependent on others, first her parents and then her husband. In an effort to deal with conflict between herself and her husband, she began abusing tranquilizers about 5 years ago. She has never been employed, but has cared for her home and two children reasonably well. Seven weeks ago, her husband left her with little warning. Since then she has been so depressed that she cannot manage her household chores and often does not get out of bed until noon. The client explains this by say-

ing that her migraine headaches prevent her from functioning effectively.

Multiaxial diagnosis of sample client

Axis I   —296.22 Major depression, single episode, without melancholia

—305.91 Other substance abuse, continuous (tranquilizers)

Axis II —301.60 Dependent personality disorder

Axis III—Headaches

Axis IV—Psychosocial stressor: marital separation

—Severity: 5—Severe

Axis V —Highest level of adaptive functioning in past year: 4—Fair

Although there may be no diagnoses for particular clients under one or two of the first three axes, this client has diagnoses under all categories and, in fact, has two diagnoses under Axis I. These are listed in order of priority of treatment; the presenting problem of severe depression would receive attention first. The diagnostic categories in Axes I and II are preceded by a code number. All of the diagnostic categories in the *DSM-III* are identified by their own 5-digit code number. The numbers generally should be listed along with the diagnostic label, especially for record-keeping or insurance purposes.

THE DIAGNOSTIC CATEGORIES

Diagnoses in the *DSM-III* are divided into 17 broad categories, with each category subdivided into specific diagnoses. Familiarizing the reader with all the specific diagnoses is beyond the scope of this chapter. However, the 17 broad categories will be reviewed so counselors can understand and more effectively use the framework of the *DSM-III*.

I. Disorders Usually First Evident in Infancy, Childhood, or Adolescence

This category generally is used for diagnosing difficulties in individuals under the age of eighteeen. However, diagnoses of adults can be drawn from this group if the difficulty (such as mental retardation) appeared when the individual was under eighteen and the difficulty has persisted since.

This broad category can be subdivided into five subcategories: *Intellectual, Behavioral, Emotional, Physical, and Developmental.* Specific diagnoses are encompassed by each of the five subcategories.

A. The Intellectual subcategory includes the gradations of mental retardation. To be diagnosed as mentally retarded, an individual must score an IQ of 70 or below on an individual intelligence test and must show accompanying adjustment deficits evident before age eighteen. Psychological testing is nearly always required as part of the process of diagnosing mental retardation and determining its severity (mild, moderate, severe, or profound). Determination of etiology is not needed for diagnosis but can certainly contribute to effective treatment planning. In mild cases, counseling with the child via play therapy, behavior modification, or other means can promote emotional and behavioral adjustment. Counselors also can help the parents of children diagnosed as mentally retarded to understand, accept, and interact with their children effectively and can work with relevant schools or agencies to ensure the provision of needed services (Reid, 1983).

B. The Behavioral subcategory includes a number of diagnoses that fit under the headings of attention deficit disorder or conduct disorder. Attention deficit disorder, formerly known as "hyperkinetic reaction of childhood" or "minimal brain dysfunction," is characterized by symptoms such as a brief attention span, hyperactivity, impulsiveness, irritability, emotional lability, and learning disabilities (Kaplan & Sadock, 1981). The disorder is 10 times more common in boys than girls. Psychiatric and psychological evaluations are indicated, especially since medication often is the primary treatment modality. Here, too, however, family counseling can help parents and child to understand the disorder and maintain needed environmental structure (Reid, 1983).

Conduct disorders involve a "repetitive and persistent pattern of conduct in which either the basic rights of others or major age-appropriate societal norms or rules are violated" (e.g., thefts, truancy, substance abuse) *(DSM,* 1980, p. 45). Four subtypes of the disorder are described: undersocialized, aggressive; undersocialized, nonaggressive; socialized, aggressive; and socialized, nonaggresive. Treatment of those with conduct disorders can be difficult since the clients often are hostile and mistrustful of adults. Family therapy, leading to increased supervision of the client and improvement in the family system, seems helpful, especially when combined with Reality Therapy in an individual or peer-group setting (Kaplan & Sadock, 1981). Adjunct services such as group homes, drug abuse treatment programs, or academic remediation also may be useful.

C. *The Emotional subcategory* is subdivided into the disorders listed below. Brief information on diagnosis and treatment of the most common of these is included.

1. Anxiety disorders of childhood or adolescence

a. *Separation anxiety disorder*—Inordinate anxiety is manifested upon separation from parents, important others, or familiar environment. Accompanying physical complaints, fear of disaster, and high attention needs are common. This can result in "school phobia" or refusal to attend school. Family counseling, behavior therapy, and supportive counseling designed to increase the child's sense of security, competence, and independence have been effective treatments (Kaplan & Sadock, 1981).

b. *Avoidant disorder*—Severe anxiety and withdrawal are manifested upon contact with strangers but not with family and familiar figures. Treatment as above has been effective with this relatively rare disorder.

c. *Overanxious disorder*—This common disorder is characterized by pervasive anxiety and worry about a broad range of events and experiences, especially those in which the client must meet expectations or wants approval. Self-consciousness, self-doubts, and perfectionism are likely. A supportive and consistent counseling approach that promotes self-awareness can be helpful (Kaplan & Sadock, 1981).

2. Other disorders of infancy, childhood, or adolescence

a. *Reactive attachment disorder of infancy*—This is characterized by poor emotional development in infancy.

b. *Schizoid disorder*—Such children are reserved and isolated, having little interest in or facility for forming peer relationships. Behavior modification and other counseling approaches designed to gradually reinforce and encourage increased social contact, with family support, can be helpful (Kaplan & Sadock, 1981).

c. *Elective mutism*—This is a relatively rare disorder involving the refusal to speak in almost all social situations.

d. *Oppositional disorder*—Clients with this disorder manifest "disobedient, negativistic, and provocative opposition to authority figures" (*DSM,* 1980, p. 63), commonly resulting in family conflict and poor school performance. Client-centered and Adlerian models have been found effective with such clients, along with an effort to reduce confrontation and family conflict (Reid, 1983). The process of increasing self-esteem, independence, and insight in the client also can be helpful (Kaplan & Sadock, 1981).

e. *Identity disorder*—This client is confused about self-image, values, wants, and future goals, leading to impaired functioning in social or other areas. Accompanying depression or anxiety is common. Counseling to develop self-awareness and self-esteem and to restore social and occupational functioning can be useful (Reid, 1983).

D. Physical disorders.   Inclusion of these disorders in the *DSM-III* implies that emotional determinants as well as physical symptoms are present.

1. *Eating disorders*—This subclass includes disorders characterized by severe disturbances in eating behavior.

   a. *Anorexia nervosa*—This involves the refusal to maintain normal body weight out of a distorted body perception and fear of becoming overweight. This potentially life-threatening disorder is particularly common among adolescent girls. Behavior modification, development of client self-awareness, family counseling, and education, often combined with medical treatment, hospitalization, and monitoring of food intake, are recommended (Reid, 1983). Clients are likely to be resistant to treatment. Consequently, counseling to encourage insight and analysis is unlikely to succeed (Kaplan & Sadock, 1981).
   b. *Bulimia*—This disorder is characterized by a pattern of binge eating. Like clients with anorexia, such clients may control weight through induced vomiting, excessive use of laxatives, or fasts. Recommended counseling is similar to that for anorexia.
   c. *Pica*—This is a rare disorder, involving persistent ingestion of nonnutritive matter (e.g., paint, hair, dirt).
   d. *Rumination disorder of infancy*—Symptoms of this disorder include repeated regurgitation of food, leading to subnormal weight gain.

2. *Stereotyped movement disorder*—This subcategory includes a variety of abnormal gross motor movements, generally recurrent, involuntary, rapid, and purposeless (e.g., tics, persistent head banging). Tourette's disorder is an unusual subcategory that often involves both physical tics and coprolalia ("the irresistible urge to utter obscenities") *(DSM,* 1980, p. 76). Medication often is effective in controlling such disorders. Counseling can help the family cope with any accompanying embarrassment or misunderstanding.

3. *Other disorders with physical manifestation*—These include stuttering, functional enuresis (involuntary voiding of urine beyond a certain age level), functional encopresis (passage of feces in inappropriate places), sleepwalking disorders and sleep terror disorder. These disorders have physical manifestations but often are precipitated or accompanied by affective disturbances such

as high anxiety or a strong need for attention. Medical consultation often is indicated for such disorders, although counseling can successfully reduce the emotional difficulties.

E. Developmental. This subcategory includes pervasive developmental disorders such as infantile autism (early impairment in social and communication skills and responsiveness, highly unusual reactions to environmental stimuli) and circumscribed or specific developmental disorders such as reading, arithmetic, or language disorders. While counselors may be involved as part of a treatment team working with such clients or their families, counselors will almost never work with such clients alone. Medical or educational specialists should be consulted and psychologists may be needed to conduct assessments. Educational and behavioral interventions are more indicated than is intensive therapy.

This first category of the DSM-III is perhaps the broadest of the 17 categories because it is defined by the age of the client rather than by the nature of the difficulty. However, this simplifies the diagnosis of emotional difficulties in children since, when diagnosing a child, a counselor can refer immediately to the above category of diagnoses and, by selecting the most applicable of the five subheadings, can rapidly diagnose most childhood disorders. However, it is acceptable to use categories outside of this group to diagnose disorders in children as long as the diagnostic criteria are satisfied.

II. Organic Mental Disorders

This category encompasses psychological or behavioral abnormalities associated with transient or permanent damage or dysfunction of the brain tissue. This could be caused by chemical agents (e.g., alcohol, barbiturates), metabolic disturbances, disease, injuries, or aging. Typical symptoms include a significant decline in intellectual functioning, memory loss, impaired judgment, shallow affect, or confusion. When organic mental disorders coexist with other mental disorders, the diagnosis in this category generally is viewed as the first or primary difficulty.

It would be unusual (and probably inappropriate) for counselors to have total responsibility for diagnosis and treatment of clients with organic mental disorders. Generally, psychologists and psychiatrists also would be involved in assessing and working with such clients since extensive testing, medication, and possibly other medical or surgical procedures would be involved. However, counselors may become involved with the families of such clients, providing information, facilitating adjustment, helping them to use community resources and modify the client's environment, and helping them to make decisions about the treatment or possible institutionalization of the client. Counselors also may work directly with the client in an attempt to reduce accompanying emotional difficulties (e.g., anxiety, depression, insomnia) (Reid, 1983).

III. Substance Use Disorders

This category is used to describe clients who engage in excessive or maladaptive use of a wide range of substances that affect the central nervous system such as alcohol, drugs, and tobacco. Simple use of such substances does not warrant a diagnosis; rather, criteria such as dependency, frequency and duration of use, and substance-induced behavioral, social, and occupational impairment of functioning need to be investigated to determine whether abuse is present. Often, clients with substance use disorders also have a related substance-induced organic mental disorder in which both maladaptive behavior and central nervous system damage result from the excessive substance use. This can be as mild as intoxication or withdrawal or can be less transient.

Disorders in this classification are categorized by severity (abuse or dependency), nature of substance (alcohol, barbiturates or related sedatives, opioids, cocaine, amphetamines, cannabis, or tobacco), and the course of the disorder (continuous, episodic, or in remission). Abuse of other or mixed substances also may be diagnosed.

Treatment of substance use disorders often is multifaceted. Initial detoxification may be needed. Clients may be given medication to neutralize or change their physical reactions to the substance (e.g., Methadone for opioid abuse, Antabuse for alcohol abusers). Clients may be referred to Alcoholics Anonymous for peer support and socialization. Individual counseling, often of a behavioral nature, may be included in the treatment plan. Family counseling can help repair any damage to the family, help the family support the client's efforts to change, restructure their own lives, and improve family dynamics. Education and information on substance abuse also can be helpful to client and family. Relapse rates of clients with substance use disorders are high, but a present-oriented, multifaceted, active approach seems to provide more effective treatment than long-term counseling focusing on insight and analysis (Greist, Jefferson, & Spitzer, 1982). Gestalt Therapy, Reality Therapy, and other directive, confrontational models also have been used with such clients but results have been mixed. Clients with substance use disorders often are dependent and defensive, responding best to counselors who are caring, yet firm and realistic, and who help clients build strengths, motivation, and interests while maintaining sobriety (Reid, 1983).

IV. Schizophrenic Disorders

Schizophrenia, as defined in the *DSM-III* (1980), is a disorder that appears before age forty-five (generally first manifests itself in early adulthood), has been present for at least 6 months, and involves some demonstration of florid psychosis (most commonly, auditory hallucinations), and deterioration from previous level of functioning. Accompanying symptoms might include a low level of functioning, withdrawal, thought disorder, delusions (often persecutory in nature), loose associations, a flat affect, extreme self-centeredness, confusion, and loss of goals and boundaries. Clients with schizophrenia often present a family history of such disorders and typically reflect considerable social and occupational impairment. The *DSM* (1980) desribes four types of schizophrenia: disorganized, paranoid, undifferentiated, and residual. In diagnosing schizophrenia, the course of the illness also is specified according to criteria in the *DSM*.

Many counselors receive little training in dealing with severely disturbed clients and thus may feel flustered and incompetent when confronted with a schizophrenic client. Some of this feeling is appropriate. Counselors should not assume full responsibility for the diagnosis and treatment of schizophrenic clients since they generally will require projective testing and, often, at least brief hospitalization. Medication almost always is used, at least temporarily, to reduce and control symptoms. However, it is acceptable for counselors to be part of a multi-faceted team approach to helping a severely disturbed client; the counselor might conduct an intake interview, provide information and counseling, or work with the client's family. Counselors also might work with schizophrenic clients in therapeutic milieus (halfway houses or day treatment centers), helping clients to develop self-confidence, social skills, and future plans and also might lead supportive groups with such clients. In such capacities, counselors should continue to use all the skills they use with other clients and should inquire about the history of a client's schizophrenic symptoms, just as counselors would ask about work history. Supportive, behavioral, present-oriented approaches generally will be most effective rather than confrontational or analytic models (Kaplan & Sadock, 1981). Cognitive retraining has also been helpful (Meyer, 1983). As the counselors' expanding role brings them into more contact with very troubled clients, the counselors should be careful not to reject or stigmatize clients through their own apprehensions or self-doubts. Many clients who have suffered from schizophrenia make great progress in recovering from the disorder and can lead productive and rewarding lives.

V. Paranoid Disorders

Paranoid disorders are relatively rare. However, they are a separate diagnostic category and must be distinguished from paranoid schizophrenia, one of the specific diagnoses in category IV. Clients suffering from paranoid disorders show less impairment of their daily functioning than do clients with paranoid schizophrenia. They do not manifest obvious hallucinations but, rather, have a set of delusions that seem unlikely rather than impossible. For example, the paranoid schizophrenic client may imagine that her supervisor is undermining her effectiveness at work by beaming electronic rays at her typewriter while the client with a paranoid disorder may believe that his supervisor is deliberately making grammatical errors in the letters the supervisor gives the client to type in order to make the client look incompetent. The first belief is impossible; the second, possible but not likely. Delusions of clients with paranoid disorders typically are persecutory (someone is out to get me) or jealous (I am being betrayed). Close examination by the counselor of both the delusions and the client's history and life-style often is needed in order to diagnose a paranoid disorder. Such disorders often are precipitated by environmental stressors. Counselors can reduce clients' resistance and anxiety by accepting rather than disputing the presented delusions. However, they should not participate in developing or discussing them at length (Meyer, 1983).

With this category of disorders, too, counselors may be involved as members of a treatment team, generally including psychiatrists and psychologists. Counselors may be involved in helping such clients reduce and manage stress and in helping family and relevant others, especially those who may be the subject of the delusion, to understand and relate to the clients more effectively.

VI. Psychotic Disorders Not Elsewhere Classified

This category includes four diagnoses: schizophreniform disorder (schizophrenia-like symptoms but of shorter duration), brief reactive psychosis, schizoaffective disorder (characterized by a relatively equal mix of schizophrenic and affective symptoms), and atypical psychosis. This category encompasses disorders that, on the surface, may look like schizophrenia but that fail to meet one or more of the criteria needed for a diagnosis of schizophrenia.

Some sources divide schizophrenic and other psychotic disorders into process (endogenous) and reactive (exogenous) types. Process schzophrenia tends to have a gradual, often insidious onset and does not have an apparent precipitating event. Reactive schizophrenia, on the other hand, generally has a more rapid onset and often occurs shortly after the client experiences a traumatic event (e.g., death of a family member, combat experience during war). The prognosis is better for clients with short-term reactive schizophrenic disorders than for those with lengthy process disorders, and counseling is likely to have a greater impact on the former group. Although some clients diagnosed in this category are showing the early signs of a process schizophrenia (leading to a later revision in diagnoses), others need only some short-term supportive and structured counseling to help them reorient their lives and overcome their symptoms (Reid, 1983). Here, too, a team approach is advised for diagnosis and treatment planning.

VII. Affective Disorders

Affective disorders, particularly depression, are the most common form of mental disorder among adults (Kaplan & Sadock, 1981). All of the diagnoses grouped under affective disorders are characterized by a disturbance in mood, with an accompanying manic or depressive syndrome. However, they vary with respect to the nature and severity of the mood change. This category is subdivided into *major affective disorders, other specific affective disorders,* and *atypical affective disorders.*

Major affective disorders include bipolar disorder and major depression. Bipolar disorders, formerly known as manic-depressive illnesses, involve vacillation between an extremely elevated or irritable mood and a normal or depressed mood. A major depression, either recurrent or single episode, involves a severe and pervasive mood change of at least 2 weeks' duration. Both of these disorders may be accompanied by psychotic features or melancholia (loss of pleasure in almost everything) indicated by the fifth digit of the code number for the disorder.

A manic syndrome is typically characterized by excessive euphoria, irritablility, hyperactivity, incoherence, grandiosity, distractibility, and mood change. Clients experiencing such a syndrome may sleep little, talk rapidly and persistently, and become intrusive and demanding of others. They may engage in excessive spending, an unusually high level of sexual activity, flamboyant dressing and makeup, and reckless driving *(DSM,* 1980). The syndrome appears suddenly and may last anywhere from a few days to several months.

A depressive syndrome, on the other hand, tends to be characterized by discouragement, sadness, loss of pleasure or interest in nearly everything, loss of energy, disturbances of sleep and appetite, low self-esteem, and indecisiveness. Thoughts of death or suicide often are present *(DSM,* 1980). Recurrences of bipolar disorders and major depressions are fairly common. Depression is more prevalent in women than in men.

Full syndromes of manic and depressive disorders have a considerable impact on clients' functioning. However, clients in a manic phase are often not aware of their need for treatment while those who are severely depressed may be too debilitated to seek treatment quickly. Consequently, friends or family often become involved in encouraging such clients to obtain help. Causes of major affective disorders vary and can be genetic or biochemical, can be situational, can result from individual or interpersonal traits, or can be linked to family background. Generally, the prognosis for these disorders is good. Clients suffering from a manic syndrome seem to respond well to treatment with drugs such as lithium, which can reduce the severity of recurrences as well as prevent them. Behavioral counseling and training in decision-making can also be helpful (Meyer, 1983). Depressive symptoms also are amenable to drug treatment (e.g., tricyclic antidepressants) as well as to electroconvulsive therapy (ECT) (Kaplan & Sadock, 1981).

Counselors, too, play an important role in the treatment of clients with severe manic or depressive syndromes. According to Kaplan and Sadock (1981), ". . .psychotherapy is absolutely central to the treatment of those patients suffering from depression or mania who seem to have psychological illness in addition to the physiological illness" (p. 371). Rapid intervention is indicated to relieve symptoms and prevent self-destructive behavior. Cognitive therapy, psychodynamic counseling, and behavioral counseling can be effective (Reid, 1983). Clients also may need help in improving social skills, dealing with stressful situations, and testing reality. Effectiveness of counseling is likely to be maximized if the client is not in a manic phase and is not undergoing ECT, which can cause temporary organic changes.

Other specific affective disorders include cyclothymic disorder (a milder version of the bipolar disorder) and dysthymic disorder (formerly, depressive neurosis), a milder form of major depression. This category diagnoses less-pervasive and disruptive disorders involving depressed or elated moods without psychotic features. However, their duration may be considerable, although it is often episodic. For example, a diagnosis of dysthymic disorder requires that symptoms have been present for at least 2 years. Disorders in this subcategory generally have less impact on the lives of those who experience them than do the major affective disorders. However, these, too, can be accompanied by prolonged unhappiness, suicidal thinking, and reduced levels of social and occupational functioning.

Hospitalization and medication are not often indicated for treatment of these disorders. Rather, counseling tends to be the primary mode of treatment (Kaplan & Sadock, 1981), especially with depressed clients. (Lithium is being studied as a treatment for cyclothymic disorders.) Several approaches to counseling have been found to be effective with clients diagnosed as having a dysthymic disorder: cognitive, interpersonal, behavioral, and psychodynamic counseling models have worked (Greist et al., 1982; Kaplan & Sadock, 1981; Reid, 1983). Clients with the disorder generally need help in handling stress, building self-esteem, taking control of their lives, and developing their interpersonal and coping skills. Group and family counseling also can enhance treatment effectiveness. A high percentage of counselors' caseloads are comprised of clients suffering from depression. Therefore, it is important for counselors to become knowledgeable about the diagnosis and treatment of depression.

VIII. Anxiety Disorders

Diagnoses under this category typically include symptoms such as motor tension, anxious and repetitive thinking, vigilance, and autonomic changes such as increased perspiration and heart rate. This category is divided into two subcategories: phobic disorders and anxiety states (including post-traumatic stress disorder).

A. *Phobic disorders* can take many forms such as agoraphobia (fear of public places), social phobia, fear of snakes, or fear of heights. Agoraphobia, which may keep people housebound for years, has been receiving considerable attention in the media.

All the phobias involve considerable unreasonable dread of a particular object or situation. The dread has an undesirable impact on the mood and life-style of the client while the client is seeking to avoid the feared situation. Behavioral counseling, using techniques such as desensitization, thought-stopping, and flooding has relieved the symptoms of clients suffering from phobias. Other forms of counseling, including psychodynamic and cognitive therapy and development of social and life management skills, also have been useful (Reid, 1983).

B. The second category of anxiety disorders, *anxiety states* (formerly anxiety neuroses), includes a variety of disorders in which there is prominent anxiety but where the activating event is less clear than it is in phobic disorders. This diagnostic category is further subdivided as follows:

1. Panic disorder—This is characterized by a series of apparently unpredictable anxiety attacks with accompanying physical changes (e.g., palpitations, sweating, faintness) and feelings of apprehension between attacks. This is a fairly common disorder.

2. Generalized anxiety disorder—Symptoms of anxiety, both physical and emotional, have persisted for at least 1 month. Client-centered counseling can be particularly helpful to clients with this disorder (Meyer, 1983).

3. Obsessive compulsive disorder—Clients experience recurrent, involuntary, uncomfortable thoughts or impulses (obsessions) or engage in apparently senseless repetitive behaviors or compulsions (e.g., frequent handwashing, avoiding cracks in sidewalks). These are distressing to the client and may impair functioning. Thought-stopping and paradoxical intention are specific interventions which have ameliorated these symptoms (Meyer, 1983).

4. Post-traumatic stress disorder—This diagnosis has been employed in recent years to characterize the emotional difficulties experienced by many veterans of the Vietnam War. Post-traumatic stress disorder is a maladaptive reaction to a traumatic event (e.g., flood, rape, accident) that involves re-experiencing the trauma in memory or dreams, withdrawing from daily experiences, and suffering symptoms of anxiety. Accompanying symptoms can be numerous and varied (e.g., hyperalertness, sleep disturbance, distractibility).

Counseling that is both supportive and insight-oriented has been found effective in treating anxiety states (Kaplan & Sadock, 1981). Counseling that involves discussion and clarification of fears, accompanied by strategies such as relaxation therapy, desensitization, covert conditioning, meditation, biofeedback, or stress management offers a good prognosis for clients with such disorders. Group counseling with clients who have experienced similar events can be helpful to those with post-traumatic stress disorder and has been used extensively with rape victims and Vietnam veterans.

IX. Somatoform Disorders

Somatoform disorders, similar to what once were called psychosomatic disorders, are diagnosed in clients who present a long history of physical symptoms (often many and varied) that seem to be linked to psychological factors. Since this diagnosis presumes that there is no organic basis to the physical complaints presented, counselors need to work with medical doctors in diagnosing and treating clients who seem to have somatoform disorders. Four subcategories of this disorder have been identified.

A. Somatization disorder.   This is characterized by a long history of numerous physical symptoms with no apparent physical causes.

B. Conversion disorder (formerly hysterical neurosis, conversion type).   This disorder is characterized by an involuntary loss of or impairment in physical functioning not explained by a physical disorder. Circumstances of the ailment suggest that psychological factors are the cause. Examples are blindness or paralysis of a limb without physical cause, which result in needed family attention being given to the client. The prevalence of this disorder seems to have declined markedly over the last 25 years.

C. Psychogenic pain disorder.   This is typified by severe and prolonged pain that seems to have a psychological rather than a physical etiology.

D. Hypochondriasis.   Clients with this disorder are unduly preoccupied with the possibility of illness and often attribute normal physical sensations to disease or illness.

Treatment of clients having somatoform disorders often is difficult; clients tend to be resistant and to emphasize physical rather than psychological factors (Kaplan & Sadock, 1981). However, a supportive and accepting counseling relationship can help clients find better ways to meet their needs, thereby reducing frequency, intensity, and persistence of physical complaints. A variety of counseling techniques has been used successfully with such clients, including behavioral counseling, hypnosis and suggestion, group and family counseling, information-giving (Greist et al., 1982), biofeedback, pain management, controlled medical treatment, and techniques to relieve accompanying anxiety and depression (Reid, 1983). Insight-oriented counseling generally has not been effective with such clients.

X. Dissociative Disorders

This category includes psychogenic amnesia, psychogenic fugue, multiple personality, and depersonalization disorder. Those diagnoses are characterized by a sudden change in the normal integration of consciousness, identity, and motor behavior. The symptoms generally are temporary and are not the result of organic causes. A common misconception is that clients with multiple personalities (e.g., the classic cases of Eve and Sybil) are suffering from schizophrenia. This is not the case, as can be seen by the placement of multiple personality under dissociative disorders. Schizophrenia involves considerable loss of contact with reality and poor functioning. Each of the personalities of an individual with a multiple personality is typically in reasonable contact with reality and functions satisfactorily. The difficulty is caused, of course, by the shifts in personality and the client's lack of awareness and control over that phenomenon.

Despite the attention they attract, dissociative disorders are relatively rare. Medical consultation and treatment by experienced practitioners is indicated for these disorders. However, counselors may participate as members of a treatment team.

Hypnosis, life review, cognitive and behavioral counseling, family counseling, and stress management in the context of a supportive counseling relationship have been effective in treating dissociative disorders (Greist et al., 1982).

XI. Psychosexual Disorders

Psychosexual disorders are subdivided into four categories: gender identity disorder, paraphilias, psychosexual dysfunctions, and other psychosexual disorders. These diagnoses describe individuals who have difficulty either in their sexual functioning or in their feelings about their sexual identity. Diagnoses in this category seem to allow a broad definition of normal sexual functioning. Paraphilias, for example, are only diagnosed when an unusual source of sexual arousal is *primary*. The diagnoses grouped under psychosexual dysfunctions seem particularly useful to counselors in that they provide a brief but clear and comprehensive overview of concerns related to sexual functioning.

The following outline lists the disorders included in this category with definitions provided when necessary.

A. Gender identity disorders

1. Transsexualism—sense of discomfort about own sex.
2. Gender identity disorder of childhood—rejection of own sex, desire to become a member of the opposite sex.

B. Paraphilias

1. Fetishism—use of objects (e.g., shoes) to achieve sexual excitement.
2. Transvestism—cross-dressing for sexual arousal.
3. Zoophilia—active or fantasized sexual activity with animals.
4. Pedophilia—active or fantasized sexual activity with children.
5. Exhibitionism.
6. Voyeurism.

7. Sexual masochism.
8. Sexual sadism.

C. *Psychosexual dysfunctions*

1. Inhibited sexual drive.
2. Inhibited sexual excitement.
3. Inhibited female orgasm.
4. Inhibited male orgasm.
5. Premature ejaculation.
6. Functional dispareunia—genital pain during intercourse without apparent physical cause.
7. Functional vaginismus—involuntary vaginal spasms when coitus is attempted.

D. *Other psychosexual disorders*

1. Ego-dystonic homosexuality—an unwanted and troubling pattern of homosexual arousal.
2. Psychosexual disorder not elsewhere classified.

Behavioral counseling, coupled with anxiety reduction, generally is the treatment of choice for psychosexual disorders (Kaplan, 1974). If the client has a frequent partner, couples counseling often is used. Support groups (e.g., for pre-orgasmic women or for men suffering impotence) can be useful. The counselor treating such clients should have expertise in sex therapy as well as in general counseling. A medical referral often is indicated to rule out a physical determinant of presenting concerns.

Prognosis for most psychosexual dysfunctions is excellent (Kaplan, 1974). However, clients with paraphilias and some of the other disorders tend to be resistant to treatment because their behavior is gratifying to them although perhaps not to their family or society.

XII. Factitious Disorders

Diagnoses under this category are characterized by the client's desire to be a patient. Symptoms presented may be physical, emotional, or a combination of the two. The symptoms often have a bizarre and unusual quality and reflect the clients' voluntary efforts to simulate and report concerns that will enable them to receive care and treatment. This disorder often is seen in prisons. Factitious disorders can be distinguished from somatoform disorders in that symptoms associated with the latter are not under the client's voluntary control. Factitious disorders differ from malingering in that the malingerer's goal generally is to avoid something, not simply to become a patient.

Treatment methods are not yet well-established for factitious disorders, a relatively rare condition. Reid (1983), however, recommended treatment of the underlying concerns and dynamics. Reality Therapy has also been recommended (Meyer, 1983). This disorder often emerges in response to a severe stressor and may remit spontaneously when the stressor no longer is present.

XIII. Disorders of Impulse Control Not Elsewhere Classified

This category of disorders includes pathological gambling, kleptomania, pyromania (recurrent fire setting), and explosive disorders (loss of control, resulting in aggressive and violent outbursts). These disorders are characterized by failure to resist the temptation to perform harmful acts and a buildup of tension that is released through the impulsive act. Although the act is not typically compulsive in nature and usually is consistent with the client's overall personality, the act generally is harmful to the self or to others and may lead the client to feel considerable remorse afterwards.

Clients in this category tend to be resistant to treatment. However, they may become involved in counseling because of legal or family pressure. Despite the difficulty in treating such clients, several treatment modalities have been used with some success. Both insight-oriented treatment and peer support groups (e.g., Gamblers Anonymous) have been effective, especially with clients engaging in excessive gambling. Behavior modification (e.g., aversion therapy) and environmental change also have produced desirable results. Biofeedback, exploration of accompanying feelings (e.g., rage, depression) and development of techniques of impulse control also can be useful. Because of the strong impact such disorders are likely to have on clients' families, family counseling often is part of the treatment plan (Kaplan & Sadock, 1981). Clients' social and occupational circumstances also may be adversely affected by this disorder and may require counseling intervention. Because of the potential danger inherent in these disorders, rapid and active intervention often is indicated to promote behavioral self-control.

XIV. Adjustment Disorders

Adjustment disorders are relatively minor maladaptive reactions to identifiable stressors in clients' lives. The disorders follow the stressor by no more than 3 months and may be accompanied by a broad range of symptoms including anxiety, depression, withdrawal, conduct disturbance, work or academic inhibition, social impairment, or a combination. Typically, the symptoms subside after the stressor has passed or been handled. Numerous subclassifications in this category facilitate the diagnosis of emotional and behavioral changes accompanying the adjustment disorder.

Clients who are having difficulty adjusting to life events such as unemployment, divorce, bereavement or academic failure comprise approximately 5 percent of mental health professionals' caseloads (Greist et al., 1983). Counselors can be highly effective with these clients by using a crisis-intervention model; clients are helped to use their own strengths and resources to cope with or adapt to immediate stressors. Counseling may combine supportive and interpretive elements, depending on the degree of emotional disruption that the client is experiencing. Counseling generally would focus on the present and would attend to both affective and environmental factors. Group or family counseling can supplement treatment and help develop clients' support systems (Reid, 1983). Although hospitalization or medication are rarely indicated for such clients, suicidal thinking or severe symptoms may be present. Most clients with adjustment disorders recover once the stressor has passed, but counseling can accelerate that process and help strengthen the client so that future challenges can be met more effectively (Greist et al., 1982).

XV. Psychological Factors Affecting Physical Conditions

This category describes a combination of physical and emotional conditions in which the physical disorder (coded on Axis III) is exacerbated by the emotional difficulty. Physical conditions often associated with emotional factors include obesity, ulcers, and asthma. As with somatoform disorders, collaboration between counselors and physicians is indicated in treating such clients. Counselors may teach relaxation skills or perform family therapy with clients while physicians treat the medical ailment. However, somatoform disorders can be distinguished from psychological factors affecting physical conditions in that in psychological factors affecting physical conditions there will be a medically diagnosed physical ailment; physical complaints of clients with somatoform disorders generally will not be verified by medical tests and examinations.

XVI. Personality Disorders

Personality disorders are pervasive patterns of maladaptive functioning that often are evident by adolescence. These typically cause some distress as well as impairment in social and occupational functioning. However, personality disorders typically are deeply ingrained, long-standing, and ego-syntonic. Consequently, clients with personality disorders may not be highly motivated toward treatment. Family, friends, and others may be more bothered by the behaviors and attitudes than are the clients themselves. The *DSM-III* lists 11 widely differing personality disorders. These have been divided into Group A, appearing odd or eccentric; Group B, emotional, histrionic, or unpredictable; and Group C, anxious and frightened.

Group A

1. *Paranoid personality disorder*—This is characterized by "unwarranted suspiciousness and mistrust of people, hypersensitivity, and restricted affectivity. . ." *(DSM, 1980, p. 307)*.
2. *Schizoid personality disorder*—This is a new diagnostic category, describing individuals who are emotionally dis-

tant, cold, and indifferent and who have no more than one or two close relationships.

3. *Schizotypal personality disorder*—Another new category, these individuals are not schizophrenic but tend to be superstitious, suspicious, isolated, anxious, and inadequate in social situations. They may have ideas of reference and a vague and confusing manner of speech.

Group B

1. *Histrionic personality disorder*—Individuals with this disorder generally are attention-seeking and emotionally excitable. They have high needs for activity and typically have disturbed interpersonal relationships. They often are perceived as superficial, self-centered, dependent, and manipulative.

2. *Narcissistic personality disorder*—This disorder describes individuals with an exaggerated sense of their own importance, pervasive thoughts of great success, a self-centered need for attention, and poor interpersonal relationships.

3. *Antisocial personality disorder*—Before age fifteen, individuals with this disorder begin a long history of antisocial behavior, violating the rights of others (e.g., lying, stealing, fighting, substance abuse). Irresponsibility and instability at work, in parenting, and in social relationships probably are evident.

4. *Borderline personality disorder*—Pervasive instability, evident in behavior, mood, relationships, and self-image, characterizes individuals with this disorder. Feelings of emptiness and self-damaging behavior often are noted.

Group C

1. *Avoidant personality disorder*—This typifies individuals who are low in self-esteem and fearful of rejection; consequently, they avoid social relationships despite a desire for closeness.

2. *Dependent personality disorder*—These individuals have little self-confidence and tend to give others responsibility for their lives. Their own needs are secondary and they generally defer to others.
3. *Compulsive personality disorder*—Clients diagnosed as having compulsive personality disorders tend to be perfectionistic, controlling, emotionally withholding, and indecisive. They often are absorbed with work and neglect personal relationships.
4. *Passive-aggressive personality disorder*—This disorder describes individuals who often express anger and resist demands in passive and indirect ways (e.g., forgetfulness, procrastination, tardiness), resulting in social and occupational difficulties.

Clients also may be diagnosed as having atypical, mixed, or other personality disorders. Another variation on this category is "personality traits," diagnosed when clients manifest significant characteristics of one of the personality disorders but either the pervasiveness or the breadth of the disorder is insufficient to warrant a diagnosis of a personality disorder. In such cases, these are listed on Axis II without the use of a code number (e.g., Narcissistic traits).

Treatment of personality disorders varies, of course, depending on the nature of the disorder. Extensive writing has been done in this area and is beyond the scope of this text. In general, however, treatment of personality disorders tends to be difficult because of client resistance and the long-standing nature of the disorder. Long-term therapy may be indicated if motivation can be maintained (Reid, 1983). A directive approach such as Reality Therapy with a warm, empathic, and genuine counselor has been recommended, with behavior being shaped through modeling and reinforcement (Greist et al., 1982). The social and occupational difficulties of these clients may call for interventions such as career counseling and the development of interpersonal skills. Family and group counseling can effectively supplement individual counseling. Client-centered counseling or medication usually are not helpful.

It should be borne in mind that personality disorders are

coded on Axis II and that their treatment may not be covered by health insurance since they are not viewed as "clinical psychiatric syndromes."

XVII. Conditions Not Attributable to a Mental Disorder

Conditions listed in this category are not due to a mental disorder. Diagnoses are indicated by a code number beginning with V, such as V65.20 Malingering. Many of these conditions reflect a client who is having difficulty with an external situation (e.g., occupational problem, uncomplicated bereavement) or with relationships (e.g., parent-child problem, marital problem). Because these conditions are, by definition, not the result of a mental illness, their treatment typically is not covered by health insurance. However, the conditions often respond to counseling, especially when it is supportive and directed at the present concerns. Information-giving and adjunct treatments (e.g., career counseling, communication skills) may be particularly helpful in relieving distress associated with these conditions (Greist, et al., 1982).

The concluding section of diagnoses in the *DSM* is entitled Additional Codes. These codes provide counselors a way to defer a diagnosis, to indicate that the mental disorder is unspecified due to lack of information, or to indicate that no mental disorders or diagnoses on Axes I or II are present.

DIAGNOSTIC DISCRIMINATION

Although the descriptions of mental disorders may sound clear on paper, the diagnosis of a disorder often is challenging and difficult. A number of guides and resources are available to facilitate the diagnostic process.

Differential Diagnosis

A section headed *Differential diagnosis* is contained in the descriptions of many of the diagnostic categories in the *DSM*. This section lists disorders that bear a resemblance to the one under consideration and highlights the difference among the disorders, in order to promote accurate diagnosis. For example, reviewed in the description of paranoid disorder are the differences between that disorder and organic delusional syndromes; schizophrenia, paranoid type; schizophreniform disorders; and paranoid personality disorders. Counselors can double-check the accuracy of their diagnoses by reviewing the descriptions of those similar disorders.

Atypical Disorders

Most of the major diagnostic categories contain a final category for atypical and mixed versions of that disorder (e.g., atypical somatoform disorder; atypical, mixed, or other personality disorders). Counselors should not use such diagnoses as catchalls or as excuses for not getting enough information; rather, they should try to make as precise a diagnosis as possible and should reserve use of these diagnostic categories for cases that genuinely and clearly differ from those described by the more specific diagnoses.

Decision Trees

The *DSM-III* contains seven decision trees. These are designed to facilitate the process of differential diagnosis and help the diagnostician to make fine diagnostic distinctions. These tools are provided for diagnosis of the following areas:

1. Psychotic features
2. Irrational anxiety and avoidance behavior
3. Mood disturbance (depressed, irritable, or expansive)
4. Antisocial, aggressive, defiant, or oppositional behavior
5. Physical complaints and irrational anxiety about physical illness
6. Academic or learning difficulties
7. Organic brain syndrome

The tree for the differential diagnosis of psychotic features, for example, helps the counselor determine which diagnostic category out of 16 possibilities is the correct one for a client suffering from "delusions, hallucinations, incoherence, marked loosening of association, poverty of content of thought, markedly illogical thinking, behavior that is bizarre, grossly disorganized or catatonic" *(DSM,* 1980, p. 340). The tree for the differential diagnosis of mood disturbance helps counselors to discriminate among major depression, dysthymic disorder, adjustment disorder with depressed mood, and other disorders involving depression.

The use of the decision trees is fairly clear and straightforward, needing no further explanation. Counselors are encouraged to spend some time familiarizing themselves with these useful tools as part of their efforts to understand the *DSM-III* and refine their diagnostic skills.

Supplements to the DSM-III

Several worthwhile resources have been developed to help the diagnostician to master the *DSM-III.* A companion volume to the *DSM-III* is the *Quick Reference to Diagnostic Criteria from DSM-III* (1980). This is a pocket-sized summary of the *DSM-III,* containing the salient features of each diagnostic category. It is an invaluable reference and facilitates diagnosis. Another useful book is the *DSM-III Training Guide* (Webb, DiClemente, Johnstone, Sanders, & Perley, 1981). Finally, the *DSM-III Case Book* (Spitzer, Skodol, Gibbon, & Williams, 1981) provides interesting and useful examples of clients with various disorders.

CASE EXAMPLES

The following brief cases are provided to offer readers an opportunity to practice their diagnostic skills. Cases should be considered in light of both the *DSM-III* and information provided in this chapter. Suggested primary diagnoses and the criteria used for arriving at each diagnosis are provided at the end of this chapter.

Case 1 — Milton

Milton, age sixty-seven, is married and has four children, all of whom live away from home. Milton is a retired accountant; he receives Social Security and a pension that provide him and his wife an adequate standard of living. He is in fair health but suffers from arthritis. Milton's wife Lucy recently had a stroke. Although she is at home, she is partially disabled and needs a great deal of help. She had focused her life on her role as wife and mother while Milton worked long hours to support the family. The couple attended church frequently but had few shared recreational activities and a limited social life.

During an initial interview, Milton complained of feeling unhappy and fearful. These feelings seemed to begin at his retirement the previous year and worsened with Lucy's stroke. Milton is particularly bothered by his feelings of anger toward Lucy. He reported that he used to be decisive and capable but has not been handling the recent changes in his life very well. There is no history of previous mental disorder.

Case 2 — Chuck

Chuck is a seventeen-year-old high school junior. He lives with his mother and twelve-year-old sister. His parents were divorced 3 years earlier. Chuck was referred for counseling after he was stopped by the police for speeding and he and the two friends with him were found to have marijuana in their possession. Chuck has been doing poorly in school for 2 years. He often is tardy and has many unexcused absences. On several occasions his mother has returned home from work unexpectedly to find Chuck at home playing pool and drinking beer with friends when he should have been in school. He has repeatedly violated curfews and lies to his mother about his whereabouts. His mother believes that Chuck's friends are a bad influence on him but he strongly defends his companions.

Case 3 — Jill

Jill, age thirty-four, was seen in couples counseling with her husband, Fred. Jill was a plump woman, dressed in a gypsylike red dress. She wore a great deal of jewelry that clanged when she waved her hands, something she did frequently. Jill recently had learned that her husband was having an affair with a co-worker and was thinking about ending their marriage. She responded by breaking a set of dishes and threatened to jump off a bridge if Fred left her. Jill acknowledged that she, too, had had affairs but said they didn't matter because she didn't care for the men and was only trying to relieve her boredom, whereas Fred really seemed to care for his new partner. Fred had difficulty making himself heard since Jill dominated the session but he did say that he was fed up with his wife's demanding and self-centered behavior and wouldn't be manipulated by another suicide threat.

Case 4 — Uta

Uta is an unattractive thirty-three-year-old single woman. She was born in Germany but has been living in the United States for 12 years since completing college. She was brought to counseling by her mother. For nearly a year, Uta has been expressing the belief that her mother is an imposter and that Uta is the daughter of Hitler. She believes she is constantly followed by both protectors and enemies who know her background. She also has heard Hitler talking to her and addressing her as his daughter.

Case 5 — Edwin

Edwin, a forty-nine-year-old male, sought counseling because, for the past few months, he has been feeling tense and irritable almost constantly. He found himself worrying about his social life, his job, and his health. Recent symptoms of trembling, heart pounding, and light-headedness led him to consult a physician but no physical cause was found for his complaints. The physician referred Edwin for counseling. Edwin has a long history of disturbances in his relationships with women and expressed the fear that he would never marry. There had been no unusual recent event in his life that seemed related to his presenting concerns.

Diagnoses

Case 1 — Milton

Diagnosis: 309.00 Adjustment disorder with depressed mood

Criteria:

1. Reaction is maladaptive
2. Results in impairment in functioning
3. Occurred in response to identifiable stressor (retirement, wife's stroke)
4. Not a worsening of a previous disorder
5. Symptoms of depression are evident
6. Duration of disorder does not justify diagnosis of dysthymic disorder

Case 2 — Chuck

Diagnosis: 312.21 Conduct disorder, socialized, nonaggressive

Criteria:

1. Persistent pattern of nonaggressive behavior that violates societal norms and rules (truancy, substance abuse, lying)
2. Social attachment and loyalty to friends; long friendships
3. Symptoms present more than 6 months

Case 3 — Jill

Diagnosis: 301.50 Histrionic personality disorder

Criteria:

1. Overly dramatic behavior, including craving for excitement, self-dramatization, and tantrums
2. Disturbed interpersonal relationships in which client is manipulative, demanding, and shallow

Case 4 — Uta

Diagnosis: 295.31 Schizophrenic disorder, paranoid type, sub-chronic

Criteria:

1. Grandiose delusions with persecutory content
2. Auditory hallucinations
3. Symptoms present for more than 6 months but less than 2 years

Case 5 — Edwin

Diagnosis: 300.02 Generalized anxiety disorder

Criteria:

1. Generalized persistent anxiety
2. Motor tension (trembling)
3. Autonomic hyperactivity (heart pounding, light-headedness)
4. Fear and worry
5. Symptoms present for more than 1 month

Chapter 3

THE USE OF ASSESSMENT IN DIAGNOSIS

THE ASSESSMENT PROCESS

"The meaning of diagnosis is 'to know' the client in terms of both internal and external perspectives" (Blocher & Biggs, 1983, p. 186).

Chapter 2 presented an approach to diagnosis that involved the determination and classification of clients' traits and symptoms, culminating in the naming or labeling of the clients' emotional disorders. Viewed in this way, the process of diagnosis can seem dehumanizing and destructive to the development of counselor-client rapport. However, as the quotation opening this chapter suggests, the process of diagnosis can be approached in a way that enables counselors to develop a good understanding of their clients and their environments and, through the process of assessment, formulate a diagnosis and treatment plan as well as enhance the counseling relationship.

Most clients are in pain and eager for help. Consequently, they generally respond well to a genuine and sensitive counselor who wants to get to know them better in order to help them. The assessment process should be a way of recognizing the importance and uniqueness of each client, a way of saying to the client, "You are special and I want to get to know you and understand why you are the way you are." This attitude can help clients feel optimistic and committed to the counseling process. The assessment process is, ideally, a collaboration between counselor and client in which both gain in knowledge and understanding while their working relationship is developed.

The assessment process can occur at several points in a counseling relationship. Some sort of assessment almost always will occur at the outset of the counseling process. Typically, an intake interview will be conducted, perhaps accompanied by psychological testing, so that an initial diagnosis and treatment plan can be developed. Chapter 4 discusses the intake process in detail.

Assessment also can occur during the middle stages of counseling. It can be occasioned by the counselor or client feeling that little progress is being made in counseling or that new issues and dynamics have come to light, calling for a reconceptualization of the original diagnosis and treatment plan. Such an assessment also can result from the client's health insurance company requesting a progress report and review (often done after the twelfth and fiftieth counseling sessions). The mental health agency where treatment is being provided also may mandate regular evaluations of client progress. Such mid-counseling assessments may be global, a way to provide an overview of the client's development and level of functioning, or they may be specific, seeking to clarify a particular aspect of the client's life (e.g., career development, intellectual ability, or level of assertiveness). Assessments also may be conducted toward the end of a counseling relationship as a way of measuring progress and determining the appropriateness of termination.

According to Shertzer and Linden (1979), there are four purposes of assessment: classification, evaluation, selection, and prediction. All four may be involved in diagnosis and treatment planning. Evaluation and classification generally are most important as the counselor seeks to explore the cognitive, behavioral, emotional, and interpersonal aspects of a client and classify the findings according to some framework (e.g., the *DSM*, developmental stages, or levels of intellectual ability). Assessment, as part of treatment planning, may be used to select appropriate clients for certain therapeutic programs (e.g., counseling groups, day treatment centers). Assessment as a means of making predictions about an individual client typically has modest reliability. However, predicting the likelihood of such events as a client's succeeding in a particular field or engaging in violent behavior can play an important part in treatment planning. This will be discussed further in this chapter.

Wolman (1976) specified four criteria of mental health, which may be explored during the assessment process.

1. ability to actualize physical and mental potential
2. ability to maintain an emotional balance and react in proportion to stimuli
3. maintenance of healthy cognitive functioning; having good contact with reality
4. effecting a positive social adjustment involving cooperation and friendly interaction.

The rest of this chapter, as well as chapter 4, will elaborate on the facets of the client to be explored and the tools and approaches for conducting the exploration.

TOOLS OF ASSESSMENT

Assessment tools can be categorized as qualitative or quantitative. Qualitative tools tend to be more subjective in nature; their interpretation, more ambiguous and challenging. They yield data of limited reliability and validity but provide important information that cannot be obtained in any other way. Quantitative tools, on the other hand, yield numerical data on clients, thereby facilitating comparison with other individuals and allowing for a clear measurement of change. Generally, both qualitative and quantitative approaches to assessment are used with a given client to provide a picture that has depth and richness as well as adequate reliability. Selection of the best approaches to the assessment of a particular client will be discussed later in this chapter.

Qualitative Approaches

Interviews probably are the most important qualitative approach to assessment. They are nearly always part of the process of diagnosis and treatment planning and tend to be the first method used to get acquainted and build rapport with a client. Sundberg (1977, p. 63) called interviews a "conversation with a purpose." The challenge for the counselor is to have a clear purpose in mind and conduct an interview that will achieve that purpose. However, interviews, as well as other forms of qualitative data, are prone to contamination from interviewer bias, client resistance, and other factors. Interviews are discussed further in chapter 4.

Observational data provide another source of qualitative information. Shertzer and Linden (1979) described three methods of observation:

1. *Systematic*—Client is observed during a predetermined period or event. For example, a student might be observed for the first 15 minutes of his English class every day in order to assess frequency of disruptive and cooperative behaviors. Frequently, systematic observation involves counting behaviors, making the observation a quantitative as well as a qualitative measure.

2. *Controlled*—Client is observed in a structured environment or situational test such as a leaderless group discussion.

3. *Informal*—Such observations are conducted in casual and unobtrusive ways. Data obtained typically will be anecdotal rather than numerical. Counselors might gather such data by observing a client in the waiting room, making a home visit to the client, or observing the client engaged in play.

Observations provide insight into clients' environments and can help counselors understand how clients behave outside of the counseling setting. In structuring observations and collecting observational data, however, damage may be done to the counseling relationship if deception of the client is involved. This should be considered when observations are planned.

Secondhand reports or observations are another source of qualitative data. These might be provided to counselors by clients' teachers, employers, friends, or family members as well as by other mental health professionals. Sometimes counselors will seek out such data. For example, counselors working with young children will almost always interview the parents and perhaps also the children's teachers. At other times, secondhand reports will be unsolicited and even unwelcome when they are offered. For example, the counselor may want to minimize contact with the overprotective parents of a twenty-five-year-old man who is trying to establish his independence. However, the parents may try to make contact with the counselor to share their perception of their son's difficulties. In interpreting and evaluating secondhand reports, counselors should take into account the possible bias and personal needs of the observer. Such sources can, however, provide important and otherwise unavailable material.

Autobiographies, written by clients, can be useful in providing information, especially in the case of clients who are not comfortable with discussion. Autobiographies also can be used to promote client self-exploration. Clients may be given little or no direction in writing the narrative (e.g., "Write an overview of your life in no more than 10 pages") or the client may be given guidelines or questions to direct the development of the autobiography. A comparison of interview and autobiographical data acquired on a client can be a fruitful source of information; the counselor can take note of similarities and differences in content, the items included, and the tone, emphasis, and organization. Errors and distortions may come to light as well as areas of consistency and repetition.

Products made by the client can be another valuable source of data as well as a way of promoting discussion with a quiet or hostile client. These might include drawings, poems, photographs, crafts projects, letters, homework assignments, songs, and other items that have importance to the client and reflect an investment of the client's time and energy. Discussion of the creation of these items and the meaning they have for the client can reveal much about the client's values, feelings, and abilities.

Time lines are yet another way of obtaining client data. A line can be drawn, representing the client's life to date as well as his or her future. Ages might be indicated on the time line to provide guidance. The client then can be asked to indicate on the time line developmental milestones or significant events, writing them next to the age at which they occurred. Projections also can be made of future happenings or realization of goals. Discussion of this information can give counselor and client a good sense of the client's history and objectives.

Unvalidated Quantitative Approaches

Unvalidated quantitative approaches to acquiring information yield some kind of number, score, or rating but do not have established validity and reliability. Consequently, such instruments do not allow predictions to be made with any confidence nor do they permit a meaningful comparison of one client to another. However, these approaches can be useful for measuring changes in the behavior or attitude of an individual, for clarifying areas needing further exploration, or for promoting discussion between client and counselor. These approaches may be commercially available, standardized questionnaires or they may be homemade and informal modes of gathering data.

Checklists, semantic differentials, and rating scales are common forms of standardized tools of assessment that often have limited or undetermined validity. However, they do provide a common frame of reference and a convenient method of obtaining data. Shertzer and Linden (1979) describe these approaches: "A behavioral continuum is defined as precisely as possible, and a rater is asked to evaluate and to allocate samples of the specified behavior either along an unbroken continuum or in ordered categories along the continuum" (p. 401).

The Mooney Problem Check Lists (Mooney & Gordon, 1950) are extensive lists of problems or difficulties likely to be experienced by certain age groups. These lists have content validity, but they lack construct and criterion-related validity. Counselors cannot, therefore, conclude that the client who checks 40 problems is more troubled than the client who checks 12 problems. The inventory does, however, provide counselors an estimate of how individuals feel about themselves and their lives at a particular time.

Like checklists, the *semantic differential* is a common format for inventories that may have only face or content validity. These typically consist of pairs of items placed on a bipolar, 7-point continuum, that can measure potency (strong–weak), activity (fast–slow), or quality (good–bad) (Shertzer & Linden, 1979). An example is:

Bad   1   2   3   4   5   6   7   Good

Clients indicate where on the scale they would place themselves or some aspect of their lives. Counselor-made semantic differential scales can be useful in assessing client self-images and attitudes. Several administrations of the same scales over time can provide some indication (albeit imprecise) of client change.

Numerical rating scales provide an alternate method for quantifying behavior. These typically consist of five to seven graduated descriptions for the rater's use. A common format describes frequency of behavior:

I am able to assert myself with authority figures

    5—almost always
    4—generally
    3—frequently
    2—sometimes
    1—rarely

This format often is used in unvalidated inventories that appear in popular magazines.

Rank-ordering is another approach to assessment. Clients are provided with a set of objects, activities, or events and are instructed to arrange them from high to low based on interest, preference, or another variable. For example, clients might be given a list of occupations to rank-order according to level of interest.

The Q-sort technique is a variation of rank ordering. The rater is presented with a set of cards containing descriptors, pictures, statements, or other stimuli and is asked to divide them into a predetermined number of stacks, according to their relative standing on a particular criterion (e.g., importance, applicability to the client). The number of cards to be sorted into each pile usually is specified.

All of the formats described in this section (checklists, semantic differentials, numerical rating scales, rank-orders, and Q-sorts) have been used for standardized inventories with high reliability and validity and for experimental, unstandardized, or counselor-made inventories used for exploration and discussion.

Another approach to quantifying information on client behavior involves gathering *base-line data* on a particular behavior and then determining change in frequency. For example, a child with a conduct disorder might be observed by her teacher in order to determine frequency of aggressive behavior (e.g., hitting other children, throwing objects) prior to counseling and again 3 months after counseling has begun. Although such measures have limited validity or reliability, they can provide a useful indicator of the nature and severity of clients' concerns and their response to treatment.

Counselor-made *questionnaires* also can be useful in gathering information. Most mental health agencies use questionnaires as a way of gathering demographic and introductory information on clients. However, counselors may want to supplement those with either general or individualized questionnaires on clients' concerns or on particular aspects of their development (e.g., marital adjustment, career development, social history). Providing written rather than oral responses can help some clients to lower their resistance and anxiety about the counseling process and can promote self-disclosure.

Validated Quantitative Approaches

Inventories that have been standardized and have been shown to have a satisfactory degree of validity and reliability can enhance the counseling process by providing an objective source of data, allowing comparison of the client with others, facilitating the uncertain process of prediction, and providing access to information that might otherwise be unavailable. The process of administering and interpreting standardized tests requires counselors to develop some relevant skills and knowledge. The counselor should become familiar with the types of tests that are available and should become comfortable using Buros' mental measurements yearbooks, *Tests in Print,* and other references designed to simplify test selection. Some knowledge of the statistical aspects of testing are needed when counselors evaluate the appropriateness and worth of a standardized inventory and when counselors are interpreting clients' inventoried scores. Counselors also should be informed on optimal procedures for test administration and should become accustomed to observing clients' test-taking behaviors, another source of information on their adjustment and attitudes.

Types of Inventories

Standardized and established inventories can be divided into three categories, depending on what they intend to measure: ability, interests, or personality. Although it is beyond the scope of this book to provide detailed information on specific tests or on the statistical aspects of test evaluation and interpretation, an overview of the categories of available inventories is provided to help counselors determine when testing is in order and what types of inventories might be most useful.

Measures of Ability

Ability tests measure a combination of innate abilities and learning acquired through formal and informal education. These tests can be threatening to some clients because they raise the possibility of poor performance; the impact of such instruments on the client-counselor relationship should, consequently, be considered carefully before they are administered. However, such tests can provide important information on clients' intellectual abilities and suitability for further education or career planning.

Achievement, intelligence, and aptitude tests are categorized as measures of ability. The three types of tests may appear indistinguishable, consisting of a series of questions or tasks with predetermined correct answers. However, the development, scoring systems, and normative samples of the inventories differ, enabling them to serve three different, though related, purposes (Seligman, 1980).

Achievement tests are designed to measure the previously attained degree of mastery or ability in a particular area. These tests generally are used to assess the impact of academic experiences, to indicate academic strengths and weaknesses, to provide an objective measure of learning, or to indicate the relative standing of a person's level of learning in a sample or normative group (class, school, nationwide sample).

Achievement tests typically are of limited interest to the counselor engaged in diagnosis and treatment planning. However, students' records may include achievement test data that will need to be understood and interpreted by the counselor. Increasing numbers of high schools are requiring satisfactory performance on proficiency or achievement tests as a prerequisite for graduation and counselors dealing with adolescent clients may consequently become involved in the process of assessing achievement. Also, counselors may make use of a broad-based achievement test such as the Wide Range Achievement Test (WRAT) as part of a test battery. The WRAT, which evaluates achievement in spelling, arithmetic, and reading, is a much-used inventory, designed to measure the basic academic skills of young people and adults.

Intelligence tests are more likely to become part of the diagnostician's repertoire. Group and individual tests of intelligence are available. The individual tests generally are more valid and informative as well as more time-consuming and complicated to administer. Counselors are qualified to administer group tests of intelligence such as the Otis-Lennon Mental Ability Test and the Culture Fair Intelligence Test, but few counselors have the specialized training needed to administer individual intelligence tests (e.g., the Stanford-Binet Intelligence Test, the Wechsler Intelligence Scale for Children, and the Wechsler Adult Intelligence Scale). Consequently, a referral often will need to be made to a psychologist when a highly reliable measure of a client's intellectual functioning must be obtained. This is most likely to occur when a diagnosis of mental retardation is suspected and needs to be confirmed or disconfirmed by an individual intelligence test.

Intelligence tests also might be used when it is suspected that a client's academic experiences have not provided an accurate reflection of his or her academic achievement (i.e., the client is an "underachiever") or when career counseling is part of the treatment plan. Under the latter circumstances, a group intelligence test, administered by the counselor, may well provide sufficient information.

Aptitude tests are designed to evaluate a person's potential for learning or profiting from a given educational experience or the probability of that person succeeding in a given occupation or course of study. Aptitudes are described as simple or complex. A simple aptitude such as clerical speed is readily defined and measured and bears an obvious relationship to success in certain clerical or secretarial occupations. A complex aptitude, on the other hand, tends to be difficult to define. An aptitude for law school is a complex aptitude, although a test has been developed to measure it (e.g., the Law School Aptitude Test). Aptitude test scores tend to be highly correlated with school grades and scores on other inventories of ability. Therefore, counselors often can infer information on clients' aptitudes without administering these inventories.

However, as with achievement tests, counselors may need to interpret aptitude test scores supplied with a client's record or may decide to include an inventory of aptitudes as part of a battery of tests administered to a client contemplating a career change or experiencing academic difficulties. Aptitude, as well as achievement and intelligence tests, also can be important aids in the diagnosis of specific developmental disorders.

Interest Inventories

Interests may be defined as constellations of likes and dislikes and are manifested through the activities people pursue, the objects they value, and their patterns of behavior (Seligman, 1980).

Information on client interests may be gathered through discussion (expressed interests), an examination of behaviors and activities (manifest interests), and scores on questionnaires (inventoried interests). Research has shown that interests often are the major determinant of educational and occupational choices (Scharf, 1970; Thomas, Merrill, & Miller, 1970) and that interest in one's occupation is significantly correlated with enjoyment of and persistence in that occupation (Super & Bohn, 1970; Zytowski, 1970).

A large variety of interest inventories are available. They range from self-administered and self-scored inventories (e.g., the Self-directed Search) to extensive questionnaires that provide a computer-scored measure of clients' interest in more than 200 occupational areas (the Strong-Campbell Interest Inventory). Although a great deal of information can be obtained from exploring clients' expressed and manifest interests, counselors involved in career assessment, leisure counseling, or preretirement counseling may seek to obtain additional information by administering interest inventories. These instruments, which have no right or wrong answers, typically are less threatening to clients than are tests of ability. However, scores on interest inventories, like their answers, tend to be less clear-cut and more difficult to interpret than those of ability tests. A high interest score in the occupation of musician, for example, should not be automatically interpreted to mean that the client should become a musician. Exploration is needed to determine the client's preparation for the field, the degree of congruence between the life-style of a musician and the client's preferred life-style, and what it is about that occupation that appeals to the client. Related occupations that involve music, creativity, and the experience of performing also should be explored as well as the option of satisfying the client's musical interest through leisure rather than occupational activities. Client-counselor dialogue, then, is critical to the effective interpretation of interest inventories.

Personality Inventories

Personality inventories may be global in scope and designed to provide an overall picture of a client's emotional style or they may be specific, focusing on particular aspects of personality (e.g., self-concept, career maturity, values, interpersonal skills, level of risk taking, or motivation). Measures of personality can be very helpful to counselors involved in diagnosis and treatment planning. The measures can provide a clear and well-organized picture of a client's personality, highlight strengths and weaknesses, and provide material the client may be unwilling or unable to provide.

Inventories of personality can be divided into projective and objective measures. Projective instruments have been described as, "A relatively unstructured personality test in which an examinee responds to materials such as ink blots, ambiguous pictures, and other objects by telling what he sees, making up stories, or constructing and arranging objects. Theoretically, since the material is fairly unstructured, whatever structure the examinee imposes on it will be a projection of his own personality" (Aiken, 1976, p. 328). The administration and interpretation of projective personality tests require specialized training and supervised experience. Such training generally is not a part of counselors' preparation and most counselors are therefore not qualified to do projective testing. However, it is important that they become familiar with projective tests since they may want to refer clients to psychologists for projective testing and often will receive client records and intake reports that contain an analysis of projective material.

Projective personality tests are intended to provide a global picture of clients' emotional makeup. It is believed that they can effectively bypass many of a client's defense mechanisms and reflect unconscious feelings and motives as well as pathology that may thus far have been controlled on the conscious level. Such tests can be particularly helpful in determining the presence of schizophrenic symptoms (e.g., thought disorders, ideas of reference, confusion). The most widely used projective personality tests are:

1. Rorschach Psychodiagnostic.   Developed by Hermann Rorschach in 1921, this test consists of 10 ink blots. Clients are asked to report what they see and where it is located on the blot. An analysis of the content, form, determinants, and quantity of clients' responses yields information on their wishes, attitudes, and perceptions of the world (Beck, 1961). This is the most widely used of the projective tests (Sundberg, 1977).

2. Thematic Apperception Test (TAT).   The TAT, developed by H. A. Murray, consists of 20 pictures (1935). Generally, clients will be shown 10 of them, selected by the examiner for relevance to the client's age, sex, and areas of concern. The client is asked to make up a story to explain each picture, provide information on what is happening, what led up to the scene in the picture, and what the outcome will be. The nature of the clients' responses, their underlying themes and degree of accuracy can be analyzed to provide information on the test-taker's needs, conflicts, relationships, experiences, and overall personality dynamics.

3. Sentence Completion.   Several varieties of this inventory have been developed, the best-known being that of J.B. Rotter (1946). Rotter's format consists of 40 sentence stems (e.g., I like . . .). The client is instructed to complete each stem with the first words that come to mind. In this way, data is provided on clients' concerns, feelings, and attitudes.

4. House-Tree-Person.   Clients are instructed to draw a house, a tree, and a whole person. Variations on this have been developed and studied, notably by Goodenough and Machover. Some examiners ask clients to draw only one human figure while others ask for drawings of both male and female figures. The drawings provide insights into clients' self-images and perceptions of their families as well as their overall emotional development and intelligence.

5. Bender Visual-Motor Gestalt Test.   Known as the Bender Gestalt, this is primarily a measure of visual-motor development and learning disability. However, it also has been widely used and studied as a projective personality test. The Bender Gestalt consists of nine designs (each on a separate card) that the client is asked to copy onto a blank sheet of paper. Analysis of the designs for accuracy, size, placement on the page, and other variables offers data on clients' interpersonal relationships, areas of concern, and emotional development (Bender, 1938).

A complete psychological assessment is likely to include most or all of the above inventories as well as an individual intelligence test. It also might include the Minnesota Multiphasic Personality Inventory, discussed in the next section. The ambiguity inherent in the interpretation of projective tests is reduced by giving the client several of these tests. The examiner can then base interpretations on recurring patterns and themes rather than on isolated responses and can produce a more detailed and reliable report.

Although counselors generally cannot administer and interpret the projective personality tests discussed here, there is a wide range of objective or standardized personality inventories that are available for use by counselors. These generally are paper and pencil tests in which clients respond to multiple-choice items. Scoring is standardized and numerical values, attached to predetermined aspects of personality, are provided when the test is scored. Little skill is involved in the adminstration and scoring of these inventories. However, their interpretation can require considerable skill and knowledge of behavior and personality.

Following are some of the well-established standardized personality tests that are available for counselor use:

1. *California Psychological Inventory (CPI).*   The CPI, developed by Gough (1969), is a broad-based, standardized test consisting of 480 true/false items, yielding scores on 18 scales. The scales are divided into four classes: measures of poise, ascendancy, self-assurance and interpersonal adequacy; measures of socialization, maturity, responsibility, and intrapersonal structuring of values; measures of achievement potential and intellectual efficiency; and measures of intellectual and interest modes (psychological-mindedness, flexibility, and femininity). Normative data available for the CPI are based on large and heterogeneous sample groups. The CPI is a well-regarded inventory, providing a comprehensive view of the adolescent or adult client's patterns of social interaction.

2. *Edwards Personal Preference Schedule (EPPS).*   The EPPS was developed to measure 15 normal personality variables (achievement, deference, order, exhibition, autonomy, affiliation,

intraception, succorance, dominance, abasement, nurturance, change, endurance, heterosexuality, aggression, and consistency). The EPPS, based on Murray's needs theory, consists of 200 pairs of items. Respondents choose the statement in each pair that they believe to be more descriptive of their personality. The EPPS does not have well-established validity but is a much-studied inventory that can provide insight into clients' motivation and behavior (Kline, 1975).

3. *Sixteen Personality—Factor Questionnaire (16 PF).* The 16 PF consists of 187 items, measuring 16 bipolar personality factors (reserved/outgoing, less intelligent/more intelligent, affected by feelings/emotionally stable, humble/assertive, sober/happy-go-lucky, expedient/conscientious, shy/venturesome, tough-minded/tender-minded, trusting/suspicious, practical/imaginative, forthright/shrewd, placid/apprehensive, conservative/experimenting, group-dependent/self-sufficient, casual/controlled, and relaxed/tense). A shorter version, form C, also measures motivation. Available in alternate forms as well as in forms to measure children's personality (the Children's Personality Questionnaire and the Early School Personality Questionnaire), the 16 PF is still being studied and developed. Although some questions have been raised about its documentation (Shertzer & Linden, 1979), it is gaining wide use in clinical evaluation and career and individual counseling.

4. *Minnesota Multiphasic Personality Inventory (MMPI).* Published in 1942, the MMPI is the most widely used and investigated of all personality questionnaires (Shertzer & Linden, 1979). Unlike the other inventories discussed in this section, it was designed specifically for use in the diagnosis and treatment of mental disorders. Consisting of 566 true-false items, the MMPI includes the following clinical scales: hypochondriasis, depression, hysteria, psychopathic deviate, masculinity-femininity, paranoia, psychothenia, schizophrenia, hypomania, and social introversion. Over 400 additional special scales have been developed, making the MMPI an extremely flexible and useful inventory. Its scoring and interpretation are complex, however, and require special training and experience. Its use by counselors is limited.

5. Myers-Briggs Type Indicator (MBTI).   The MBTI, based on Jungian personality theory, has been gaining increasing attention in recent years. It consists of 166 forced-choice items and provides scores on four bipolar continua: introversion/extroversion, sensing/intuition, thinking/feeling, and judgment/perception. Used with adolescents and adults and in general, career, and marital counseling, the MBTI can provide insights into clients' personalities. As with several of the other inventories, however, it is still being studied and considerable research is in progress on its theoretical and practical use.

As a general rule, standardized personality inventories are untimed, forced-choice questionnaires that require approximately 45–60 minutes of client time. Quite a few standardized personality tests with fairly well-established reliability and validity are available. None thus far has conclusively shown a high level of reliability and validity, however. Differences in theoretical orientation and content among inventories are apparent; consequently, counselors are encouraged to review many so they can select those that best suit the needs of their clients and are compatible with the counselors' own theoretical stances.

Other Types of Inventories

This section has focused primarily on broad-based tools of assessment, designed to provide information on an individual. However, many inventories that are outside this scope also are available. They include those designed to assess environment, marital or family dynamics, or the structure of a group. Tests also are available that focus on a particular aspect of a client's development. Reference books cited earlier, as well as catalogs published by test publishers, can help counselors select the most appropriate inventories.

PLANNING THE ASSESSMENT

The interview is the core of the process of diagnosis and treatment planning. Through an interview, counselors have an opportunity to observe and become acquainted with clients, to explore their concerns and histories, and to formulate diagnoses and treatment plans. Sometimes, however, the intake interview is not enough. There are many situations in which this might be the case: a client who has difficulty with self-expression, a hostile or resistant client, a confused or severely disturbed client, or a client presenting ill-defined or unusual symptoms. In such cases, testing may well be in order. However, testing can be threatening or arduous for the client and can damage the client-counselor relationship. Consequently, counselors should try to ensure that the assessment process is both effective and expeditious; testing should not be routine or gratuitous, but should only be used to answer questions or fill in important gaps that cannot be resolved in less obtrusive ways.

Some of the most important areas that can be elucidated by testing are:

1. self-image and self-esteem
2. degree and nature of motivation
3. intellectual and academic strengths and weaknesses
4. presence and extent of brain damage or learning disability
5. needs and values
6. patterns of interpersonal relationships
7. view of the world
8. mood
9. nature and degree of pathology
10. leisure and career interests
11. attitudes toward and relationships with significant others
12. likelihood of responding to particular modes of treatment
13. overall pattern of personal strengths and deficits.

Ideally, counselors should know the areas in which further information is needed before testing is begun. Especially if the client is to be referred to another mental health professional, counselors must clarify the reasons for the testing and communicate them as specifically as possible to the examiner. Providing the examiner with questions to answer seems particularly likely to yield the needed information. Precise questions, such as the following, are typical of those asked when clients are referred for testing:

1. Does this client need hospitalization or can she be treated on an outpatient basis?
2. What interpersonal patterns seem to be undermining this client's social relationships?
3. Can this client perform satisfactorily in a regular classroom or is a special placement in order?
4. Does this client seem to be a suitable candidate for group therapy?
5. What personal strengths can be developed to help this client through his current crisis?

Often, however, such specific questions cannot be formulated and a client will be referred for a general psychological assessment. In such cases, a battery of tests typically will be used, combined with a brief interview, in order to provide a comprehensive picture of the client. A battery of tests might be used even when specific questions are posed, since the answers to diagnostic questions such as the examples cited here can rarely be derived from the results of only one inventory. Rather, the answers will emerge from the nature and patterns of responses that a client gives to a number of inventories.

Some typical test batteries are:

1. Overall assessment conducted by a counselor
    a.   California Psychological Inventory
    b.   Tennessee Self-concept Scale
    c.   Otis-Lennon Mental Ability Test
    d.   Wide Range Achievement Test
2. Overall assessment conducted by a psychologist
    a.   Rorschach Test
    b.   Thematic Apperception Test
    c.   House-Tree-Person
    d.   Bender Gestalt
    e.   Wechsler Adult Intelligence Scale
3. Assessment of a client with career confusion
    a.   Strong-Campbell Interest Inventory

   b. Edwards Personal Preference Schedule
   c. Career Maturity Inventory
   d. Differential Aptitude Test
4. Assessment of a client with interpersonal concerns
   a. Myers-Briggs Type Indicator
   b. Sixteen Personality-factor Questionnaire
   c. Thematic Apperception Test (optional or if examiner is qualified)

In planning the testing process, the intake interviewer or case manager should provide the client with some general information on the purpose of the assessment, clarifying how it will benefit the client. Counselors can help assuage client anxiety about the testing process by providing details on the testing site, the length of the testing process, the nature of the tests to be administered, the name of the examiner, and what information (if any) the client can expect to receive from the testing.

FRAMEWORKS FOR ASSESSMENT

Once data has been gathered on a client, the counselor has the challenging task of organizing and analyzing the data. The organization and interpretation of the data generally can be facilitated by the use of frameworks. These are established standards or pervasive patterns that can be compared with the client's individual history and traits. Such a comparison can provide information on how patterns evidenced by the client in question do or do not coincide with pre-established patterns. This can lend structure and confidence to the counselor's interpretations.

Which framework to use depends on several factors—the orientation of the counselor, the nature of the client's difficulties, and the approaches to treating emotional difficulties espoused and offered by the agency where treatment is taking place. A variety of frameworks will be considered in this section. This list is by no means exhaustive and counselors should feel free to use alternate frameworks or develop individual frameworks that are helpful to them in assessing their clients.

Developmental

Perhaps the most basic frameworks for assessing clients are developmental ones. These come in many varieties and the counselor will need to decide which is most useful and relevant to a particular client. Because the frameworks are readily available in other sources, they will only be mentioned here.

Classic and well-established developmental frameworks are exemplified by those of Sigmund Freud (Brill, 1938) and Erik Erikson (1963). Such frameworks enable counselors to assess clients' psychosocial and psychosexual development, with particular emphasis on the early years.

More recent models of development facilitate analysis of the adult years and of periods of children's development. Spock (1964) and Fraiberg (1959), for example, offer well-established models for looking at children's physical and social maturation. Books and journals (e.g. *Child Development*) on later childhood and adolescence abound. The Brooks/Cole life-span human development series is a good basic example (Minuchin, 1977; White & Speisman, 1977). Adult development has been receiving considerable attention since the 1970s, with recent literature on the subject ranging from Sheehy's (1974) popular book *Passages* to the scholarly *Middle Age and Aging* (Neugarten, 1968).

Models also are available to help counselors assess special areas of development. For example, Super (1957) and Ginzberg (1972) have developed well-documented theories of career development. Havighurst (1972) described age-related tasks. Piaget (1948, 1969) provided guidelines for assessing the moral development of children as well as their growth in cognitive skills. *The Family Life Cycle* (Carter & McGoldrick, 1980) extended the concept of development beyond the individual and provided a framework for examining the growth and history of a family.

Social, Economic, Ethnic Frameworks

Another way to view clients is within the context of their social, economic, and ethnic backgrounds. This provides another norm or reference point with which clients' individual patterns can be compared. Literature is available to help counselors draw these comparisons (Atkinson, Morten, & Sue, 1983; Carter, Pearce, & Giardano, 1982; Stone & Shertzer, 1971). Most counselors probably also have fairly good awareness of common patterns of many ethnic and socioeconomic groups and can draw on their own knowledge in assessing their clients. Such information should be used with caution, however, and counselors should seek verification in the literature of any guidelines or patterns that they use for assessment of clients.

Psychological Aspects—General

Of particular importance to counselors and clients is the analysis of psychological variables, especially those that provide information on the short-term course of the client's disorders, the urgency of their situations, and their receptivity to counseling. Chapter 4 provides detailed information on the mental status examination that yields some of this information. Generally conducted (formally or informally) during the intake or initial interview, the mental status examination provides the counselor a structure for assessing a client's current level of emotional and intellectual functioning. Signs of psychosis such as delusions, hallucinations, incoherence, markedly peculiar behavior, or extremely inappropriate affect should be noted during the initial interview and should prompt the counselor to consult with a psychiatrist on the client's difficulties. Other psychological aspects requiring early assessment include the client's potential for suicidal or violent behavior and the client's system of defenses.

Psychological Aspects—Suicidal Behavior

Whenever clients express feelings of significant depression and discouragement or express thoughts of suicide, counselors should consider the clients' potential for self-destructive behavior. There are approximately 50,000 suicides annually in the United States (Wolman, 1976). Most of these are depressed clients who have given some warning of their intent (Lamson, 1978) and who might well have been prevented from committing suicide

Table 3-1

Rank-order of variable	Indicators of Suicidal Portential Content of item	Direction for suicide
1	Age	Older
2	Alcoholism	Yes
3	Irritation, rage, violence	No
4	Lethal prior behavior	Higher
5	Sex	Male
6	Accept help now	No
7	Duration of current episode	Longer
8	Prior inpatient psychiatric treatment	No
9	Recent loss or separation	No
10	Depression (somatic)	Yes
11	Loss of physical health	Less
12	Occupational level	Higher
13	Depression (affective)	No
14	Suicidal ideas repeatedly discarded	No
15	Family available	Less

by a combination of counseling and medication. Table 3-1 above enables counselors to identify clients who are high suicide risks (Litman, Farberow, Wold, & Brown, 1974, p. 141). The typical high-risk-for-suicide client is forty-five and over; male; divorced, widowed, or separated; and living alone. He chooses a highly lethal weapon (e.g., gun) (Kaplan & Sadock, 1981). Common behaviors of clients contemplating suicide include social withdrawal, giving away their important possessions, persistent insomnia, loss of appetite, a decline in occupational or academic performance, previous suicidal attempts, and feelings of hopelessness, failure, defeat, shame, and guilt (Walker, 1981).

As uncomfortable as it might seem, counselors suspecting suicidal thinking in a client should ask directly whether the client has contemplated suicide. This line of questioning is not likely to initiate thoughts of suicide if such thoughts have not been present already. Rather, the questioning should enable clients and counselors to accept and explore the clients' feelings and to take preventive measures.

A discussion of clients' suicidal thoughts should explore the following areas:

1. Duration of suicidal feelings—Generally, a suicidal crisis is relatively brief. It may last only a few hours, is most severe at its onset, and has usually passed within 6 weeks (Hipple & Cimbolic, 1979).
2. Nature of the plan, the availability of the means, and likelihood of rescue—Clients who have a clearly formulated plan for suicide, including the use of a lethal weapon that they possess, are high risks. For example, a client who plans to take a large quantity of aspirin sometime in the future is less worrisome than a client who intends to shoot him/herself with an available gun next weekend when the family is out of town.
3. History—Clients with suicide in their family backgrounds (especially suicides by their mothers) and a background of their own aborted suicide attempts are at high risk (Hipple & Cimbolic, 1979). Exploration of this information should help counselors avert future suicide attempts.
4. Mood—Feelings of anxiety, depression, hopelessness, and guilt have a strong association with suicide. However, clients in deep despair sometimes are too discouraged and debilitated to attempt suicide. It may not be until their mood begins to improve (just when the counselor thinks they are showing progress), that they have the energy to act on their suicidal thoughts (Walker, 1981). Counselors should, therefore, pay particularly close attention to clients with suicidal thoughts when their depressions begin to lift.
5. Motivation—Clients do have a reason for contemplating suicide, as irrational as that act may appear to outsiders. They may want to end their suffering, to punish others, to find peace in an afterlife, or may hope that a suicidal gesture will bring them attention and change in the behavior of others. Understanding the clients' motivations is important; through knowing what clients' needs are, counselors can help them find alternate routes to meeting those needs.

Although all suicidal thoughts and gestures should be taken seriously because of their potential lethality, people who are contemplating suicide almost always are conflicted or ambivalent (Lamson, 1978). No matter how discouraged they are, there is likely to be a part of them that wants to be helped. Counselors often can make contact with that part through a combination of empathy, hopefulness, and active intervention. A contract can be made in which the client promises not to commit suicide for a predetermined period. Hot lines, hospitalization, and other emergency resources can be made available to the client. Support systems and the client's own coping mechanisms can be strengthened through the counseling process.

Suicidal ideation, like psychosis, can be frightening to counselors. However, the assessment of suicide risk and prevention of suicide is a very important aspect of the counselors' roles as diagnosticians and treatment planners, drawing on their helping skills and their ability to take an active stance.

Psychological Aspects—Violence

Although it is relatively rare for clients to engage in actual acts of violence (Schoenfeld & Lehmann, 1981), counselors should be alert to the possibility that their clients might engage in physically harmful or destructive acts against others. The most important predictor of violent behavior is a past history of violence; history-taking is therefore of great importance whenever destructive or harmful behavior is suspected. Clients who are accident-prone and who drive recklessly also may be liable to engage in self-destructive or violent behavior. Violent clients are likely to be male, to make excessive use of drugs or alcohol, to have feelings of failure and low self-esteem, and to have both psychological and neurological difficulties. Psychotic disorders and paranoid disorders, in particular, often are associated with violent client behavior.

Detecting neurological disorders and referring clients for relevant testing are skills that should be possessed by all counselors, particularly those who are dealing with potentially violent clients. Although counselors generally are not trained to diagnose neurological impairment, they should watch for the following clues (Adams & Jenkins, 1981): visual or auditory hallucinations, difficulties in impulse control, memory disturbances, confusion, inability to learn new material, extremely concrete thinking patterns, reported visual field abnormalities, a history of head injury, prolonged alcohol or drug abuse, frequent headaches, seizures, or language disturbance. Especially when several of these disorders are noted in a client, counselors should request a psychiatric or neurological evaluation of that client.

Psychological Aspects—Defense Mechanisms

All people use defense mechanisms. Defense mechanisms are unconscious psychological processes that help people achieve some balance between their instinctual drives and the demands of reality. Defense mechanisms assist in coping with reality, in deferring gratification, and in meeting needs in socially acceptable ways.

A broad range of defense mechanisms have been identified. Individuals can be described by the types of defense mechanisms they are most likely to use. Their styles of defense, in turn, provide important information on the nature of their difficulties, the prognosis of their conditions, and their receptiveness to counseling.

Kaplan and Sadock (1983) developed a fourfold classification of defense mechanisms that can be useful to mental health professionals. It is listed below, with brief definitions provided:

Narcissistic defenses

1. Denial—refusing to acknowledge the presence of a situation or concern.
2. Distortion—extreme reshaping of external reality to meet inner needs.
3. Projection—attributing own characteristics or feelings (often persecutory) onto others.

Immature defenses

1. Acting out—direct expression of unconscious wishes or impulses, often in a socially unacceptable or aggressive way.

2.   Blocking—inhibition (usually temporary) of feelings, thoughts, or impulses.
3.   Hypochondriasis—transformation of negative feelings toward others into complaints of pain or illness that are exaggerated or have no physical basis.
4.   Introjection (or Identification)—internalization of characteristics of a loved or feared individual in order to reduce anxiety, increase closeness with that individual.
5.   Passive-aggressive behavior—indirect expression of anger and aggression.
6.   Projection (defined above).
7.   Regression—returning to an earlier situation or previous stage of development to avoid present or future anxieties or concerns.
8.   Schizoid fantasy—using fantasy and extreme withdrawal to avoid conflict.
9.   Somatization—converting impulses into sensory or neuromuscular symptoms.

Neurotic defenses

1.   Controlling—extreme attempts to manage or direct events, people, or objects in one's environment.
2.   Displacement—changing the object of an impulse, attitude, or feeling without changing the impulse, attitude, or feeling itself.
3.   Dissociation—temporary but extreme modification of self or personal identity to avoid stress (e.g., fugue states).
4.   Externalization—perceiving aspects of one's own personality in the environment and in external objects.
5.   Inhibition—limiting or renouncing specific ego functions (e.g., overt sexual involvement) to avoid conflict and anxiety.
6.   Intellectualization—controlling feelings and impulses by thinking about them and analyzing them rather than by experiencing them.
7.   Isolation—intrapsychic splitting of emotion from content and experience, leading to repression or displacement.

8. Rationalization—justification of attitudes or behaviors by selecting the most favorable motives or reasons and ignoring others.
9. Reaction formation (or Overcompensation)—managing unacceptable impulses or feelings by expressing their opposites.
10. Repression—excluding thoughts, impulses, feelings, and events from consciousness.
11. Sexualization—attributing unwarranted sexual significance to an object or activity to ward off anxiety connected with unacceptable impulses.
12. Somatization (defined above).

Mature defenses

1. Altruism—constructive and gratifying service to others.
2. Anticipation—realistic planning to deal with future anxiety and inner distress.
3. Asceticism—engaging in a gratifying moral rejection of most sources of pleasure.
4. Humor—using wit and humor to make uncomfortable feelings more tolerable.
5. Sublimation—modification of unacceptable urges into acceptable ones by changing the object or vehicle of expression (e.g., sexual tension may be discharged through sports).
6. Suppression—conscious or semiconscious postponement of gratification of an impulse.

Clients engaging in immature, narcissistic, or neurotic defenses are more likely to be seen in counseling than are those using predominantly mature defenses. With all clients, analysis of the nature of their defense mechanisms can facilitate understanding of client dynamics and can contribute to their increased use of mature defense mechanisms.

INDIVIDUAL FRAMEWORKS

Sundberg (1977) suggested that there were three ways of thinking about a person's characteristics: types, traits, and transactions. Types can be determined through the diagnostic process, by applying the *DSM-III* or other diagnostic system to the client's history and presentation. Traits, as defined by Sundberg, are characteristics of the client that are assessed through comparison with others. These have been considered from many perspectives in the preceeding sections of this chapter.

Gathering information on transactions involves looking at clients in the context of their environments and examining their interactions with people, objects, and events in their environments. This perspective, especially when approached in a longitudinal fashion, allows clients to provide their own frameworks for analysis. Counselors can then define typical patterns of response and behavior that characterize particular clients and can take note of changes in typical patterns. Characteristics of clients and their environmental systems also can be compared, for example, by looking at objective pressures and norms within the social system and clients' responses to them. Once the counselor has a sense of the client's history and repeated patterns, prediction of future patterns is possible. Patterns and longitudinal trends typically provide more reliable and important information about clients than do acute episodes or isolated pieces of information (Shertzer & Linden, 1979). Consideration of types, traits, and transactions, then, is important in gaining a complete and reasonably accurate picture of clients and in minimizing the likelihood of unjustified labeling or the drawing of unsubstantiated and unwarranted conclusions.

PROCESS OF ANALYSIS

Analyzing and interpreting the data gathered on a client probably is the most challenging and the most creative part of diagnosis and treatment planning. The process involves developing hypotheses about the significance and importance of the data in order to provide insight into the client. Sundberg (1977) defined assessment as ". . . the set of processes used . . . for developing impressions and images, making decisions, and checking hypotheses about another person's pattern of characteristics which determine his/her behavior in interaction with the environment" (pp. 21–22). This definition captures the scope of the analytic process and the way in which it draws on a broad range of counselor abilities.

Key Questions

Assume that an intake interview has been conducted and that data from that interview are available on tape, in the counselor's notes, and in the counselor's memory. The counselor can begin the process of analysis by asking the following questions about the data:

1. What underlying themes or repeated issues were present during the interview? These may be obvious, such as a client's repeated negative references to men (e.g., a demanding and critical father, an abusive first husband, an alcoholic second husband, and a temperamental male supervisor). Often, however, these patterns are more subtle. For example, the client may describe a recent car accident, a forgotten appointment, a series of errors at work, and a failed dinner party. Such clients may be prone to self-destructive behavior or may be so confused and anxious they feel overwhelmed and out of control.

2. What items or issues were given greatest importance by the client? Counselors tend to focus on certain aspects of a client's narrative that they believe to be of particular relevance in characterizing the client. These might include the client's family situation, thought processes, or previous emotional difficulties. While this process of selective attending and exploring is sound and provides the counselor a structure for information-gathering, it also is important that the counselor step into the client's shoes and determine what the client perceives as important. The client, for example, may talk at length about home repair projects. The counselor should take note of this and try to determine what the projects mean to the client. Do they represent a constant source of stress, a gratification, or do they represent the client's feeling that all aspects of life, the house included, are falling apart?

3. What unusual pieces of information, reactions, or thoughts are presented by the client? An old newspaper adage was that if a dog bites a man, it is not news but if a man bites a dog, it is news. The same principle holds true for interpretation of client

data. If the client simply reports that he owns a dog, that piece of information might not be worth mentioning in the intake report. If, however, the client talks at length about her five dogs, 14 cats, six gerbils, and pet hyena and states that she wishes she didn't have to work full-time so that she could provide her animals with her companionship, this certainly is noteworthy and should be explored to determine what has motivated the client to become so absorbed with her animals.

4. What omissions or abbreviations appeared in the client's presentation? In reviewing the tape of an intake interview, the counselor may note that a particular client said almost nothing about her mother, although she talked extensively about her father. Another client may talk easily about his sports activities but say little about his job. Counselors should attend to these omissions and, if possible, explore them with the client. However, the client may resist discussing these subjects or the omissions may not be noted until after the client has left. This might make analysis of the omissions difficult and the counselor should be cautious about premature interpretations. One cannot be sure, for example, whether the client said little about her mother because the two have a conflicted relationship or because that relationship is comfortable and the client wanted to spend her time on areas in which she needed help. However, significant omissions should be noted in the intake report as areas needing further exploration or, if substantiating information is available, as highly charged or conflicted areas for the client.

5. How does a given piece of data fit in with the client and his or her environment? Interpretations should rarely be made on the basis of a single piece of information. Rather, the counselor should seek to develop a comprehensive and coherent picture of the client that integrates and makes sense of the presented data.

6. What frameworks help make sense of this data? A previous section of this chapter discussed frameworks for analysis. Counselors may consider the frameworks described there to determine which ones seem to fit the client's data or are relevant to the client's major concerns. Those frameworks then could be used to enhance the process of interpretation.

Guidelines for Interpretation

Perhaps the biggest pitfall of the process of interpretation is the counselor becoming judgmental. While the counselor should not just report the facts, those interpretations that are made should not condemn, criticize, or stigmatize the client; they should be well-substantiated; and they should generally be cautious and tentative in nature. It is preferable to talk in terms of possibilities and likelihoods rather than absolutes.

The following are four hypothetical reports by counselors, offering their analyses of the same situation, the first few minutes of a counseling session with Joan B. and her four-year-old son Kevin. The four analyses are quite different and represent distinct approaches to the process of report writing:

Example 1

Joan B. and her four-year-old son Kevin arrived for their appointment approximately 15 minutes late. They walked in and Ms. B. took the chair by the desk, pointing out some toys in the corner for Kevin to play with. While Ms. B. and I began to talk, Kevin raced around the room, waving a toy airplane, and simulating airplane noises. He then climbed on and off Ms. B's lap several times, knocking her purse to the floor. When his mother told him to be quiet while we spoke, Kevin returned to the toys and began noisily pounding blocks against each other. Ms. B. ignored this behavior.

Example 2

Joan B. and her four-year-old son Kevin arrived for their appointment approximately 15 minutes late. Ms. B. seemed oblivious to the fact that she had kept me waiting. Ms. B. took the chair by the desk and encouraged Kevin to play with some toys in the corner. Unfortunately, he chose to play with the toy plane and became quite noisy and irritating as he raced around the room, making airplane noises. Kevin then climbed on and off his mother's lap several times, knocking her purse to the floor.

Ms. B. was ineffective in her efforts to quiet Kevin and seems unaware of how to control her child's behavior. Kevin continued to make a nuisance of himself by noisily pounding blocks against each other.

Example 3

Joan B. and her four-year-old son Kevin arrived for their appointment approximately 15 minutes late, suggesting Ms. B.'s resistance to the counseling process. Ms. B. attempted to assert her control over her son by taking the chair by the desk and telling him to play with the toys in the corner. Kevin chose to play with a toy airplane, and raced around the room with the plane, simulating airplane noises. His selection of the plane seemed to represent an effort to assert his masculinity and to defy maternal control. When ignored by his mother, however, the Oedipal needs typical of his age group emerged and he approached his mother in a rather seductive way, climbing on and off her lap. Still not receiving the affection and attention he craved, Kevin knocked Ms. B.'s purse from her lap in an apparent passive-aggressive gesture. At this point, his mother tried to quiet him, but her weak ego strength and apparent fear of her son got in the way, and she was ineffective. Kevin then expressed his anger and frustration with his mother's vague and ambivalent responses to him by noisily pounding blocks against each other.

Example 4

Joan B. and her four-year-old son Kevin arrived for their appointment approximately 15 minutes late. Ms. B. did not seem aware that they were late. She took the chair by the desk and told Kevin to play with the toys in the corner. Kevin selected a toy airplane and ran around the room with the plane, simulating airplane noises. He kept glancing at his mother, as though wanting something from her, either control or attention. Ms. B. did not respond to Kevin, but seemed to focus on our conversation. Apparently losing interest in the plane, Kevin put it aside and began to climb on and off his mother's lap. This seemed further indication of his wish for her attention. Only when Kevin knocked her purse from her lap did Ms. B. tell him, in an almost fearful voice, that he should be quiet. She seemed reluctant to exert control over him until he manifested behavior which could not be ignored. When she did attempt to modify Kevin's behavior, she seemed uncomfortable and ineffective. Kevin then began noisily banging blocks against each other, apparently ignoring his mother's direction and continuing his pattern of seeking her attention through acting-out behaviors. Although Kevin is at the age when his mother's attention typically becomes very important, especially for boys, he seems unusually active for a four year-old and does not seem to be meeting his needs consistently through his interactions with his mother.

Discussion

These four examples illustrate a number of both desirable and destructive approaches to analysis of client information. While none of them is perfect, it can readily be seen that some are both more useful to the counselor and more helpful to the client.

In example 1, the counselor is presenting little more than a factual description of the scene. He is performing almost the same role as a tape recorder or video camera. While there is little in example 1 that could be viewed as damaging or inaccurate, the data is not organized in a meaningful way and is not used to provide insight into the dynamics of Ms. B., her son, and their relationship.

The counselor in example 2 loses too much of his objectivity and communicates a negative and judgmental picture of the clients. Words such as "oblivious," "unfortunately," "irritating," "ineffective," and "nuisance" are inappropriate as used here. This counselor seems more concerned with his own rights and feelings than he is with understanding the clients. Consequently, not only is this analysis inappropriately pejorative, it fails in its effort to provide understanding of these clients.

Although the analysis presented in example 3 is thought-provoking and may even be accurate, this counselor is overinterpreting the limited amount of information available and is leaping to premature conclusions. The author has used a psychoanalytic framework to make sense of the experience and the use of that structure does provide coherence to the interpretation. However, the counselor seems to be forcing the observations to conform to that framework. Conclusions are drawn in absolute terms, based on isolated incidents rather than trends or patterns, and motivations are inferred with little justification. Descriptions such as "assert his masculinity," "defy maternal control," "passive-aggressive," and "weak ego strength" might be justifiable after lengthy data-gathering and observation of these clients, but are inappropriate, based on this small sample of behavior. Such interpretations might be very useful to the counselor during the process of diagnosis and treatment planning, but only if they are well-substantiated and their accuracy more certain.

Example 4 seems to be the best of the four. The counselor remains relatively objective, makes use of a developmental framework to assess Kevin's behavior, is tentative in the conclusions drawn, yet does provide some understanding of these clients and their interactions. Emphasis is placed on observable behaviors rather than motivations that can only be surmised. Efforts have been made to substantiate all interpretations by describing the observations that justified them. This example is useful to both counselor and clients in that areas needing further exploration emerge clearly, working hypotheses for interpreting the dynamics of this situation are presented, and the clients are described in such a way as to increase empathy and insight.

Clearly, the process of interpretation can be a challenge. Some counselors are most comfortable with the noninterpretive stance assumed by the counselor in example 1, while others feel that they should try to make the sort of rapid interpretations presented in example 3. Both of these approaches do a disservice to clients and do not make good use of the special skills of counselors: their knowledge of human development and behavior, their empathy and sensitivity, their insight into clients, and their understanding of human relations. By drawing on these skills during the process of interpretation, counselors can facilitate diagnosis and treatment planning and can present their clients as full human beings who seem to come alive and whose lives and experiences have coherence and importance.

The next chapter contains information on the process of gathering information through an intake interview. It also includes the transcript of an interview and an accompanying analysis that should provide further clarification of many of the points presented in this chapter.

Chapter 4

INTAKE INTERVIEWS AND THEIR ROLE IN DIAGNOSIS AND TREATMENT PLANNING

Nature of the Intake Interview

Purpose

In most mental health agencies, clients are seen for an intake interview before treatment is begun. These interviews generally are designed to serve the following purposes:

1. Determining suitability of client for agency's services.
Generally, clients or their referral sources are knowledgeable enough about the range of mental health services that they present themselves for treatment at the sort of agency that can meet their needs. Occasionally, however, clients seek or need a particular service that is not provided by the person or agency they have consulted. For example, a severely disturbed man may present himself at an agency specializing in career counseling or a woman seeking abortion information may seek assistance from a religious-affiliated agency that does not provide such information. In cases such as these, the counselor should advise the client of the unsuitability of the agency and make a referral as discussed in chapter 6.

Sometimes clients request a specific form of treatment (e.g., biofeedback, assertiveness training) not available at an agency. Upon hearing such a request, the counselor should not immediately stop the interview and discuss a referral. Rather, the nature of the client's request should be explored to be sure the requested treatment modality is well-understood by the client and seems to be a sound method of treatment for him or her. Only then should a referral be considered.

2. Assess and respond to urgency of client's situation.

A client in a crisis situation, perhaps having suicidal thoughts following a marital breakup, generally should receive help as soon as possible. Similarly, a severely disturbed client, perhaps one who is actively hallucinating or spending money wildly during a manic episode, also needs immediate attention. One goal of the intake process is to assess the urgency of the client's situation and, if immediate intervention is warranted, to see that it is provided.

3. Familiarize client with agency and counseling process.

Many clients are apprehensive and unsophisticated about counseling. Presenting themselves for counseling may be viewed as an admission that something is wrong with them. Fantasies of the counseling process recently expressed to me by new clients included "having to lie on a couch and dredge up unpleasant dreams and memories," being hypnotized and "forced to tell the truth" about themselves, and being given electroconvulsive therapy.

Clients' preconceptions of the counseling process should be aired and any fears or distortions alleviated by a clear, concise description of the counseling process. Clients also should be informed of any relevant agency policies such as scheduling, fees, confidentiality, presence of a waiting list, and additional screening procedures. Clients also should be given some information on what will happen next in the treatment process.

4. Begin to engender positive client attitudes toward counseling.

Part of the process of helping clients to feel comfortable with the agency and its procedures is the development of some positive counselor-client rapport and the communication of a sense of optimism. Even clients who will not see the intake interviewer again should leave that interview with a sense of having gained something from the interview, of having been heard, and of hopefulness that counseling will help them. The intake interviewer, as a representative of the counseling agency, plays a key role in determining whether clients will return for counseling and whether they will be ready to make a commitment to counseling.

5. *Gather sufficient information on presenting problem, history, and dynamics to allow formulation of diagnosis and treatment plan.*

The focal task of the intake interview is to gather enough information on the client to allow the formulation of at least a provisional diagnosis and treatment plan. Although most agencies have a recommended procedure for inquiring about client data and a form on which intake workers are to write a summary and interpretation of the data they have received, it is the responsibility of the intake interviewer to determine what information is needed, to attempt to obtain it from the client, and to terminate the interview when appropriate.

Process

Clients come in for initial or intake interviews in a variety of ways, depending on the individual client and on the nature of the agency and its procedures. Clients may be voluntary or reluctant, motivated or hostile. More wil be said about interviewing challenging clients in the next section. Intake workers generally have little background or preparatory information on the clients they will be seeing for an interview and so must be flexible, resourceful, and experienced enough to handle a broad range of clients. Often, new workers at an agency conduct most of the intake interviews as a way of filling their time, building up a caseload of clients, and freeing more established counselors to spend more time on treatment. This should not be interpreted to mean that conducting intake interviews is easier than counseling. Rather, the intake interview often is more challenging and demanding than a typical counseling session because it involves dealing with an unknown client who may not be familiar or comfortable with counseling.

At some agencies, appointments for intake interviews are scheduled. At other agencies, however, intake workers cover predetermined blocks of time. For example, a worker may interview any new clients who present themselves on Mondays between 9 a.m. and 1 p.m. That enables an agency to provide immediate service to clients, but can be more taxing for the counselor who may see no clients one week and five on another week.

Generally, the duration of an intake interview is more flexible and variable than that of the counseling session, traditionally 45 or 50 minutes long. Intake interviews often are as brief as 20 to 30 minutes or as long as 2 hours, depending on the nature of the client, the schedule of the counselor, and the depth of material that is produced by the client and desired by the counselor. Sometimes, intake interviews extend over more than one session or may involve more than one interviewer. The original interviewer may, for example, refer the client to a psychiatrist for a medical evaluation or to a psychologist for an intelligence test.

There are many ways to begin an intake interview. Some mental health workers start with an ice-breaker or a series of social amenities: "How's the weather out there? . . . Did you have any trouble finding a parking place? . . . It's nice to see you today." Others go to an opposite extreme and begin with, "Tell me what your problems are." Most authorities agree that the social approach is counter-productive because it does not set the proper tone for a counseling interview, can mislead the client as to the nature of the counselor-client relationship, and can increase clients' anxiety since they have come to see an expert, not a friend. On the other hand, what might be called the problem-oriented approach may clash with clients' perceptions of why they are seeking counseling and may promote resistance if they are reluctant to see themselves as having "problems." A compromise approach that is professional, businesslike, and relatively nonthreatening is to open the interview with something such as, "What brings you in today?" or "What sorts of things were you looking for help with?"

Once the counselor-client dialogue is under way and some idea of the client's presenting problem has been obtained, the counselor usually should orient the client to the purpose, nature, and duration of the intake interview. If the intake counselor is not necessarily the counselor who will be treating the client, this should be stated, lest the client feel misled.

After establishing the ground rules for the intake process, the counselor typically will then spend most of the interview further exploring the client's presenting concerns, gathering information on history and life circumstances, and gaining insight into the dynamics of the client. Detailed information on categories of inquiry and aspects of analysis encompassed by an intake interview are provided later in this chapter.

Techniques used by the interviewer will not differ radically from techniques used in a counseling session: open and closed questions, reflection of feeling, restatement, minimal encouragers, interpretation, and summarization are likely to be the primary modes of intervention. However, the percentage of each type of intervention used in intake interviews probably will differ from its percentage of use in counseling sessions. Counselors typically take greater control of intake sessions than they do of counseling sessions, so they tend to be relatively directive and intervene fairly frequently. More questioning probably will be done than in a counseling session because information gathering is under way. Since clients generally will not be familiar with the counseling process, interviewers select interventions that seem likely to elicit meaningful client input. Open questions seem to be the best tool for accomplishing this. (Open questions are those that call for more than a very brief response.) For example, the intake interviewer might ask, "How do you feel about your work?" rather than "Do you like your work?" It might seem that reflection of feeling and interpretation would have little place in an intake interview and, in fact, those modes of intervention probably would be used less in an intake interview than in a counseling session. However, those techniques are important in giving clients the sense that they are heard and understood by someone who has something to offer them, so those approaches should not be shirked by the intake interviewer. Neither should the interviewer avoid asking questions about areas that seem very personal, such as inquiries about hallucinations, suicidal ideation, sexual activity, and financial circumstances. Most clients expect such questions and will respond openly to direct and clear questions such as, "Have you thought about hurting or killing yourself lately?" or "Do you ever see or hear things that seem strange or that other people do not see or hear?" While beginning counselors, in particular, may feel they are violating societal conventions by asking such questions, they should bear in mind the difference between counseling and socializing. Most clients are relieved to have these difficult areas discussed in an open and nonjudgmental fashion.

Because a great deal of information probably will be gathered in a fairly short time, most intake interviewers use either note-taking or tape-recording to assist their recall. There are pros and cons to both approaches.

The client's permission must be obtained before a session is recorded. Although few clients object to being taped, this can be viewed as an intrusion into the counseling process and makes some clients uneasy, despite assurances of confidentiality. It also will take as long to review a tape recording as it will for the counselor to conduct the intake interview. However, taping has the important advantage of preserving the intake interview without distortion. Also, once the mechanics of discussing and starting the recorder are past, most clients become oblivious to the recording. During the session, then, it is less obtrusive than note-taking.

Note-taking generally is less threatening to clients and requires little or no discussion in most cases. However, it has several important disadvantages. Note-taking prevents most counselors from giving clients their full attention. Notes will almost inevitably be incomplete, possibly leading to significant omissions or distortions. Also, clients are sometimes distracted by note-taking and may attribute significance to the instances of note-taking, perhaps even focusing more on topics that seem to precipitate note-taking.

Most counselors have become familiar with tape-recording counseling sessions as part of their training and are not uncomfortable with the process. Whether to tape or take notes is an individual decision, however, determined by counselor-preference and the nature of an individual client.

Since the intake interview may not be of predetermined length, it is incumbent upon the interviewer to decide when it is time to end the interview and to inform the client that termination of the interview is imminent. The counselor should do this in a positive way and should allow at least a few minutes for client additions and questions. A typical closing interaction might be:

Counselor: You've certainly told me a great deal about yourself. I think I have the information I need to move ahead on planning your counseling. Is there anything you'd like to add to what we've talked about?

Client: No, I don't think so.

Counselor: All right. Let me fill you in on just what will happen now and how long that will take. There will also be some time for you to ask any questions you might have before we wrap up for today.

The interview would then end, with the counselor being sure to inform the client about the steps for arranging for treatment and the timetable to be followed if there will be a delay. The counselor also should be sure that the client is familiar with any procedures to be followed before leaving the agency (e.g., paying the bill, completing forms, scheduling another appointment).

TYPES OF INTAKE INTERVIEWS

Nearly all agencies and mental health practitioners in private practice make use of an intake procedure. It serves the purpose of orienting the client to the counseling process and providing enough information so that treatment can begin. Beyond that, however, intake procedures can vary according to a number of dimensions. Some of the most important of these follow.

Role of the Intake Interviewer

Key variables affecting the role of the intake interviewer include:

1. *Degree of responsibility*—Is the intake interviewer one of several people involved in screening and orienting a particular client? Does the intake interviewer have full responsiblity for treatment planning or will that be done at a staff meeting or case conference?
2. *Extent of contact with client*—Will the intake interviewer also become the counselor for the client or is it likely that the client will be referred to another helping professional for treatment?

These variables determine the optimal level of rapport between client and counselor and the degree of separation between intake and treatment procedures. If there will be no further contact between the intake interviewer and the client after the initial interview, a clearer line will have to be drawn between intake and treatment, and the degree of rapport should be limited. It can be upsetting to clients to speak openly and at length to a counselor and to begin to build trust, only to discover that they will never see that person again. Counselors should be sure, then, that their role is clarified for clients and that clients do not feel misled or confused by the intake process. Clients need to understand how they will benefit from an intake interview, but should see it as only one phase of treatment.

Nature of the Intake Process

The intake process itself varies from one agency to another depending on:

1. *The personnel involved in the process*
2. *The process of data gathering*
3. *The format used by the agency*

In some agencies, a single intake interviewer has the responsibility of gathering data on and evaluating clients' mental status, the nature and dynamics of their presenting concerns, and relevant history. However, in other agencies, clients meet with several mental health professionals as part of the intake process. The mental health counselor might gather information on the presenting problems. A psychiatric social worker might interview clients on their family backgrounds. A physical and mental status examination might be conducted by a psychiatrist. A referral also could be made to a psychologist for projective testing and an assessment of intelligence. Clearly, then, the nature of the intake process will vary, depending on who is involved in the intake process.

The manner in which data is gathered is another aspect of the intake process. Some agencies rely exclusively on data provided by clients. Interviews certainly will be used and physical and psychological tests also may be employed to acquire information. Other agencies advocate a broad-based approach to collecting intake information and, depending on the particular client, may interview family members and close friends of the client, may request academic and medical records, and may call teachers, employers, and others for additional information.

Both the manner in which data is gathered and the personnel involved will be reflected in the format of the intake interview. Nearly all agencies make use of an outline or standardized procedure for intake. While some flexibility in these procedures is necessary, it probably is the format that will exert the greatest influence over the intake process. Samples of such formats will be provided later in this chapter.

Depth and Duration of Intake Process

Intake procedures may be as brief as a 20-minute triage procedure in which clients in crisis and those who are actively psychotic are referred for immediate treatment while others are placed on a waiting list. On the other hand, intake procedures may take 4 hours or more, especially if psychological testing is involved, and may involve three or more sessions, scheduled on different days. The depth of the interview, as with its duration, is largely determined by agency policy and practice. In some agencies, intake interviewers function as selective and intelligent tape-recorders; they sift through information presented by clients, sort important from unimportant data, and present relevant material in a concise format. They do little interpretation or analysis, viewing that as either more appropriate in treatment than in intake or not part of the counseling process at all. Other agencies assume a much more analytical role and view the interviewer as an interpreter whose goal is to understand the underlying dynamics of the client's concerns. Both models of interviews will be illustrated later in this chapter.

Nature of Client Referral

In examining the nature of a client referral, counselors should consider:

1. *Who referred the client*
2. *The stated purpose of the referral*
3. *The client's presenting concerns*
4. *The level of the client's motivation*

Clients may be referred by other agencies or helping professionals who do not provide the services needed. The referral sources may be transferring full responsibility for the client to the second agency or may be seeking only a specific form of treatment for a client (e.g., career counseling, hypnotherapy for weight loss) while the referring agency continues to provide and oversee the client's treatment. Generally, the intake interviewer will have contact with the referring agency to determine why the referral was made and whether collaborative treatment is indicated.

Clients also are often referred or encouraged to seek counseling by family or friends. These referral sources may have a vested interest in the clients' seeking counseling. Such clients may have sought counseling because of pressure from another person, perhaps a spouse who threatens marital separation unless counseling is begun. These clients may be resistant and have limited motivation toward treatment. Attitudes toward treatment usually have to be addressed in the intake interview if productive counseling is to be undertaken.

Externally motivated clients comprise only one of the types of clients who may prove very challenging to the intake interviewer. Others include the severely depressed client, the schizophrenic client, the hostile and angry client, the seductive or manipulative client, the client in a crisis, and the client expressing suicidal ideation. With such clients, the interviewer's efforts to follow a standardized format and develop a comprehensive picture of the client may be frustrated. Intake interviewers must take into account the nature of clients' presenting concerns and the attitudes they bring into the intake interview so that the interview can be appropriately individualized. With depressed clients, for example, the interviewer might need to assume a more active and directive role, relying on clear and concrete questions and interventions that would facilitate client self-expression; hostile clients might require limit-setting and confrontation as an early part of the interview, while the client in a crisis often will require some immediate assistance and only a minimal intake phase.

It is evident that one of the most challenging roles of the intake interviewer is to individualize the intake process so that, at the end of the intake process, the client is motivated and optimistic and the counselor has a useful understanding of the client's difficulties. Although agencies may have standardized intake procedures, there is no way to make the process a uniform one. It is a process that is unique to each client and each counselor and is integral to the overall treatment process.

Follow-Up Procedures

An important determinant of the intake process is the nature and pacing of what happens next. The following are some common procedures used after the intake is completed:

1. The intake interviewer will expeditiously begin to see the client for counseling.
2. The client will soon begin treatment with another mental health worker.
3. The results of the intake interview will be presented and discussed at a staff or case conference and a treatment plan developed at that time.

4. The client will be placed on a waiting list until an appropriate treatment person has some available time.
5. If alternatives 3 or 4 are followed, some agencies will simultaneously assign clients to an intake group to provide interim treatment. These groups can offer some continuity of treatment, bridging the time gap between the intake interview and the assignment of the client to an appropriate treatment person or group.
6. The client might be referred to a more suitable agency or source of assistance.
7. Clients, with or without the concurrence of the intake interviewer, might discontinue contact, perhaps feeling that they really do not have an interest in further treatment from that agency at present.

Whichever of these outcomes occurs, the intake worker should make efforts to ensure that the following procedures are followed:

1. The client leaves the intake interview with an understanding of what will happen next.
2. Urgent client needs are met quickly.
3. The process of treatment planning is under way.
4. Both client and intake worker have a sense of closure and comfort at the end of the intake process.
5. The intake worker ensures that referrals and follow-up will be accomplished. If clients need time to decide whether to continue treatment or if they want to delay treatment, the intake worker arranges for the client to be contacted at a later date. If the client severs contact with the agency unexpectedly, further contact is made to ensure that the client has every opportunity to receive help and that the intake process was not excessively stressful or uncomfortable for the client.

The Extended Intake Interview

This section of the chapter will familiarize readers with the content and process of a typical extended intake interview that might be conducted by a counselor. The section includes the categories of analysis and inquiry that might be part of such an interview, a transcript of an extended intake interview, and an extended intake report based on the transcript. The next section will provide categories of inquiry and examples of *brief* intake interviews.

An extended intake may require several hours of interview time. The interviewer has a multifaceted role: establishing rapport, asking appropriate questions, making effective interventions, and analyzing the entire process. Such interviews often have overt and covert agendas. The overt agenda involves gathering useful information on the nature of clients' concerns and on relevant history. Most of the questions aimed at acquiring this material will be direct; their goals, apparent. At the same time, the counselor also is gathering information on clients' mental status. This process is more subtle and often involves using observational or inferential data rather than factual material provided by the clients.

Sometimes, in an extended intake, the interviewer will make use of checklists, inventories, or questionnaires to supplement, focus, and standardize the interview process. These might be comprehensive inventories designed to help the interviewer gather a broad range of information on a client's level of functioning, presenting problems, and history. Examples of this type of inventory are the Behavioral Inventory Battery (Cautela & Upper, 1976) and the Multimodal Life History Questionnaire (Lazarus, 1977). Numerous more specific questionnaires are available to facilitate the interviewer's exploration of a particular aspect of a client's life. Questionnaires of this nature have been developed to explore such areas as nature of problems, level of children's self-sufficiency, degree of depression, nature of client's fears or phobias, sexual adjustment, level of assertiveness, and nature of marital concerns. Whether such instruments are used depends on agency policy, counselor preference, and client concerns.

Mental Status Examination

The purpose of a mental status examination is to obtain information on how clients are functioning and presenting themselves to others. When drawing conclusions about the mental status of clients, intake interviewers will rely heavily on their observations of clients and their knowledge of normal functioning as well as on data provided by clients.

The mental status of clients can be viewed in terms of the following eight categories (Kaplan & Sadock, 1981):

1. Overall appearance. This will be assessed by observing how clients present themselves physically and interpersonally. The counselor should take note of:

a. *Client's presentability*—neatness, cleanliness, style and appropriateness of dress, weight, physical characteristics.

b. *Attitude toward counselor and intake interview*—friendliness, openness, interpersonal skills, appropriateness of interaction, apparent level of motivation.

c. *Speech patterns*—presence of accents or speech impediments, clarity, communication skills.

2. Sensorium. This category includes clients' levels of attention and concentration, their alertness and responsiveness, and their memory. This can be assessed indirectly by observing how clients handle the interview process. Can they focus on and respond clearly to questions? Do they seem attentive or are they easily distracted by outside noises? Can they recall important events and people in their lives?

3. Thought processes. In assessing thought processes, counselors should examine the organization and coherence of thoughts expressed by clients. Do clients respond directly and clearly to questions or are responses delayed, confused, or tangential? Are clients' thinking skills active and responsive or do thoughts seem minimal and labored? Problem solving and language usage provide keys to understanding thinking. Counselors should take particular note of confusion or peculiarities in speech. Use of homemade words and an unusual fascination with words that rhyme or sound interesting but make little sense when combined (called "word salad") are often indicative of thought disorders.

4. Thought content. Thought content can be subdivided into the following subcategories.

a. Orientation to reality—Is the client in good contact with reality and aware of what is happening or are there indications of hallucinations, delusions, excessive suspiciousness, or other signs of thought disorder?

b. Intelligence—It is difficult to estimate accurately clients' level of intellectual functioning without standardized testing. However, because intelligence, insight, and level of verbal skills are important considerations in treatment planning, counselors should make a rough guess as to the nature and extent of clients' intellectual abilities. These can be inferred by considering clients' academic and employment histories as well as the nature of their communication.

c. Interests and values—A review of the topics and ideas expressed by clients offers insight into their values and interests. Understanding what is important to a client and how the client prefers to spend time is an important way to understand that individual. The client's history also can provide a great deal of information about interests and values.

5. Sensory-motor and perceptual processes.   Data on this area also will be gathered from history and presentation of the client. This category encompasses clients' visual and auditory capacities and their level of motor skills. Does the client seem to hear the interviewer easily? Can the client get around without assistance? Is the client unusually clumsy or awkward? Finding answers to questions such as these requires counselors to draw on both their own perceptions of clients as well as clients' history. Although mental health workers generally have only a limited understanding of sensory, motor, or perceptual aspects of functioning, they can note disturbances in these areas and, if appropriate, request a medical consultation for more information. Such disturbances can reflect or exacerbate emotional difficulties and should be considered when formulating a comprehensive picture of a client.

6. Nature and regulation of affect.   This category refers to the nature and appropriateness of clients' emotional expressions. Well-functioning individuals generally have the capacity to express a broad range of emotions and to manifest them in a way that is appropriate to the topic or situation at hand. Such clients would not, for example, smile broadly when discussing the death of a close relative. Troubled clients, on the other hand, often manifest a poverty of affect (limited range and depth of feelings), a volatile or labile (quickly changing) affect, or an unresponsive affect (e.g., client seems sad no matter what is being discussed). Emotional expression commonly plays an important role in understanding the diagnosis and dynamics of clients. Therefore, assessing affect is one of the most important aspects of the intake interview.

7. *Self-regulation.* Self-regulation is the clients' capacity to manage their own lives effectively. In assessing immediate self-regulation, counselors should take note of whether clients arrive on time for their appointments, how they negotiate finding the office and any hurdles presented by receptionists. A broader view of self-regulation can be obtained from discussion of how clients handle stress and unexpected change, what their occupational and educational history has been like, their financial situation, and the nature and duration of their interpersonal relationships. Self-regulation often provides valuable clues to clients' ability to establish a committed and consistent counseling relationship, to follow through on appointments and assignments, and to see the treatment to an appropriate termination.

8. *Bodily functions.* Clients experiencing emotional upset, especially depression, often suffer disturbances in sleeping and eating patterns. Weight and sexual activity also may be adversely affected by emotional difficulties. Use of potentially harmful substances (e.g., alcohol, cigarettes, tranquilizers, laxatives) also may increase at times of stress. Intake interviewers should ask clients to describe patterns and recent changes in bodily functions. Interviewers also should ask about a client's medical history.

Substance of an Extended Intake Interview

The following is an outline of the categories of inquiry in an extended intake interview. Guide questions and topics are provided to help mental health workers to conduct an interview. Although this outline can be useful in providing a structure for such interviews and in helping to ensure that important areas of inquiry are not omitted, this outline should be viewed as a suggestion. Each interview will be unique and the effective interviewer will conduct intake sessions with flexibility and sensitivity to the clients' needs. Questions and topics considered will be individualized to suit the concerns and level of motivation of each client.

I. Identifying information

A. Demographic data

1. Age
2. Sex
3. Nationality, race, religion, native language (if pertinent)
4. Marital and family status
5. Educational level
6. Occupation
7. Place of residence and cohabitants
8. Referral agency

B. Observational data (generally inferred by interviewer)

1. Physical appearance
2. Nature and appropriateness of dress
3. Presentation of self
4. Description of affect
5. Visible habits, eccentricities, behaviors
6. Interaction with interviewer

II. Presenting problem

This is a brief statement of the client's chief complaints and difficulties, the clients' perceptions of what has brought him or her to seek treatment at the time and what kind of help is sought. The presenting problem may not coincide with the interviewer's assessment of a client's difficulties; clients sometimes are not fully aware of what is really bothering them, they have difficulty stating their concerns clearly, or they may be using a less threatening presenting problem (e.g., career uncertainty) as a comfortable way of seeking help with a more highly charged or less socially acceptable concern (e.g., marital infidelity, child abuse).

III. Present difficulties and previous disorders

In this section of the interview, greater exploration of clients' concerns is undertaken. Stated and implied concerns will be explored, and the interviewer will begin to formulate hypotheses about the nature and dynamics of clients' concerns. For all problem areas explored, interviewers should obtain information about:

A. Nature of concern
B. Time of onset and circumstances surrounding inception of concern
C. Accompanying symptoms
D. History of concern (initial or recurrent, frequency, duration)
E. Dynamics of concern (What seems to cause it to develop, change, or abate? What does the client do to modify it? How do close friends and family deal with the concern?)
F. Secondary gains (What benefits does the client seem to derive from this concern?)
G. Previous treatment for concern
H. Impact of concern on client's life-style, activities, relationships, bodily functions, mood
I. Precipitating factor(s) in client's seeking help at present time

IV. Present life situation

Next, interviewers should attempt to obtain (and present in their reports) a sense of the client's life-style and daily activities. The overview presented here will be explored further and elaborated on in later sections. The goal of this section is to capture and transmit the uniqueness and individuality of clients, the fabric of their lives, and the nature of their suffering.

The following topics are likely to be covered in this section:

A. Family relationships and vicissitudes
B. Other interpersonal relationships
C. Occupational/educational activities
D. Social and leisure activities
E. Physical living situation
F. Sources of satisfaction
G. Sources of stress
H. Typical day in client's life

V. Family

A. Background data
    1. Social origins and influences
    2. Economic origins and influences
    3. Ethnic origins and influences
    4. Genetic/historical patterns
    5. Significant crises or episodes
    6. Patterns of physical or emotional illness in family
B. Nature of family constellation
    1. Power structure of family
    2. Degree of closeness
    3. Family values
    4. Parenting styles
    5. Birth order and impact on client
C. Relationships
    1. Father
    2. Mother
    3. Sibling(s)
    4. Spouse(s)
    5. Children
    6. Other significant relatives

In discussing each of the above relationships, the following topics might be explored:

A. How is that individual perceived by the client?

B. What is the nature of the current relationship with that person?
C. What is the history of the relationship?
D. What impact or influence has that person had on the client? What sort of role model has the person provided?

Although this section might involve considerable history-taking, data should be gathered not for its own sake but rather to shed light on the dynamics of the client's current situation.

VI. Developmental history

In obtaining a developmental history, interviewers should be selective and focus on times of greatest significance in terms of the client's current situation. For example, little attention would typically be paid to infancy and early childhood in an interview with a thirty-five-year-old client experiencing a brief depression. However, understanding those early years might be very important to gaining insight into the dynamics of a fire-setting eight-year-old. The following outline of developmental history is, then, a comprehensive one, provided to give direction, but intended to be used selectively.

A. Infancy

1. Birth history
    a. What were the ages and health of the parents at the time of the birth?
    b. Were there medical complications?
    c. Was the child wanted at that time?
    d. How did the parents seem to feel about the sex of the child?
    e. Were there any birth injuries or defects?
2. Infant history
    a. What was the nature of early family relationships?
    b. How was child care provided?
    c. How were feeding and weaning accomplished?
    d. How was toilet training accomplished?

    e. How did overall development progress (e.g., walking, speech, physical growth)?

    f. Were any significant health problems present?

    g. Was there any significant history of habit disorders, inordinate fears, problem behavior?

    h. How was discipline provided?

B. Early childhood (preschool years)

    1. What were the child's living conditions like?

    2. What was the composition of the family?

    3. What were the child's roles and relationships in the family?

    4. What was the nature of the child's early social relationships?

    5. What was the child's personality like?

C. Middle childhood

    1. Describe the child's early educational history. When was school begun and how was it handled?

    2. How did the child relate to schoolmates?

    3. How did the child relate to teachers?

    4. What subjects and activities did the child particularly enjoy or do well at?

    5. What subjects and activities did the child particularly dislike or have difficulty with?

    6. What changes or patterns were observed in the child's family relationships?

    7. What behavioral problems, if any, were present?

    8. Describe the child's sense of initiative, level of self-confidence, and capacity for accomplishment.

    9. What was the child's personality and emotional development like during these years?

D. Late childhood/puberty

    1. What was the timetable of the child's pubertal bodily changes (e.g., growth, breast development, menstruation, appearance of facial and body hair)?

2. How did the child react to these changes?
3. Describe the child's peer relationships, especially close friendships. Was the child isolated or involved?
4. What patterns of sexual activity and interest were manifested?
5. How did the child deal with authority figures?
6. Describe the child's academic performance.
7. What social and leisure activities were preferred?
8. What were family relationships like?
9. What were the child's career aspirations?
10. What emotional or physical problems emerged?

E. Adulthood

1. Describe the client's educational aptitudes, accomplishments, and areas of difficulty.
2. What has the client's career history been like? Consider sequence of jobs, successes and failures, special skills, work attitudes, level of responsibility, relationships with supervisors and coworkers.
3. What are the client's current educational and occupational goals?
4. What are the client's leisure and cultural activities? How much time is spent on these? Is there over- or under-investment in leisure pursuits?
5. Describe the client's social relationships. Consider nature, number, duration, and intensity. What role does the client seem to assume in social relationships?
6. Describe the client's adult sexual development. How are sexual and interpersonal relationships intertwined? Is the client satisfied with his or her sexual involvements and activities?
7. Is the client married? If so, what is the marital relationship like? What are its pressures and joys? What is the chronology and developmental history of the marriage? What was the courtship like? If the client is not married, is this anticipated or hoped for?
8. If the client has children, what are their sexes and ages? Are more children planned? How was the marital re-

lationship affected by the children? What have the client's relationships been like with the children? What approach is taken to parenting?

9. Are there in-laws? What are the client's relationships with them?

10. How have the client's relationships with members of the family of origin been modified in adulthood?

11. What is the client's current financial situation?

12. What goals or future dreams are important to the client? What does he or she think his or her life will be like in 5 or 10 years?

13. Does the client have a record of arrests, incarcerations, or lawsuits? What is their nature?

VII. Medical history

A. What past and current illnesses and accidents of significance has the client experienced?

B. Is the client currently receiving medical treatment or medication? If so, what is its nature and purpose? (Interviewer also should investigate potential side effects of any medication in use.)

C. Describe the nature of any hospitalizations.

D. Has the client received previous treatment for emotional difficulties? If so, when, for what duration, and of what type? What impact did the treatment have on the client's complaints? Why was treatment terminated?

Nature of an Intake Report

The report of an extended intake interview typically will consist of the following three sections:

1. Analysis of mental status
2. Summary and analysis of client's history and dynamics of current concerns
3. Formulations of the interviewer

The first two sections have been outlined in the previous pages. They may be organized and presented according to the format offered in this chapter or the format may be varied to meet the needs of a particular client, interviewer, or agency. The third section contains the conclusions drawn by the intake interviewer and sets forth the treatment plan. The section might consist of the following categories:

A. Summary of data from consultants, records, referral sources
   1. Medical and psychiatric evaluations
   2. Psychological assessment
   3. Other available data
B. Diagnostic impression
   1. Client's strengths and weaknesses
   2. Concerns which call for therapeutic intervention
   3. *DSM-III* diagnosis
C. Treatment plan (See chapter 5 for additional details on this section.)
D. Prognosis
   1. What is the likelihood that the client will make significant improvement? (Is the prognosis guarded or optimistic?)
   2. What factors seem most important in determining prognosis?

In the following pages, readers will be provided with a verbatim transcript of an extended interview, a report written on that interview, and two additional brief intake reports. The interview format roughly follows that presented in the preceding pages and illustrates how such an interview might be conducted and subsequently analyzed.

TRANSCRIPTION OF EXTENDED INTAKE INTERVIEW

Interviewer: Ann, can you tell me a little bit about what brings you into the community mental health center today?
Ann: Well, some problems have come up with my daughter and I am feeling like I need somebody to talk to about them.

Interviewer: Tell me a little more about them.

Ann: I am a single parent and have been for the last 9 years. My daughter is just twelve this month. She's adopted, and I'm beginning to feel like that's become an issue. I'm not sure if I'm crediting the adoption with being responsible for more than it really is. Maybe what I would like you to tell me is that this is just what I can expect with a twelve-year-old girl and that what's been happening really isn't related to the fact that she's adopted and that I'm divorced. But my own life was so difficult during the years before and after my daughter's coming into my life, I'm afraid that maybe I let that affect her. I guess I wonder about the impact that's had on me, too.

Interviewer: So it sounds like you have got some concerns about the impact of some difficulties you've had on your daughter and yourself. You want some reassurance or maybe some sense of direction in how to handle some issues that have arisen now.

Ann: Yes.

Interviewer: The way we usually operate here at the mental health center is to start with a long interview, what's called an intake interview. In doing that, I'll be gathering a lot of information about your background, about what led up to this point, so we can understand as well as possible what is going on with you now and try to figure out how we can help you at this time. How does that sound to you?

Ann: Just fine.

Interviewer: We'll be spending most of our time today on this intake interview and then I'll be getting back to you in a week or two and letting you know what the staff's recommendation is for your continued counseling. We'll probably set up future appointments at that point.

Ann: Uh, huh.

Interviewer: Let's start by talking about your present situation. You mentioned you are a single parent and you have a twelve-year-old daughter.

Ann: That's right.

Interviewer: Is there anyone else in the home?

Ann: No. My ex-husband lives in Pittsburgh and my daughter visits with him a couple of times a year. He is pretty much out of the picture otherwise. We have a lot of family and friends around but there isn't anybody else who lives with us.

Interviewer: And you have been divorced for 8 years, you said?

Ann: Almost 9.

Interviewer: Almost 9.

Ann: My daughter was just about eighteen months old when my husband and I separated so she doesn't even remember living with us both.

Interviewer: At what age was she adopted?

Ann: At 10 days.

Interviewer: So she's been with you since just after her birth.

Ann: Yes.

Interviewer: You said you had family living in this area. Who are the family members whom you're close to?

Ann: Well, my mother and her second husband, my brother and his wife, and I have a cousin who is a couple of years younger than me who is as close to me as a sister could be, probably even closer because there isn't any rivalry with her. And a lot of extended family: my mother's sister, cousins that I'm not terribly close with but they are available, and I do see them a couple of times a year.

Interviewer: So extended family is pretty important to you.

Ann: Yes, it always has been.

Interviewer: Maybe we can talk a little more later about your family. Are you working at this time?

Ann: Yes, I am. I am an interior designer at a local department store.

Interviewer: How do you feel about your work?

Ann: I really enjoy it. It's creative, challenging, a lot of fun.

Interviewer: And you work full-time?

Ann: Yes, and I go to graduate school at night.

Interviewer: What are you studying?

Ann: For a master's degree in art education.

Interviewer: And what other kinds of activities are you involved in?

Ann: I really have a lot of friends. And I see them for dinner and get together with them and their kids. I take an exercise class and that's pretty much on a regular basis. But I'm always open to trying new things.

Interviewer: Sounds like you really keep busy.

Ann: Uh, huh, I do.

Interviewer: Let's go back to talking about your family and let's begin with your parents. Can you tell me something about your mother and father?

Ann: Did you want to know about their marriage?

Interviewer: Their marriage, what kind of people they were, and how you got along with them.

Ann: My parents got married when they were both about twenty and my father was a bright, attractive man. My mother was not particularly attractive. My mother says they had a good marriage; I don't really see how that could have been. But she still continues to say that. When I was eighteen years old, my father died after having been sick for about 2 years with cancer. They didn't tell me, though, what he had and just talked about a kind of a blood problem. My mother was very dependent on my father, didn't have a checking account, couldn't even write checks, never learned to drive but surprisingly carried on quite well when my father died. I never would have expected it. I imagined since he made every decision—

Interviewer: What was it like for you when he died?

Ann: Well, I just remember lying in bed and crying because I had not been able to talk with anyone about it. I had seen him just before he died and it was only a week before he died that I even knew he had cancer and that he would be dying. Nobody really ever talked about that or anything else really in my family when I was growing up so we were just very isolated and alone.

Interviewer: And you had to handle the grief alone, from the sound of it.

Ann: Right, yes, I have a brother who is 9 years younger but we have never been very close and still are not.

Interviewer: He was too young to really be a support to you?

Ann: Oh, yes, if anything he was just an annoyance.

Interviewer: You raise some questions about the quality of your parents' marriage. What concerned you about that?

Ann: Well, my father had such a good sense of humor and kind of enthusiasm and zest for life. My mother is kind of dowdy and dull and interested in only socializing with her extended family. That was pretty much all their social life was. I even remember my father and I going out to eat because my mother would never try any new foods in restaurants. So from the time I was about thirteen until the time he was too sick to go out, he and I used to go out alone and try a new restaurant, which my mother didn't seem to mind. I can't really think of anything they did together. I only remember us going to a movie as a whole family maybe once or twice. Her whole life centered around being a home-maker.

Interviewer: Then you had a very special bond with your father.

Ann: Yes, I did.

Interviewer: Tell me a little more about your parents.

Ann: Well, my father never made a terribly good living. We had all of the necessities, no luxuries, and it was with great effort that they would be able to buy me a particular sweater or some-thing that they wanted me to have, but it really was difficult for them.

Interviewer: The family got by all right but didn't have many ex-tras. And it sounds like your father was a kind of outgoing, take-charge sort of person and your mother, more the homebody.

Ann: Uh, huh.

Interviewer: What did she do to occupy her time?

Ann: Nothing that didn't relate to homemaking. She cooks a lot, not that she is a particularly wonderful cook, she is not even a particularly good housekeeper. Even with limited funds, she al-ways had a domestic once a week. Except for seeing her family (she is the youngest of four).

Interviewer: And how about your father's family, what was that like?

Ann: Well, his mother had died having an abortion when he was about four years old and he then went to live with her parents (his grandparents) and then his mother's brothers and sisters who weren't that terribly much older than he. He didn't see his father again until he was quite a bit older. When he finished high school, he was expected to work and help support the grandparents. And he went into the Marines and that's when my parents got married. He did take some college courses then. But he went into selling cars when he left the Marines.

Interviewer: He was an only child then?

Ann: Yes.

Interviewer: Were there family circumstances that led to the abor-tion?

Ann: Yes, his mother was very unhappy. When she found out

she was pregnant, she knew she couldn't have another child with her husband. He had, I think, physically abused her.

Interviewer: Um. What is your brother like?

Ann: Well, even today, I wouldn't say he is terribly exciting. He is a nice fellow but we certainly don't have anything in common. I'm not particularly close to him. If he moved away, I know I'd never see him again. There is nothing terribly remarkable about him.

Interviewer: It sounds like you are not very connected to him.

Ann: Uh, huh.

Interviewer: Tell me some more about him.

Ann: He's an accountant. He does very well financially. He owns a lovely house out in the suburbs. He is very nice to my daughter, by the way. And I guess that's the part of him I really do respond to.

Interviewer: So there is that one strength in your relationship with your brother.

Ann: Yes, I really appreciate the interest and time he shows my daughter.

Interviewer: How often do you see him?

Ann: Oh, never, if my mother doesn't arrange it.

Interviewer: Uh, huh.

Ann: She will invite us and we'll all come for dinner. There is a standing invitation that any time you want to come is just fine.

Interviewer: How long ago did your mother remarry?

Ann: I guess it's about 5 years. It's a lovely marriage and she's a new person. It's really brought a lot of joy to all of us. I really adore my stepfather. He couldn't be finer to me if I were his daughter, or more generous or love my daughter more.

Interviewer: I can see that means a lot to you.

Ann: Yes, it does.

Interviewer: What sort of person is he?

Ann: He is a pharmacist. He's just nice and warm and generous and was considerably more worldly than my mother and so it has made a lot of nice changes in her life. She has traveled, which is something she had never done. She lost about 60 pounds and is quite attractive and much more stylish now. She works full-time which is something she started to do after she remarried. They just have a very nice life.

Interviewer: What is your relationship with your mother like now?

Ann: Well, I have a lot of bitterness about what she didn't do when I was a child, though I think she did the best she could with the limited parenting skills she had. I guess I appreciate how kind she is to my daughter and she's always available for her and she loves her very much. I know she would be there if I needed her. But I try to keep my distance, because I don't want to lose any of my independence, which is something I really value.

Interviewer: Uh, huh. And you are concerned that somehow she could take that away from you?

Ann: Well, I guess I just like to keep the relationship exactly where I want it, instead of letting her encroach on any of my freedom, which I think she would. When I first came back to Dallas after separating from my husband, she was, you know, very eager to do things for me; and if I had really let her, I think she could have taken over. I mean, like, she was perfectly willing to do my laundry and any way she could be helpful. But I had a sense, even then, that I ought to keep my distance or it could get a little overwhelming.

Interviewer: She would want more closeness than you are comfortable with.

Ann: Yeah. But right now, it's just fine.

Interviewer: Are there other family members who are especially important to you now?

Ann: Yes. I have a cousin who's a little bit younger than me. I had mentioned her earlier to you. I said we are certainly as close as sisters would love to be. She's just always been a wonderful friend, even when we were little, and has continued to be when I had problems in my adult life. I really value her friendship now.

Interviewer: She gives you a lot of support.

Ann: Yes. And now I have had the chance to reciprocate. Her oldest daughter was killed in a car accident unfortunately, and not that I wanted her to have any problems, but I am happy to be there for her now since she has always been very supportive of me.

Interviewer: Let's go back and talk about what it was like for you growing up as a young girl. When you think back to before you went to school or your early elementary school years, what sorts of thoughts do you come up with?

Ann: Well, my father looms enormously in my memories. I adored him, I have a lot of wonderful memories about him. It was always fun to be with him. I remember getting sick when he would go away. He would cut short his business trips. He would travel a lot and would cut short his trips when I was sick and eventually stopped traveling, seeing that I didn't feel well when he was away. Of course, I loved that. I just remember spending a lot of time with my aunts and uncles every single night, sitting in the kitchen. As long as I was quiet, I could stay up and listen.

Interviewer: Your biggest memories were about family. You mentioned being ill a lot?

Ann: Well, my mother told me I had been a sickly baby and there seemed to be some period when they thought I might not live. And then I guess I got the most attention when I was sick and so it was kind of nice to be sick. And I was sick a lot. As I got older, I would get sick so I didn't have to do something at school or get out of going some place I didn't want to.

Interviewer: So there was a very positive side to being sick for you.

Ann: Uh, huh.

Interviewer: How about school and activities during those early years? What were they like?

Ann: Well, I remember being an extremely good student, say up until the third grade, and then after that I was a little better than average. And it felt nice to have the teachers praising me although I think I liked it a little better when I wasn't so especially good that anyone noticed me. I kind of liked it better when I was just there—being good—but not attracting any attention. My parents never really expected anything of me or pushed me in any way except, "We know you are doing the best you can." I never felt any encouragement to try anything new or experiment with anything. I didn't feel very popular. I had some friends from the neighborhood but I don't ever remember feeling especially sought after by other kids.

Interviewer: How about methods of discipline in the home? If you did something your parents disapproved of, how was that handled?

Ann: Believe it or not, I never did anything bad. I was so bent on being perfect that I was perfect. The few times that something would come up, my father would yell at me and that was horrifying that he would be that angry. I don't really remember him doing anything more than raising his voice. I remember my mother smacking me once or twice, but I was always so good, it rarely happened.

Interviewer: So it was very important for you to be good and almost all the time you could carry through on it.

Ann: Uh, huh.

Interviewer: Let's go on until you're a little bit older and you have matured physically, junior high and high school years. What were they like?

Ann: Well, I still didn't feel very attractive. My nose was too big, and my hair was stringy; I had bad skin. So I generally had a poor self-image. I was an OK student and had friends. But I was always surprised that I had them. I felt, if they really knew me they wouldn't want to be friends with me. I was more surprised than anybody that I had been accepted into these clubs in junior high and high school. I knew it was for a reason. One time it was because my cousin was in it, like I really wouldn't have gotten into it on my own. I have forgotten now what the reasons were but I always had a feeling that I had put something over on everybody.

Interviewer: A big masquerade—if anyone ever saw through it, you would be finished.

Ann: Exactly.

Interviewer: It must have been pretty uncomfortable.

Ann: It was.

Interviewer: And in terms of your academic achievement in junior high and high school, how did you do?

Ann: Always about average. As I said, my parents never really acted like I ought to be pushing myself, and so I just went along that way. They really didn't direct or guide my actions in any way. As long as I was good and didn't make any problems, that was fine. I guess what I didn't mention—I told you my brother was 9 years younger and when he was born, everything changed in terms of attention or interest in me. So I had the normal jealousy toward a new baby that somebody might be expected to. But he was extremely difficult for my parents to manage, so that from the moment he came into the house, all activity centered around him. I guess it just reinforced my wanting to be good.

Interviewer: I guess that was the way for you to be special in the family.

Ann: But really it didn't get me any attention. First, he was crying all the time so everyone was paying attention to that. When he got a little bit older, he was running into the street and he was always doing some kind of mischief and it was too much for my mother to handle. I somehow think she may have had some kind of a breakdown shortly after he was born.

Interviewer: You must have felt a lot of anger toward him intruding into what was a very nice situation for you.

Ann: Uh, huh. I sure did.

Interviewer: To shift back a little bit, what about your physical maturation and sexual development, how did that progress?

Ann: Well, I seemed to mature at about the same pace as most of the people I was friendly with. That wasn't a problem. I was always interested in boys and began to date in groups, I guess, at about thirteen. By the time I was fifteen, I was very involved with this fellow, Steve, and even to the point of having a sexual relationship with him when I was sixteen. I just adored him and would have done anything to keep him.

Interviewer: Uh, huh. What sort of attitudes or messages had you gotten from your parents about sexual relations?

Ann: Well, sex was always an issue in their marriage. Evidently my father had much greater needs than my mother did. I remember lying in bed at night and one time in particular, during a terrible argument, my father storming out. The next day when he did come home, my mother had gotten all dressed up and had makeup on and looked very special, considering the way she usually looked.

Interviewer: And you were aware as a teenager that sex was an issue between them?

Ann: I think I was aware of that even before I was a teenager. They were very unaffectionate. I never saw them hug each other or kiss each other. My father was affectionate with me but they were not affectionate with each other and just never touched. My "birds and bees" conversation with my mother consisted of her saying, when I was about twelve and she had gotten the Modess booklets that they were giving out in those days, "I guess you know what makes the world go round," and I said yes and she gave me the booklets. That was it.

Interviewer: How did you feel about that?

Ann: Well, I didn't expect anything else from her, I guess, at that point. I wasn't disappointed. I guess I really learned about sex from Steve.

Interviewer: Steve was your first special relationship with a boy?

Ann: Yes. He was very attractive and popular and I was very flattered he was so interested in me. We went together pretty seriously for about two and a half years. I thought I was madly in love. Looking back, he really wasn't very nice to me or not consistently very nice. I mean, today, I certainly wouldn't tolerate someone treating me with as little respect as he did. I remember him coming over one day and letting his dog sit on the livingroom couch and I didn't even say anything to him about it. He would occasionally see somebody else while I was not supposed to. It was just a lack of respect and real consideration in the relationship. But he was quite a catch and I was delighted. Then later we sort of slowed down the relationship.

Interviewer: So you can see some problems in that relationship now but it was very important to you at the time.

Ann: Yes, very.

Interviewer: How did you feel about the sexual component of your relationship?

Ann: Well, at first I was terrified. I was worried I would become pregnant, especially the first time. I was so scared, I even thought about killing myself. But Steve stayed around and the relationship continued to grow. I certainly liked the sex part—that was fine— and I thought it was making us closer.

Interviewer: Uh, huh. But there were some rough moments for you in the relationship?

Ann: Yes, definitely. Because he wasn't really caring about me as much as I cared about him. It was mostly what could I do for him.

Interviewer: What were your career goals at that time?

Ann: I didn't really have any. All I wanted to do was get married and have children and my parents certainly encouraged that. I did go to college after high school and that was just because everybody in the area that I lived in went on to college, so I just did, but my parents certainly didn't participate in that decision either. It was, um, just assumed that I would go to a city college, and that's what I wound up doing, going to a city junior college, but they didn't participate in any of the investigating with me, or talk about it, and I guess I knew financially going away wasn't a choice.

Interviewer: Yes, so it was just that was the thing to do and you didn't think about it too much. You just did it.

Ann: Right.

Interviewer: Did you have a job while you were in high school?

Ann: Oh, baby-sitting occasionally, but not to help the family.

Interviewer: Let's shift back to your social life. What other important relationships did you have?

Ann: Uh, I met my husband when I was a freshman at a junior college. Don and I were kind of attracted to each other right away. We had just the most wonderful beginning relationship, very caring, and when I look back on it now I certainly, you know, understand why I wanted to get involved with him.

Interviewer: What were some of the things that attracted you to him?

Ann: He took me to wonderful restaurants. He was from a much more affluent family and seemed to know his way around. He just knew about everything and, uh, at the time I met him, my father was dying, and when my father died, Don said, "I'll take care of you forever. I'll always be here for you." And that really meant a lot to me.

Interviewer: So you weren't really alone then. You had Don to give you some support.

Ann: I did.

Interviewer: How long did you know him before the two of you got married?

Ann: About another year, and he was in graduate school.

Interviewer: A year after your father died?

Ann: Yes.

Interviewer: Uh, huh.

Ann: Right. He was in law school. We got married just before he began his last year. So we continued to live in the area, uh, for another year, and then we moved away.

Interviewer: How did you decide to marry him?

Ann: I guess he just asked, and it seemed like the logical thing to do. It did necessitate my dropping out of school, though, and that I certainly have some second thoughts about now. I had completed my second year of the junior college and was preparing to transfer into a program at a 4-year school. I was going to go to a teachers college. Which I really don't know why I was interested in, but I guess it seemed like the thing to do then, and Don said, "Why don't you stop school now and get a job and we can be saving money and then we can think about getting married," and he said, ". . . because all you want to do is be a homemaker so you really don't need to go to school." And that sounded fine to me, even though I was loving school. And my mother was very resistant to my stopping school at that point, but I did what Don suggested and we did wind up getting married soon after I did that.

Interviewer: But it sounded like something a little different happened for you in college. That's the first time you really said you enjoyed school.

Ann: Yes, that's true, I did, and I also started feeling very popular and very attractive, now that I think of it. I, um, I don't know. I started feeling like I had a very nice figure, and suddenly my hair didn't feel like a problem any more. My skin was still a little bit of a problem, but I could use makeup. And other people seemed to seek me out. Men found me very attractive, and I sort of developed a dressing style that was all my own. I remember wearing tight jeans and high boots and V-neck sweaters and I looked very sexy and felt good about it, and there was, you know, lots of good feedback from other people.

Interviewer: So you gave up kind of a positive life-style, and yet it still felt like what you really wanted to do was to get married and have a family.

Ann: Uh, huh. Yes, I felt that Don would be the perfect husband and we would have a perfect life together. I also adored his mother, and, um, I think that was kind of an attraction, too. She's completely different than my mother, and, um, really was probably the most nurturing adult in my life. And, um, taught me a lot about being a homemaker and things that I, you know, wanted to learn. They had beautiful parties and entertained beautifully and these were things that I aspired to then. And she's a very talented woman, very creative, and she really loved being with me, and I guess that's what I was responding to. She was really the only older woman who had ever acted like it was a great joy to be with me, and I really responded to that.

Interviewer: So she was in a sense another mother to you.

Ann: More than my mother had ever been.

Interviewer: When you left school and went to work, what sort of job did you get?

Ann: It was a selling position in a women's clothing store. And it was pleasant. I knew it was just for a year or so because Don would be finishing school and we would be leaving. And I was really just biding my time until we were ready to have children.

Interviewer: What were the early years of your marriage like?

Ann: Basically fun. They really were. Though I felt a little lonely because, um, he seemed to be very, uh, most of our friends were his friends and I never felt quite as good as they, and that made me feel alone because we would be at parties or other things with them and I still felt like a little bit of an outsider, and we had had a very satisfying sex life before we were married, and then that seemed to change. Don got very critical of my not being enthusiastic enough and I guess I had been more participatory before we were married, but maybe it was the frequency and ease of availability. Now that, you know, it wasn't quite as much of a treat, he was angry a lot of the time about that.

Interviewer: Hmmm. So, there were a lot of good things but there were also things that were starting some tension between the two of you.

Ann: Yes.

Interviewer: You adopted a child how many years into your marriage?

Ann: Uh, about 5, but we had had a child of our own before that happened. After Don finished school, we moved to Washington, DC where he was offered a wonderful job with the government and that was not all wonderful. Part of it was nice. We loved being in Washington. It was the first time for either of us living away, and, of course, Washington is beautiful, and we had enough money to go out and eat and enjoy the things there were to do, so that was fun and at that point we decided to try to have a baby, but our sex life was terrible. I remember asking him a couple of times why we never had relations, and he would say, "What do you expect? I'm so tired." But I just knew then that things weren't right somehow. It shouldn't have been that way. But I did become pregnant, and we were both deliriously excited about it, and things seemed to be very positive.

Interviewer: Between the two of you?

Ann: Right, and . . . we were both very much looking forward to the baby, and, if he wasn't, at least I was so involved with it that I didn't notice. And when I was about 7 months pregnant, I developed toxemia, and so there I was, twenty-two, in an apartment, in terrible pain, very frightened. Don wouldn't let me call my mother, who really wasn't anybody that would be a particular comfort, but I did think of calling her, or even calling his mother, but he said we shouldn't bother anybody, and it would go away and the doctors at the hospital were thoroughly disinterested. I mean, they did whatever they had to do, but I didn't feel that anybody took any particular attention, you know, paid me any particular attention—

Interviewer: I don't know much about toxemia. What does that involve?

Ann: Well, it involves a lot of swelling and water retention and it can be very dangerous and I was in terrible, terrible pain and sometimes I would lie down and feel that it was this terrible weight of a building on my chest and I couldn't breathe and— I don't know how much of it was from the condition, and how much of it was, you know, accentuated by my fear and loneliness and Don being very detached. He would listen to the medical explanations, but I never felt like he was really feeling anything that I was experiencing. They did hospitalize me, which was also awful, and the food was horrible and I was crying and really totally out of control and he stayed as far away from me as possible in the hospital. So finally they concluded that maybe I'd be more comfortable at home and released me. So that was sort of how the rest of the pregnancy went, and it was just the loneliest, most awful time.

Interviewer: It does sound awful.

Ann: So of course I was feeling so sick there wasn't even time to try to make friends and the next thing I knew, our son was born, after a terrible, terrible delivery. Finally we did leave the hospital, though the baby was small, and, uh, had had some problems at first, but we went back, we got back home and my mother came and Don's mother came, and that, you know, was very nice and then they left and I was alone with the baby and—everything, you know, seemed to be going all right at that point. In the meantime, Don wanted very much for us to go away for a weekend with some people he was working with. I really didn't even know them, and the last thing I wanted to do was go away and leave this infant baby, but he always could make me feel like I wasn't being a good wife or wasn't doing something that I was supposed to be doing so, um, he made all these arrangements, and we were going to leave the baby with a couple he hired. I mean, really, when I look back, it just seems like it had to be another person doing that, because I can't believe I left a week-old baby with these people that I really didn't even know. And we went sailing, which also was ludicrous because I hate boats and the water.

Interviewer: So, it's puzzling why all this happened when you think back on it.

Ann: Well, it isn't, I guess, because I always did what Don wanted me to do but it's hard to think about, even. And there we were, in Annapolis, sailing with this couple that I really didn't know. The first night we called the baby-sitters and heard that the baby had died. I just remember getting into the car and driving for an hour back to Washington and my real concern at that point was this poor woman who was taking care of the baby, knowing that, you know, what she must be feeling, and I did, you know, go immediately to see her and tell her that I knew that she hadn't done anything.

Interviewer: What was it like for you to lose the baby?

Ann: It was just like the world had come to an end. I really just, I just couldn't believe that that happened. Except that I guess I never really expected that things would be wonderful for me. I mean I didn't really feel like a lucky, happy person, so, when bad things happened—

Interviewer: It's like it was "meant to be," as terrible as it was.

Ann: Maybe. Right. And—we got very busy with all kinds of plans at that point because we had to arrange to take the body back to Dallas and have the funeral, and in a way it was a terrific relief to get back to Dallas because I had family and friends there and at least the terrible loneliness that I felt was alleviated a little bit. I had all these people around, so the fact that Don didn't seem to be feeling the same anguish wasn't quite as apparent to me there, because there was all this activity and sympathy from all these people back in Dallas.

Interviewer: So it took your mind off what had happened—What had caused the baby's death?

Ann: Sudden Infant Death Syndrome. It didn't—nobody said I was responsible, you know, that if I hadn't gone away that weekend it would have made a difference. It isn't, you know, it wasn't that. I certainly believed that it was just meant to happen, but Don went back to DC ahead of me and said that he would arrange, you know, he would get all the baby's things packed up and put away and that sounded fine, and I came back about a week later and was very eager to become pregnant again. As a matter of fact, I remember making love in Dallas when we were there for the funeral and saying to him, "We've got to have another baby as soon as possible," and it just so happens I must have become pregnant then. Well, of course, that was something to look forward to, but it was still very painful and I felt very lonely. When I was 2 months pregnant, I can't even remember the sequence now, but it turned out that I was diagnosed as having bladder carcinoma and the doctor asked us both to come in and stated that we had these very few choices. Since I was so early in the pregnancy, I could go on and have all the radiation treatments and take a chance on the baby, on what it would do to the baby, or terminate the pregnancy and go on and have the treatments and I really didn't have too much problem making the decision that I wanted to terminate the pregnancy. After losing the other baby, I couldn't even face the possibility that there might be something wrong with this baby, or that I would go through another pregnancy and maybe lose the baby. So then I began a series of treatments. The chemotherapy, the radiation, I lost my hair, and it was just horrible. I was in the hospital and Don would stop by for a minute every once in a while. He obviously didn't want to hear about what was going on, and every night he would stop by and tell me about how busy he was at work, and he would, you know, go for the evening and leave me all alone.

Interviewer: So you were coping with many losses all at once.

Ann: And really, all alone, because I had really not even had the energy or time or wherewithal to make any kind of friendships, and many people said things that really hurt me. One day I was waiting to get a treatment and this woman told me a story. The story was that she had been talking to a neighbor who was telling her about all these troubles she was having, buying shoes, and fixing the car and everything, and this woman said to her, "You should be glad that you're not Ann Ryerson. Look at the trouble that she's had." And just the thought that people I didn't even know were discussing me and pitying me was just horrible—

Interviewer: You must have been worried about your life at that point.

Ann: I was, but, um, somewhere, while this was all going on, Don said, "Well, why don't we think about adopting a baby?" And so we did start to do that, and started the proceedings and the case manager from the adoption agency was a lovely woman with whom I was very comfortable sharing all the things that had happened and she had the confidence that the treatments were all going along fine and I wouldn't have a recurrence. They agreed to place a baby with us, and that was how we happened to adopt our daughter, and the day that we went to pick her up and they handed her to me, it was as though all the horrible things were just erased and—

Interviewer: It was wonderful.

Ann: It was wonderful. Right.

Interviewer: Could you have become pregnant again?

Ann: No, because I had a tubal ligation. Once you receive the kind of radiation I had, you shouldn't become pregnant again because the eggs are all, have all been radiated.

Interviewer: But bringing this child into your life really seemed to wipe out a lot of the pain?

Ann: Yes, absolutely. It really, I mean, my arms had just ached for all these months for the baby that had died and it was really, you know, a tremendous turning point for me.

Interviewer: What kind of impact did that have on your relationship with Don?

Ann: Well, at first he seemed to be just as delighted, but he really wasn't participatory at all in any child care and I still was trying to be perfect for him. I mean, he was very, covertly demanding, um, kind of expecting dinner at a specific hour, and expecting three-course dinners and not at all, um, sympathetic to how much time and effort a baby takes, and also to, um, my wanting him to participate, and, you know, us to be whatever I thought was a family. I mean, he just waited for me still to serve him, and after dinner he would not stay and help clean up. He would say, "Come and talk to me," but in the meantime expect me to clean up the kitchen and then—I don't know, we just seemed to grow further and further apart. What I think was nice about that time was that we had become friendly with this other couple who were very much a stabilizing influence, and when we were all together, everything seemed wonderful, and I guess I got to thinking that maybe we could have a good kind of life together. Because when the four of us were together, or when we were together with them and their baby, and our baby, it seemed, you know, right and comfortable, but they left the area after a year, and at that point things really changed. I started to suspect that Don was seeing somebody else. He was always talking about this one woman at work whom he admired so very much and it just started to register that he must be seeing her. I asked him and of course he laughed, and then he got much more innovative in our lovemaking and that certainly was a clue that he was learning something some other place, and he would, um, shower and change clothes and tell me that he was going to research something for a case he was preparing.

Interviewer: So you had a lot of signs that there were problems there.

Ann: But of course he denied them every time, and we were moving along with our plans to move to Pittsburgh. Don was going to go into practice and we had flown up there and bought a house, and one day Don called me from work and said he had to talk to me, could I get a baby-sitter and let's go out for dinner, and I did, and we went out for dinner and he told me that he was seeing somebody else and that he wanted out of the marriage.

Interviewer: What was that like for you?

Ann: Well, my first reaction was almost relief, and it gave me the one opportunity I had ever had to tell him how I felt, and or, at least, the one opportunity I ever took to tell him how I felt. It was such a relief that I said, you know, I feel the same way and I really would like to end the marriage also. And so we went back to the house and I packed myself and the baby up and got on a plane and flew back to Dallas, and no sooner had the plane taken off than I knew that had been a terrible decision and I called Don at 4 o'clock in the morning and said, "I'm coming back. This is crazy. We should, you know, we can't resolve anything with this distance between us," and he said, "No, don't. There's nothing for us to discuss."

Interviewer: So he was very clear the marriage was over for him.

Ann: Uh, huh. Absolutely, and there was never any effort at any kind of counseling, though repeatedly I tried to persuade him that this just wasn't fair and we should give it some more time.

Interviewer: So, on second thought, you had a lot of regrets about the end of the marriage.

Ann: Yes. I did. I still feel that if I had acted differently, it probably would not have ended, though I don't really regret it. I just think that it could have had a different course of events if I had acted differently.

Interviewer: So there you were without any real direction, with a young child, and your marriage at an end.

Ann: Right.

Interviewer: How did you handle that difficult time?

Ann: Well, at first I wasn't doing too well. I was staying at my cousin's house, the one that I mentioned to you that I'm so close with. And I stayed there for several months and finally took a secretarial job and decided to go back to college and moved into my own apartment, and that was what I was doing when—I developed a recurrence of the cancer.

Interviewer: That must have been a terrible time for you. How old were you at this point?

Ann: Twenty-five. That was probably the second worst time of my whole life, because I went from doctor to doctor, hearing that the last treatment hadn't been right and that they'd given me too much radiation, and it was just a confusing, terrifying thing. Sort of waiting to die, and worrying about my little girl, and maybe hoping that Don would come back, which he didn't. He never even called and asked what was happening.

Interviewer: He knew that you had the recurrence?

Ann: Uh, huh. I mean, I assumed he would have been curious, but he wasn't. And that became a real turning point for me, because somewhere in the midst of all that, thinking that I was going to die, I almost was reborn, and decided to take control of my life. I felt that I couldn't rely on the doctors and I decided to stop the treatment, against their advice, feeling that really nobody knew me better than I did and that I was in the best position to make decisions for myself about how I was feeling and what I should be doing. And, um, I stopped all the treatments. I was working at that point again, and, um—things just really changed for me at that point, as far as waiting for somebody to tell me what to do or giving away any of my power or being so vulnerable.

Interviewer: Taking control of your own life and wanting to live.

Ann: Right.

Interviewer: And the cancer went into remission?

Ann: Yes, it, um, everything changed. I really, seriously registered in this school program. Before that I had just been taking some courses, and I started to read voluminous amounts of self-help books, and kind of incorporated so much of what I read into my personality, and just acted like I had some control over what was going to happen.

Interviewer: That was about 10 years ago?

Ann: Yes. Eight or 9 years ago.

Interviewer: And you've made a great many changes in this period.

Ann: Yes. Now I feel fine, I look fine, and my life is terrific.

Interviewer: Can you kind of summarize for me some of the important things that happened?

Ann: Well, I finished an interior design program at college. Stopped thinking about work as just work, and started thinking of it as a career. And began to have some real direction as far as that went, and started to feel that I was a pretty incredible person, having come through the kinds of things that I had, and I have a very strong faith and belief that we're here for a reason, and that things don't just happen randomly, and I want to make the most of every day that I have, and basically, I guess I think the biggest change is that I don't think anybody anywhere knows any more or better what I should be doing than I do, and I just, you know, live and act in that way.

Interviewer: So the main things are changes in your attitude. Just being much more positive, more in control, and good changes in your education and career direction.

Ann: Right, and capable and powerful and extremely confident. I just wonder how I spent all that time feeling so negative about myself when I realize that I really have so tremendously much to offer.

Interviewer: It sounds very rewarding for you— Let's look further at some aspects of your present life. How have those changes been reflected in your present life?

Ann: Uh, I joined a very supportive women's group soon after I moved back to Dallas, and I have maintained my contact with those women all these years, and that's been particularly meaningful. We vacation together with the children, we celebrate holidays together, not always on the holiday time, but after a time, you know. After the actual date, but just because these people are as much like family as family to me. And, um, you know, then I try to spend as much time with my daughter as I can, so I go to movies with her, go on walks, go bike-riding, that kind of thing.

Interviewer: You've been doing a great deal, but your daughter is always a big focus. What's her name?

Ann: Claire.

Interviewer: Claire. And tell me some more about your relationship with Claire.

Ann: Well, I just adore her, and feel like she's the most wonderful, important person. I think she's a pretty terrific kid, and I feel like we've been very close. I try to be very honest with her, but I also feel a lot of pain for what I think she has to deal with because of our divorce and because of being adopted. It's been very hard to be alone with her, and this isn't what I wanted for her.

Interviewer: So it sounds like she's been a very special thing in your life. There are still some hurdles to overcome, though.

Ann: Well, now some problems have come up. That's really what brought me in, and I do have some concerns about helping her and me move through those.

Interviewer: What are the problems that especially concern you?

Ann: Well, she seems to be bothered by some things, and not wanting to share them with me. I respect her privacy, and I would, happily, you know, provide or seek some other help for her, if that was what she wanted to do. But I don't know if I'm projecting my own concerns about the adoption and the divorce onto her, so I don't want to say, "Do you want to go and see a counselor so you can talk about being adopted?" because maybe it's not a problem to her and I'm just assuming that it is. I don't know how much of the normal conflicts that we've started to have are just normal, developmental things with a twelve-year-old.

Interviewer: Tell me about one of these conflicts.

Ann: Well, the biggest one has come up over religion. I am Protestant. Just the last couple of weeks, she's started to say that she doesn't believe in God and that she's not going to religious school any more and she doesn't want to go to church and she doesn't believe any of this, and, at that point, she mentioned trying to find her biological mother.

Interviewer: This must all be very troubling to you. How did it happen that Claire was available for adoption?

Ann: Well, I don't know terribly much about it. I really just know the physical details of her parents. I really, you know, don't know what were the circumstances of their relationship. I just know that both of her parents had similar coloring to my then-husband and me and similar size and stuff, but, uh—

Interviewer: It must be very upsetting to you that your parenting and your religion, beliefs which are important to you, are being challenged by Claire in this way.

Ann: Oh, yes, because I certainly feel that she is my child. She doesn't know anything else, I mean, I recognize that she wasn't born to me, but that certainly isn't what gives us our identity.

Interviewer: And you feel that she's perhaps concerned about the adoption and about the divorce?

Ann: Well, I don't know if she's just using religion now, if she's levelling with me about the fact that that was the real issue. She may be picking on something that she thinks is more acceptable to say. She had asked about finding her biological mother earlier and I had said, you know, I understood her curiosity, certainly, and I would help her, but not until she was about eighteen. And that seemed to satisfy her at the time, but I'm wondering if some of this wasn't triggered by her recent visit with her father. Also, I was supposed to get married earlier in the year, last year, to somebody that she did not like at all. I wonder now if this isn't, you know, some repercussion from her negative feelings about that situation.

Interviewer: So you feel that might have affected Claire. Tell me about what your relationships with men have been like since your divorce.

Ann: Well, there have been a lot of men, some, you know, more significant than others. It's hard to meet men that are—well, that are available, first of all, and that don't have so many personality peculiarities that would eliminate them, and I feel now that I need a very special man, somebody that isn't going to be threatened by the independence that I exhibit. I don't need a man to do anything or give me anything that I can't give myself at this point, and so it will have to be somebody very special. There haven't been a lot of deep relationships, but a couple. And it's been painful when they have, you know, broken off. A couple, well, there were three times when I thought I would get married. One was very soon after the divorce and I think I was just taken by the fact that he had custody of his children and he had seemed to adore my little girl, and it was lovely to be together in that way, but I know that it wouldn't have worked out because he would not have been comfortable with the kind of growth that was about to take place for me, so—

Interviewer: But that seemed a way to get back into a family situation quickly.

Ann: Right, but I think I knew then that it wasn't really the answer. And I don't feel it now. I'd like there to be a man and I'd like there to be somebody special, but I can live just fine not married.

Interviewer: Uh, huh. How about these other almost-marriages that you talked about? Particularly the most recent one.

Ann: Well, he seemed to be the very special person that I was telling you about. He seemed to respect and appreciate the things that I had accomplished, and to be very delighted about my successes professionally. But some issues came up about his very negative feelings about my little girl, and also it required my moving away, and I had such a really terrific support system and comfortable life here, that I realized that I would almost be putting myself in the same situation that I had years ago when I moved to Washington and I wasn't really sure that he could give me the kind of emotional support that I might need, and I wasn't really sure that I ever want to depend that much on another person to provide that.

Interviewer: So when you looked at all the circumstances, even though he seemed very special, the whole package didn't seem to be what you wanted.

Ann: Right, right.

Interviewer: And was it your decision then to end the relationship?

Ann: Yes, but he, you know, didn't, uh, seem that uncomfortable when I said it didn't seem like it was going to work out. I have some concerns about why I haven't been able to make a relationship, another relationship, and I wonder if I'm carrying some old hurts or feelings from the first marriage, though I almost feel like I'm a different person now, and—

Interviewer: But something you might like to look at in counseling is your relationships and whether they've gone as well as they could have for you.

Ann: Yes, well, I guess with men, but certainly not with other people I have—

Interviewer: Yes, specifically with men. Anything else you can think of that you might like to work on?

Ann: No, the issues with my daughter and my social life are pretty much the prime concerns right now. I mean, I'd like to make some career changes, but I don't know that, you know, you can help me with that. I feel I just have to move along and take an opportunity when it presents itself.

Interviewer: And your medical condition?

Ann: Is fine.

Interviewer: Anything else you would like to add that you think I ought to know about you?

Ann: No.

Interviewer: Well, thank you for sharing so much about yourself.

We'll be in touch with you very soon to set up another appointment.

Ann: Thank you.

REPORT OF EXTENDED INTAKE INTERVIEW

Client: Ann Ryerson   Interviewer: Leslie Porter
Birthdate: 8/15/47   Date of interview: 9/20/83

Identifying Information

Ann Ryerson, a 36-year-old white, Protestant female was self-referred to the Southern Valley Community Mental Health Center. Ms. Ryerson and her twelve-year-old daughter Claire live in the CMHC's catchment area. The client has been divorced for 9 years. She is employed as an interior designer at Neiman-Marcus and is studying for the master's degree in art education.

Ms. Ryerson (Ann) is an attractive woman of average height and weight. She was appropriately dressed in a business suit and was carefully groomed. She seemed highly motivated toward help and seemed to respond to all questions openly and directly. Client did appear rather tense throughout the interview but not to a debilitating degree. Some depression and sadness also were evident, especially when client was discussing illnesses and bereavements she had experienced. However, she also evidenced a sense of humor and considerable warmth. Affect, then, seemed appropriate with the exception of her generalized anxiety. The client manifested no noticeable habits or behavioral abnormalities during the interview and related well to this interviewer.

Presenting Problem

Ann's primary concerns revolved around behavioral and attitudinal changes that she has recently noticed in her daughter, Claire. Claire had been adopted by Ann and her then-husband when Claire was ten days old. Over the past 6 months, Claire reportedly has become hard to get along with, has expressed an interest in locating her biological parents, and has questioned

Ann's religious beliefs. Ann is worried that her own concerns have had a negative impact on Claire and she wants to gain insight into that and improve her relationship with Claire. Ann was also concerned about her difficulty in forming a positive and enduring realtionship with a man.

Present Difficulties and Previous Disorders

Ann is seeking understanding of recent changes in her daughter, Claire, and help in coping with them. She is not sure whether to view them as a natural phase of adolescence or as a delayed and potentially serious reaction to Claire's adoption and the subsequent divorce of the Ryersons. The client stated that she and her daughter have always been very close, and Ann seems worried lest the current changes in Claire jeopardize their relationship.

Ann also acknowledged some difficulty in her social relationships with men. She apparently has dated quite a bit since her divorce and has had at least three serious relationships. She is single and seems somewhat dissatisfied with her relationships.

The client's history, to be discussed in greater detail in later sections of this report, reveals an early and extended pattern of low self-esteem, dependence on others, interpersonal difficulties, and illness. About 8 or 9 years ago, however, the client dealt very positively with an extremely stressful period in her life and, since then, seems to have become more self-confident and self-reliant. Her current concerns seem to have reminded the client of her earlier difficulties and consequently are frightening to her. In general, however, she seems to be coping well with her life and to be expressing manageable concerns. Presenting problems do not seem to be having an adverse impact on the client's life-style but rather to be troubling more for their potential to disrupt her life. It also may be that the client is feeling a conflict between the demands of her adolescent daughter and the client's own wish for a rewarding and established relationship with a man since the onset of Claire's current difficulties seemed to coincide with the client's recent thoughts of marriage to a man she had been dating.

Present Life Situation

The client seems to lead a full and active life. She reports deriving great gratification from her relationship with her daughter. She has several close women friends who serve as a surrogate family and she also maintains frequent and satisfying contact with her mother, her stepfather, and a female cousin. She seems to be successful in her work and to have a sense of career direction. She participates in an exercise class as well as other leisure activities and dates regularly.

Family

The client comes from a middle-class Protestant family and grew up in this area. Her nuclear family consisted of her parents and a brother who was 9 years younger than she.

Ann described her father as a dynamic man with a zest for life. He and the client seemed to have a particularly close relationship until he died of cancer when she was eighteen. The client seems to have been "Daddy's little girl"; when she was ill (apparently quite often), he would leave work to be with her and the two of them seemed to share many pleasurable activities. The client apparently had not been well-prepared for her father's death and seemed to receive little help from the family in handling the bereavement.

Ann's relationship with her father may have given her an early message that as long as she was a "good little girl," a man would love her and care for her. That relationship seemed to foster helplessness and dependency rather than growth and seemed to establish the pattern for her marriage.

Ann's relationship with her mother is described as oppressive and unfulfilling. The client viewed her mother as having been dull and traditional. The mother is perceived as a limiting influence for Ann and does not offer her a model of competence or independence. Ann's mother has remarried and seems to have become more individualized and approachable, but the client still seems to feel guarded and bitter toward her mother.

The client's relationship with her brother seems rather distant, though satisfactory. He was the troublemaker while they were growing up and she seemed to resent the attention his acting-out brought him. Now, although she praised him for his good relationship with Claire, Ann seems to have little in common with her brother and sees him only because their mother arranges it.

Close relationships have been established with her stepfather and a cousin. In general, then, although the client's early years did not offer a positive model for adulthood, she seems to be making good use of her family as a support system at the present time.

Ann's closest relationship seems to be with her daughter, Claire. Claire is described in what sounds like idealized terms and it is possible that the client is setting unrealistically high standards for her daughter. The years of closeness between them also may make it difficult for both of them to handle Claire's emerging need for independence.

The client seems to have little contact with her ex-husband, who resides in Pittsburgh. He does, however, have Claire visit him each year.

Developmental History

Ann's childhood years seem to have been fairly uneventful, with the exception of the birth of her brother. She describes herself as being almost perfect in her behavior and seems to have used model behavior and illness to get attention. She was a satisfactory student, although her parents did not encourage her to excel academically. She apparently had little intrinsic motivation toward school. She seems to have been brought up with the traditional view that her task in life was to marry and have children and that women's needs come second to their husbands'. Ann's primary goal, then, for a number of years, was to accomplish that task.

The client began dating and became sexually active at sixteen. Although she describes that as being very stressful, she seemed to feel that it was worth risking pregnancy and parental disfavor in order to keep her boyfriend happy. Her self-image apparently was low and was dependent on her having a boyfriend.

The client entered a community college after high school.

She seemed to have no clear career goals at that time but was simply doing what her friends did. Somewhat to her surprise, she became rather popular and attractive in college and found that she enjoyed school for the first time.

Ann met her husband-to-be, Don, during her first year of college. He seemed to be her only source of support after her father's death, and he apparently encouraged her to transfer her dependency from her father to him. Ann and Don were married after about a year of dating, and the client, following the traditional path, left school to work and put her husband through law school.

Although courtship and the early months of their marriage seemed good, problems developed when the couple moved to another state. Ann became pregnant and, after an extremely difficult pregnancy, gave birth. During the pregnancy, Ann developed toxemia and reportedly got little attention from her husband during that time. That must have been particularly troubling since illness had brought her attention in the past. Shortly after the child's birth, while Don and Ann were on a sailing trip and the little boy was left with baby-sitters, he died of Sudden Infant Death Syndrome. Ann seemed to deal well with her anger and guilt, but, even now, may not have fully gotten over her grief at the loss of the child.

Despite further deterioration in their marriage, Ann and Don decided to have another child. During that pregnancy, however, Ann was diagnosed as having bladder carcinoma. The risk of genetic damage from chemotherapy led Ann to decide to have an abortion. The chemotherapy treatment ruled out future pregnancies. It was while Ann was recovering from cancer that the couple adopted Claire. Although the adoption seemed to be extremely gratifying to Ann, Don apparently continued to withdraw from the marriage and to deny Ann fulfillment of her needs for dependency and intimacy. Eventually, Don became involved with another woman and told Ann he wanted a divorce. Ann initially agreed but later changed her mind. Don seemed to have made a firm decision and the divorce was obtained. Ann seems to have some regrets about her hasty agreement and may not have fully resolved her feelings about the divorce.

About that same time, Ann experienced a recurrence of her

cancer. The stressful combination of becoming a single parent and becoming ill apparently led to a dramatic change in Ann's approach to life. She realized that being the good little girl had ceased to work and she took control of her life, regained her health, found work, returned to school, and eventually established a comfortable life-style for Claire and herself.

Ann has continued in good health and in control of her life for about 8 years. She seems interested in remarrying at some point, but is no longer dependent on men to complete her life and shape her identity.

Mental Status

Overall, the mental status examination of this client yields positive findings. She was presentable and appropriate, related well to this interviewer, and seemed motivated toward treatment. Her attention and concentration seemed unimpaired, and client responded clearly and directly to all questions. She seemed to have good recall of the important events in her life. Her thoughts were clear and well-organized and no confusion was evident. Her problem-solving skills certainly have been exemplary since her divorce. In light of that, however, it is somewhat surprising that she has sought counseling so quickly for her daughter's recent changes. Ann is well-oriented to reality and seems to be of above-average intelligence with strong verbal skills. She has a wide range of interests and seems to have clear and strong values. No evidence of sensory-motor or perceptual difficulties were noted. Affect was appropriately varied and ranged from amusement to tearful sadness. Some underlying anxiety and accompanying depression were noted. This seems to be a client who is functioning at a relatively high level, has excellent self-regulation skills, and is currently not significantly impaired by either physical or emotional difficulties.

Dynamics and Formulations

Ann seems to be reacting strongly to some relatively minor and short-lived changes in her daughter. These changes and Ann's request for counseling followed shortly after the end of a serious romantic relationship. It is possible that Ann sees her life as being at a transition point. She has worked hard for several years and has established a comfortable situation for her daughter and herself. Now, however, her daughter may have begun the separation and individuation processes that so often occur during adolescence. This may be leading Ann to raise some questions about the direction of her own life. Fears of losing the intimacy with Claire that Ann has valued for so long may have caused some buried feelings of dependency, loneliness, and self-doubt to surface and Ann probably could benefit from some help with those feelings, as well as with her heterosexual relationships.

Diagnostic Impression

Ann is a client with many strengths: motivation, intelligence, determination, competence, interpersonal skills, and the ability to establish support systems and a rewarding life-style. However, she seems fearful of change at this point and may be overly involved with her daughter. She also seems to have difficulty discussing present self-doubts and her social relationships with men.

Ann seems an appropriate candidate for counseling at present in light of her motivation, intelligence, verbal skills, and the nature of her concerns. The following areas should receive attention during the counseling process:

1. Mother-daughter relationship
2. Client's self-image and future goals
3. Her social relationships with men

The following diagnosis is advanced:

Axis I   —309.24 Adjustment disorder with anxious mood.
             V61.20 Parent-child problem
Axis II —V71.09 No diagnosis on Axis II
Axis III—Bladder carcinoma, in remission for 7 years
Axis IV—Psychosocial stressors: Daughter's behavioral and
             emotional changes. Severity: 3-Mild
Axis V —Highest level of adaptive functioning, past year:
             2-Very good

Treatment Plan

Since Ann's presenting problem focuses on her daughter, it is felt that she would be most amenable to counseling with a family focus. However, Ann also seems to have concerns that are independent of her relationship with her daughter. Consequently, a combination of individual and family (mother-daughter) counseling is suggested, probably beginning with family counseling and interspersed with or moving toward individual counseling as Ann develops trust in the counselor and becomes more able to focus on her own concerns.

In light of Ann's high motivation, as well as her tendency toward dependency, it is felt that a client-centered approach will be most productive, focusing on communication patterns between mother and daughter, the clients' perceptions of their concerns, and their self-images. Such a model of counseling also seems conducive to the development of Ann's self-esteem.

It is anticipated that counseling with Ann generally will be present-oriented and relatively brief in duration. Exploratory and supportive techniques both seem in order. However, it is possible that unresolved past concerns will surface and will be seen to have a significant impact on the client's present situation. An example of this might be a connection between Ann's unfinished grieving over the loss of her first child and her inability to loosen her hold on Claire. Attention probably will need to be paid primarily to the affective realm with some secondary attention to cognitive issues. Choice of counselor seems open.

Prognosis

The prognosis in this case seems very optimistic. This is a client with many strengths who has maintained good control over her life. Of course, the counselor has not yet met with Claire. It is possible that Claire's difficulties will turn out to be more severe than they sound at the present time. However, based on present information, short-term, client-centered counseling, combining individual and family sessions, seems likely to restore this client's self-confidence and positive relationship with her daughter, reduce her anxiety, and help her improve her interpersonal relations.

THE BRIEF INTAKE INTERVIEW

Increasing numbers of mental health agencies seem to be moving toward a briefer approach to intake interviews. Such interviews typically last 30 to 60 minutes and culminate in a relatively brief written report (perhaps 2 to 4 pages). This approach would be particularly prevalent in agencies that are understaffed or advocate one of the brief or strategic approaches to treatment, discussed in subsequent chapters.

The primary goals of the brief intake process are similar to those of the extended process. They commonly include the following:

1. Assessing and dealing with urgency of case
2. Gathering demographic data
3. Orienting client to rules, policies, and procedures of agency
4. Understanding client's presenting problem and reasons for seeking help at present time
5. Performing a brief mental status examination
6. Obtaining information on client's current situation
7. Surveying relevant history, especially previous treatment
8. Developing a diagnosis and treatment plan

In a brief intake interview, greater emphasis is placed on presenting concerns than is typically done in the extended interview. The brief model assumes a less analytical approach, generally accepting the client's statement of his or her goals with only limited exploration. Far less attention is paid to history-taking and only limited examination of underlying dynamics is undertaken.

Information Sheet

An intake interview, whether brief, extended, or in-between, often begins with the gathering of some factual information on the client. Sometimes this information is gathered by a receptionist, clerical worker, or mental health aide rather than by the mental health professional who will be conducting the interview.

A sample of such an information sheet is provided on the next page. It has been completed with data obtained from a client whose brief interview report will be presented in the following section.

Models of Brief Intake Interview Reports

Although the content areas of brief intake interview reports are fairly consistent, the formats used tend to vary from one agency to another. What follows are two brief intake reports, completed according to two different models. The first of these was based on an interview with George Williams, the client whose data is provided on the information sheet. The second report was based on Ann Ryerson, the client whose extended interview and report were presented in the previous section.

INFORMATION SHEET

INTAKE WORKER ___ **L D** ___
DATE __ **1/11/84** __
PRIOR CASE # _____

PLEASE PRINT AND FILL IN COMPLETELY

NAME __ **Williams,** ____ **George** _____ **P.** _____
     Last   First   Middle Initial

Maiden Name _____
ADDRESS ___ **85 Trumbull Street** _____
_____ **Laurel, Md.** _____ ZIP __ **20708** __
HOME PHONE # **(301) 776-3854** OFFICE PHONE # __ **n.a.**
DATE OF BIRTH **2/19/61** _
            Mo. Day Yr.
PLACE OF BIRTH **Baltimore, Md.**
          City and state
SEX (circle one) (Male) Female   AGE __ **23** ____
RACE (circle one)
(White)   Black   Hispanic   Oriental   Other _____
MARITAL STATUS (circle one)
(Single)   Married   Widowed   Divorced   Separated

EDUCATION (circle highest grade completed)

6 7 8 9 10 11 (12)

Some College   College Graduate   Post Graduate

OCCUPATION _ **Machinist** _____ SALARY **currently**
                                        unemployed

REFERRAL SOURCE **self** _____

Have you ever been seen at this Mental Health Center before?
YES (NO)

Have you ever been seen at any mental health center?
(YES) NO   Where **Baltimore**
If YES, please give date last seen ___ **uncertain-approximately**
                                        6 years ago
Is any other member of your family being seen at this Center?
YES (NO)
NAME _____
Relationship _____ Birthdate _____

Have you ever been to a psychiatric hospital?   YES (NO)
Place of hospitalization _____
Date of hospitalization: from _____ to _____

Are you on any medication? YES (NO) If YES, what?_____

Intake Form

Intake Worker   LP

Date 1/11/84 Name of Patient George P. Williams
Referral Source Self

1.   What does client present as problem? What precipitated
      client's coming to the center?

      Client presents a 6 to 7 year history of increasing alco-
      holism. Until recently, he has maintained enough con-
      trol over his drinking so that he could complete high
      school and hold employment. Six months ago, the wom-
      an with whom he has been living became pregnant and
      suggested marriage. Mr. Williams stated that he has be-
      come increasingly confused and anxious since and has

lost control of his drinking. He was fired from his job
last week.

2.   What does the patient want from us? What are patient's
expectations?

Mr. Williams seems to want to regain his former control
over his drinking so that he can hold a job and take
care of his girlfriend and expected child. He also wants
help in reducing the anxiety and confusion he is experiencing and making a decision about whether to marry.

3.   Patient's present situation (living and working situations).

Mr. Williams is living in a rented three-room apartment
with his girlfriend, Rose Talbert. They have been involved with each other for 1½ years and have been living together for nearly a year. The couple is expecting
a child in 3 months. Mr. Williams had been employed
regularly until last week. He is currently seeking employment. Ms. Talbert has been employed as a book-
keeper but will soon go on leave to care for their child.

4.   Brief past history.

Mr. Williams describes himself as a loner who never had
many friends. He began drinking in junior high school
as a way to feel more accepted by peers. He was sometimes involved in truancy and vandalism in school and
was briefly in family therapy then. There is no record
of arrests. Mr. Williams is the second of two children.
He maintains some contact with both his sister (6 years
older, married) and his parents. Father had a history of
alcoholism but was always employed.

5.   Physical description and mental status of patient, affect,
intelligence, delusions or hallucinations, motivation,
anxieties about becoming invested in treatment, degree
of depression.

Client is a tall, slender male with a youthful, gangly appearance. He was casually but appropriately dressed. He appeared moderately depressed and anxious but maintained good contact with reality. Responses to questions were brief but direct. Alcohol could be detected on client's breath but he did not appear intoxicated. He seems to be of average intelligence. Client is in a crisis and, consequently, currently is motivated toward treatment. However, he seems reluctant to give up drinking entirely and may have difficulty making a significant commitment to treatment.

6. Recommendation, statement of mutually agreed contract on therapeutic goals, time frame or reason for none.

Client made a 2-month commitment to weekly counseling.

Stated goals: 1. Reducing or eliminating alcohol consumption
2. Making decision on marriage
3. Relief of debilitating depression and anxiety

Referral is being made for medical evaluation and consultation. A brief, behavioral model of treatment seems most appropriate. Couples counseling is anticipated, but client was reluctant to involve his girlfriend in his treatment at present. It is expected that more than 2 months of treatment will be needed but a short-term contract was made in light of client's perceived reluctance.

Diagnostic impression:

Axis I	303.91	Alcohol dependence, continuous
	309.28	Adjustment disorder with mixed emotional features
Axis II	301.82	Avoidant personality disorder (provisional)
Axis III		No medical complaints; referral made.

Axis IV   Psychological stressors: girl-
                     friend's unplanned pregnan-
                     cy, loss of employment. Sever-
                     ity: 5- Severe
Axis V   Highest level of adaptive func-
                     tioning past year: 4- Fair

INITIAL INTERVIEW

Ann Ryerson   #0364-7
Client's Name and Number

Date of Interview 9/20/83 **Name of Interviewer** Leslie Porter

**IDENTIFICATION, APPEARANCE,
BEHAVIORAL OBSERVATIONS:** Client is a 36-year-old
white Protestant female. She presented an attractive and appropriate appearance, related well to the interviewer, and
seemed motivated toward treatment. Ann generally manifested an appropriate range of emotions, although anxiety with
accompanying underlying depression was noted. Client manifested no habits or behavioral abnormalities and seemed to be
in good contact with reality.

Current Work/School & Living Situation: Client has been divorced for nine years and lives in a comfortable residence
with her 12-year old adopted daughter, Claire. Ann is an interior designer/planner and is studying for the master's degree
in art education. Family and friends offer nearby support systems.

Relevant Family/Social History: Client grew up in an intact
middle class family. She has one brother, now 27. She seems
to have been dependent on father; distant from mother. Father died when she was 18. Client married at 20 and had an
infant who died of SIDS. A subsequent pregnancy was terminated when client required chemotherapy. Client was divorced
after seven years of marriage.

Referral Source: Self-referred

STATEMENT OF PRESENTING PROBLEM:

Symptoms: Client is feeling anxious and concerned about recent behavioral and attitudinal changes in her daughter, Claire. Ann requests help in understanding and coping with these changes. According to Ann, Claire seems increasingly uncomfortable with her adoptive status and her relationship to Ann. Ann also expressed concern about her social relationship with men.

Precipitating Factors: Ann's concern about Claire's apparent changes began about six months ago when Ann was in the process of ending a serious romantic relationship.

Brief History of Problem: Ann reported that she and Claire always have been extremely close. Changes observed in Claire, however, seem to Ann to pose a threat to their relationship. There is no history of similar problems with Claire. Ann has an early history of dependency, low self-esteem, and limited goals, but seems to have functioned at a high level for the past seven years.

MEDICATION AND/OR MEDICAL PROBLEMS: Ann currently is in good health and is taking no medication. She exercises regularly and is health-conscious. She did, however, have two occurrences of bladder carcinoma (1971, 1974).

STRENGTHS & RESOURCES: Ann has many strengths, including motivation, above-average intelligence, good verbal skills, the ability to manage her life and form support systems, and a stable lifestyle. She dates regularly, has a close group of women friends, and maintains satisfactory relationships with mother, brother, stepfather, and other family members.

OTHER RELEVANT DATA: Ann seems to be reacting strongly to some relatively minor and short-lived changes in her daughter. Ann may see her life as being at a transition point. She has worked hard for several years and has established a good life. Now her daughter may have begun the process of separation that is almost inevitable during adolescence. This may be leading Ann to raise some questions about the direction of her own life. Buried feelings of dependency, loneliness, and self-doubt may be surfacing and Ann probably could benefit from some help with those feelings.

SUMMARY OF IMPRESSIONS: (Definitions of Issues)

Ann seems fearful of change at this point and may be overly involved with her daughter. She also seems to have difficulty discussing present self-doubts and her relationships with men. The following areas should receive attention during the counseling process:

1. Mother-daughter relationship
2. Client's self-image and future goals
3. Her social relationships with men

Diagnostic impression:
309.24 Adjustment disorder with anxious mood
V61.20 Parent-child problem

RECOMMENDED MODALITY: Short-term, client-centered counseling, beginning with family (mother-daughter) counseling and moving onto some individual counseling is recommended. Attention should be paid, however, to the presence of unresolved past concerns that are impinging on present mood level. The prognosis seems excellent.

Designated Counselor: Peter O'Brien

AVAILABILITY & READINESS FOR TREATMENT: Available to be seen as soon as possible. Evening or weekend appointment required.

MAKING THE TRANSITION FROM INTAKE TO TREATMENT

An intake interview generally will culminate in the formulation of a diagnosis and a treatment plan. Detailed information on diagnosis is provided in chapter 2 and on treatment planning, in chapters 5 through 8. In some agencies, the intake interviewer has the responsibility for determining the diagnosis and treatment plan while in others this is accomplished through a case conference.

Case conferences are used by many agencies to make diagnosis and treatment planning a group process, presumably increasing accuracy because input from a number of people is obtained. The case conference also often serves as the vehicle for assigning clients to mental health workers.

A typical case conference will be a regularly scheduled weekly meeting, perhaps 2 hours in duration, of all mental health workers in a particular agency or division of an agency. Each worker who interviewed a new client that week will present the group with a brief summary of the history and concerns of that client and the worker's impressions of the client. Other staff present will have an opportunity to ask questions of the interviewer and then the group will collaborate to determine a viable diagnosis and treatment plan for the client. Typically, once that has been agreed upon, the case will be assigned to an appropriate staff member, taking account of the expertise of the staff members, their interest in particular types of clients and approaches to treatment, the treatment needs of the client, and the schedule constraints of both clients and staff members.

Limitations on the case conference process may be imposed by the presence of a waiting list or by the client's financial circumstances. If there is a waiting list, a determination will need to be made as to how long a particular client can comfortably delay treatment and what sorts of interim services or referral sources might be provided in the meantime. This process is facilitated if someone is earmarked as the case manager or person responsible for ensuring the expeditious provision of services to a particular client. The delay of treatment can be a frustrating and disappointing experience for clients who often bring with them feelings of ambivalence and apprehension about seeking mental health services. It is important that clients be informed of the nature and expected duration of any delay and encouraged to maintain their commitment to treatment. It is easy for clients to fall by the wayside or be lost in the procedural intricacies of an agency and steps should be taken to prevent those outcomes.

Finances can present another potential roadblock to treatment. Some agencies have sliding fee schedules, based on clients' incomes, while others do not. Some mental health workers are eligible to recieve third-party payments from insurance companies while others are not. Some clients have medical insurance that will pay all or part of the cost of mental health services for emotional illnesses while other clients do not have such coverage. Although it is often difficult for both clients and mental health professionals to discuss fees and finances, appropriate and viable treatment plans cannot be made unless the intake interviewer obtains information on what services the client can afford. Treatment planning must take account of costs and financial resources and should seek to find a way to provide clients with necessary services at costs they can afford.

SUMMARY

This chapter considered the nature and importance of intake interviews. Outlines were provided for mental status examinations and both brief and extended intake interviews. A transcript of an extended intake interview was included as were examples of both lengthy and brief intake reports. Finally, the relationship of intake interviews to diagnosis and treatment planning was reviewed.

Chapter 5

TREATMENT PLANNING FOR INDIVIDUAL CLIENTS

SUITABILITY FOR COUNSELING

The first step in treatment planning is determining whether a client is likely to benefit from counseling. In order to assess this, counselors should look at three areas:

1. Level of client motivation
2. Characteristics of client
3. Nature of the problem

Motivation

Clients come to counseling from various referral sources and with varying degrees of motivation. Asking clients, "What led you to seek counseling at the present time?" is a good place to begin to assess motivation. A reasonable estimate of the client's motivation generally can be made by examining the following:

1. Nature of referral
2. Urgency/magnitude of difficulty and nature of precipitating event

Clients may be self-referred, other-referred, agency-referred, or some combination. Self-referred clients have taken a look at their lives and feel that some change is warranted; they have selected counseling as a way to achieve that change. Generally, a self-referral is an indication of motivation.

Often, clients are referred by their family or friends. This type of referral can take many forms. A common example is the client who says to the counselor, "You seem to have helped my friend Ann when she was going through some rough times at work, and now she's a supervisor. I'm having trouble at work now and Ann said maybe you could help me, too." In such a client, there certainly is a strong element of self-referral. However, the client may have some unrealistic expectations of what counseling can do. More exploration of the motivation of this client is needed.

Another common type of other-referral is the client who says, "I'm coming for counseling because my husband told me he would leave me if I didn't shape up. I don't want to lose my husband, so here I am." On the surface, this client's motivation toward counseling seems to be indirect at best. She does not express an interest in change to please herself but, rather, because it has been demanded by her husband. Often, however, clients have difficulty taking responsibility for seeking counseling; they may view it as an admission that something is wrong with them. Such clients may really be quite self-motivated but may need the smoke screen of an other-referral as a temporary self-protection. On the other hand, such clients may resent the source of referral (e.g., the threatening spouse) and may transfer that resentment to the counselor. While other-referred clients may be excellent candidates for counseling, the counselor should spend extra time exploring their expectations and strengthening their intrinsic motivation for counseling.

There is a similarly broad range of agency-referred clients. Some may be highly motivated and may have been referred so the client can obtain less expensive or more appropriate services. Other clients, however, may be referred for compulsory counseling. For example, some persons arrested while intoxicated are given the choice of seeking counseling or losing their driver's license. Others may be required to see a counselor as a condition of parole. Involuntary clients typically have more extrinsic than intrinsic motivation toward counseling and may manifest considerable resistance to the counseling process. Treatment planning with them must take account of the nature of their motivation. Short-term contracts and concrete, readily attainable goals generally should be established. Their progress should be assessed at regular intervals.

The urgency or magnitude of a client's difficulty often provides valuable information on the nature and level of motivation. Contrary to what one might think, urgency does not necessarily suggest high motivation. For example, Bettina, a narcotics addict, presented herself for detoxification and counseling upon learning that she was pregnant. She had been told that her drug abuse could harm the fetus, so she presented her concern as an urgent one. However, Bettina had little interest in changing her lifestyle or examining her attitudes and behaviors; she refused to continue counseling after being physically detoxified and resumed her drug use several weeks later.

Often, a crisis in clients' lives leads them to enter counseling. Experiencing a personal crisis does seem to make clients more receptive to the counseling process but is not a guarantee they will be sufficiently motivated to engage in counseling. All it does is open the door for the counselor. Whether the counselor is allowed through that door depends on the skills of the counselor and the long-standing levels of motivation and discomfort of the clients.

Occasionally, counselors encounter clients whose motivation is so low they cannot be engaged in the counseling process. Such clients may refuse to disclose more than identifying information, may be verbally abusive toward the counselor, or may have misunderstood the nature of counseling. If efforts to clarify the nature of counseling, develop rapport, and help the client to identify some goals do not succeed, the counselor probably should suggest that counseling may not be appropriate at present. A referral for other services can be made or, if warranted, an appointment for a follow-up visit in a few weeks or months can be scheduled. This is not a failure for either client or counselor but, simply, an acknowledgement that counseling is not the cure for all ills.

Characteristics of Client

Most counseling modalities are aimed toward clients who are of at least average verbal and intelligence levels and who have a reasonable degree of organization in their lives. Such clients seem most likely to keep scheduled appointments, to follow through on suggested tasks, and to engage in a dialogue about their concerns.

Clients without those characteristics tend to pose more of a challenge and call for particularly careful treatment planning. Support systems may have to be enlisted to enable them to keep scheduled appointments. Alternatively, counseling sessions may have to be held in the client's home or in inpatient or day treatment facilities. Verbal tactics may have to be deemphasized while behavioral and teaching models might be used extensively. The field of counseling today is sufficiently broad to accommodate the needs of clients who are not the affluent, articulate, and self-disciplined clients so often depicted in early case studies. However, the client who has little intrinsic motivation toward counseling, who has difficulty keeping appointments, and whose verbal skills are well below average seems likely to benefit more from other treatment modalities than from individual counseling.

Nature of the Problem

In order for clients to be suitable for counseling, they must have concerns that are amenable to treatment by counseling. Categories of common concerns are:

1. Relationship difficulties
2. Goal confusion
3. Poor or confused self-image
4. Indecision
5. Behavioral change, habit control
6. Depression or anxiety

Clearly, counseling is appropriate for a wide range of concerns. However, clients sometimes present goals or concerns that are

outside the scope of the counseling process. Examples of these
are:

1. Clients who really want to make someone else change
2. Clients seeking the counselor to be their friend or de-
   fender
3. Clients asking for information beyond the counselor's
   range of expertise (e.g., on financial affairs or divorce
   law)
4. Clients who want the counselor to force them to do
   something (e.g., lose weight)

Goals of the above clients are not too far afield from the
counseling process. For example, clients who want their counselors to be their friends can be encouraged to reflect on their
social relationships and define some ways to form better friendships outside of counseling. Unless the presenting concerns of
such clients can be redefined through the counseling process,
they will need to be referred to other sources. However, counselors should bear in mind that clients' presenting problems often
are not what is really troubling them and considerable effort
should be channeled toward elucidating their underlying concerns before it is determined that counseling is not warranted.

Frances, Clarkin, and Perry (1984) concluded, "The findings
of outcome research demonstrate psychotherapy to be, on the
average, significantly more effective than no treatment" (p. 214).
Sixty to 70 percent of clients improve in response to treatment
and some of those who do not improve would probably have
deteriorated further without help. Sometimes, however, no
treatment is the best recommendation. Frances et al. (1984) list
nine categories of clients who seem unlikely to benefit significantly from treatment:

1. Clients with a diagnosis of borderline personality disorder who have a history of treatment failures
2. Clients seeking counseling to strengthen a lawsuit or
   disability claim
3. Highly resistant and antisocial clients
4. Poorly motivated clients without incapacitating symptoms

5. Healthy clients in crisis who are improving on their own
6. Healthy clients with minor chronic or very long-lasting concerns
7. Clients with malingering or factitious illnesses
8. Extremely immature and dependent clients
9. Narcissistic or oppositional clients who might get worse in order to defeat the counselor

Although there are certainly clients in the above categories who would benefit from treatment, this list provides additional guidelines for determining clients' suitability for treatment.

APPROPRIATENESS OF THE SETTING

All counselors work in a context with parameters. These can include:

1. The expertise of the staff
2. Catchment area (geographic area from which clients can be drawn)
3. Fee schedule
4. Hours
5. Availability of particular modes of treatment at a given time
6. Level of supervision and frequency of treatment available to clients

Some of these parameters are determined by the nature of the agency's funding. For example, a career counseling program supported largely by county funds may be available only to county residents. Other parameters are determined by the objectives of the agency. For example, an agency focusing on marriage and family concerns may be ill-equipped to help a psychotic client or a client seeking to make a career change. Fee schedules and times when services are available are other parameters that must be considered. Finally, agencies almost always have some temporary and fluctuating limits on the kind and amount of services that can be offered. For example, although an agency may have groups available for divorced men, such groups may not begin for several months. Another agency may not have evening appointments available at a particular time.

In determining the best setting for a client's treatment, counselors should take particular account of the level of supervision and the frequency of treatment needed by the client. Whether treatment for a client should be provided at an outpatient facility, at a day treatment center, or at an inpatient (residential or hospital) facility can be determined by examining the following variables:

1. Severity, progression, and duration of client's symptoms
2. Threat to self or others
3. Nature and effectiveness of previous treatment
4. Cost effectiveness
5. Support systems and living situation
6. Preferences of client and significant others
7. Ability to attend outpatient sessions
8. Overall objective of treatment (e.g., symptom removal, rehabilitation, maintenance)

Available research provides little help in guiding the counselor's choice of treatment setting (Frances, et al., 1984). Clinical judgment is the best guide in making this decision as it is in determining most of the other treatment parameters.

It can be seen that clients can be suitable for counseling but unable to receive the services they need at the particular agency where they have presented themselves. It is at this time that the counselor should make a referral. The process of referral is discussed in depth in the next chapter. Referrals should not be made capriciously since they entail a risk of making clients feel rejected or discouraged about the possibility of receiving help. However, if a mental health agency cannot provide the services that are appropriate for a given client, a carefully planned and well-chosen referral probably should be made.

Goal Setting

Early in the counseling process, either concurrent with determining the suitability of clients for treatment or shortly thereafter, counselors and clients should work on the formulation of goals. Goals change as clients and counselors develop a working relationship, and new goals will supplant old ones as gains are made. Nonetheless, goals are necessary in order to develop a treatment plan, to assess progress, and to give direction to the counseling process.

Goal setting should be a mutual process, involving clients and counselors. Often, counselors feel they know what would be best for clients and know what their goals should be. Perhaps counselors sometimes do "know best." However, shared goals are most likely to facilitate the counseling process and motivate the client.

The goals selected should be clear and measurable. Clients often express goals such as "feeling better about themselves" and "getting along better with others." While such changes may well be made through the counseling process, they are vague objectives and are difficult to measure. Such objectives make developing a treatment plan and assessing progress a challenge. Consequently, counselors should not stop the goal-setting process here but should work with clients to determine, for example, exactly how they will know they are getting along better with others. Will they have fewer fights with colleagues, have lunch with friends more often, or have a longer list of people they would want to invite to a party? Regardless of the treatment modality used, goals should be defined as concretely as possible. Subjective self-report data (e.g., "I really do have more self-confidence these days") are important indicators of counseling progress. However, such feelings can be ephemeral and may not be sound building blocks in the counseling process. Clients seem to develop the soundest self-help skills and the greatest sense of their own competence and independence if they understand what they have done to effect positive changes in their lives and what the indications of those changes are.

Counselors often speak in terms of long- and short-term goals. Exactly what is meant by these terms varies greatly from client to client. For a client with many coping resources, perhaps a reentry woman who has effectively managed home and family, short-term goals might include the following:

1. Conducting four informational interviews
2. Obtaining and reviewing catalogs of area colleges

3. Discussing with her family her interest in returning to school
4. Clarifying interests and career objectives through inventories and counseling

Long-range goals might be:

1. Completing her college education
2. Obtaining employment with advancement potential
3. Continuing to have open and warm relationships with her husband and children and spending ample time with them

However, with a client with more limited resources, a different schedule will have to be established. A nineteen-year-old single parent who has not completed high school might develop the following short-term goals:

1. Calling to obtain information on the high school equivalency test
2. Asking her parents whether they would care for her child if she went to night school

Long-term goals might include:

1. Completing her high school diploma
2. Developing a budget
3. Reestablishing contact with the father of her child

In both examples, all goals can be described and measured in objective terms. All were developed in collaboration with the clients and were designed to help the clients build on their resources, taking account of their strengths and life circumstances. The schedules vary, however. Short-term goals for the reentry woman could be accomplished in a month or less while long-term goals would require several years. For the young mother, short-term goals could be accomplished in as little as a day; long-term goals, in 6 months. Short-term goals, regularly evaluated and renegotiated, provide both counselors and clients with a sense of progress and reinforcement while long-term goals guide the direction of the counseling process. Both contribute to the development of viable treatment plans.

PARAMETERS OF THE COUNSELING PROCESS

The first step in developing a treatment plan is determining the broad parameters of the counseling process. These include:

1. Duration
2. Level of directiveness
3. Supportive versus exploratory counseling
4. Cognitive, affective or behavioral counseling
5. Modality of counseling
6. Counselor variables

Once these broad parameters have been specified for a client, the counselor can move on to determining the particular approach to counseling as well as the adjunctive services which would be most helpful.

Duration and Frequency

In determining duration and frequency of treatment, counselors must decide the length of the counseling sessions, their spacing and frequency, their approximate number, and whether counseling will be time-limited. Counseling duration and frequency is determined by the interaction of several factors: the motivation of the client, the established goals, and any constraints such as the client's financial circumstances or the limits imposed by the agency on the number of client contacts. Ideally, the client's goals should be the primary determinant. However, in reality, it is necessary to look at a range of factors.

One way to view the question of duration is to assess whether counseling should be:

1. Brief and intensive (e.g., crisis intervention)
2. Brief but less intensive (e.g., short-term weekly counseling, with or without a predetermined date of termination)

3. Extended, nonintensive, and open-ended (e.g., supportive or exploratory counseling)
4. Extended, intensive, and open-ended (e.g., psychoanalysis) (Frances, et al., 1984)

Making this determination requires assessing the level of disruption, the immediacy of the problem, and the resources and motivation of the client.

A client with a recent or immediate concern, accompanied by a high level of disruption, would be a candidate for crisis intervention. Examples might be a thirty-six-year-old man with three children whose wife recently died in an accident, leaving him depressed and overwhelmed, or a fifteen-year-old rape victim, suffering from high anxiety, who has been unable to return to school. Immediate intervention is indicated to help them cope with their stressful situations. Crisis intervention techniques are designed to help them process the painful experiences they have endured, use the strengths and coping skills they have employed effectively in the past, and apply them to the present situation. Crisis counseling may be completed in one or two sessions or may continue for 10 to 15 sessions. Regardless of duration, the objective is to enable clients to emerge from stressful situations with positive affect and strengthened resources.

Short-term counseling is commonly indicated when an otherwise well-functioning client presents a relatively circumscribed concern. The widowed father in the previous paragraph, for example, might become a candidate for short-term counseling once he has dealt with his crisis; short-term counseling might help him to improve his parenting skills, to resume a social life as a single person, and to redefine his future goals.

Short-term counseling also may be indicated for a multi-problem client with limited motivation. An example would be a fifty-two-year-old female client who presented concerns about her eighty-two-year-old mother. The mother had been living with the daughter and her family for 12 years but now seemed to require a nursing home placement. The daughter sought counseling for help in deciding whether to place her mother in a nursing home and in coping with her guilt and anger toward her family. The family was insisting that the aged mother had become too great a burden for them. During counseling, it became evident the client was experiencing considerable marital strain and had been feeling some depression and lack of direction since her youngest child entered college. However, she was not motivated to look at these issues at present, but only wanted help wtih her concerns about her mother. (The client returned for career and marital counseling a year later.)

How short is short-term counseling? The definitions differ greatly, depending on the agency or counselor providing the service. Ten to 15 sessions is a common standard for short-term counseling but many counselors view a counseling contact of less than 6 months duration as short-term.

What then is the duration of long-term counseling? Again, a definition is elusive, partially because of the flexibility of the counseling process. It is not uncommon for clients to be seen weekly for 6 months or more and then biweekly or monthly for another few months. Counselors also may see clients weekly for several years. Both patterns may be viewed as long-term counseling relationships, yet they differ greatly. Counselors employed in community agency and private practice settings often see clients for long-term counseling, especially as a supportive or transitional mechanism (e.g., seeing clients monthly while they embark on a new venture).

Many counselors enjoy long-term counseling relationships. They offer counselors and clients the opportunity to develop a strong working relationship, to deal with several issues or concerns, and to see significant change. For the counselor in private practice, long-term counseling contacts offer a stable income. Because of these attractions, counselors should be particularly cautious about recommending long-term counseling. It can tax a client's finances and schedule and may lead to undesirable dependency on the counselor. Counselors should be sure that long-term counseling really is the best treatment for the client.

The duration and frequency of a counseling relationship often bear little relationship to the severity of clients' concerns. They are more related to the nature of the problem and the treatment provided. Of course, sometimes multiproblem clients have the motivation and resources required for long-term counseling, but this should not be taken for granted. Long-term counseling would be appropriate for clients with disparate and wide-ranging goals that have been mutually agreed on, with a high level of motivation, and with adequate finances and time. Also, it must be conducted in a context that permits long-term counseling. Some agencies explicitly limit the number of sessions that can be provided a client or implicity discourage long-term counseling because it curtails the number of clients who can be served.

Clients sometimes will ask how long counseling will take. Of course, it is impossible to provide a definitive answer to that question unless the counseling occurs in a time-limited context. However, the experienced counselor probably can offer the client a general idea of how long it usually takes to deal effectively with the sorts of concerns the client presents. Questions about duration typically reflect some apprehensions about counseling, and these should be explored. If the question reflects a reluctance to make a significant commitment of time and energy to counseling, the counselor might suggest that the client agree to a predetermined number of sessions, after which the counseling would be reevaluated.

Clearly, predicting the duration of a counseling relationship can be difficult. Although some studies have found a correlation between number of sessions and more positive outcome, "most studies fail to demonstrate a significant advantage of longer treatment" (Frances, 1984, p. 170). However, flexibility and change are in order and counselors may find that crisis intervention can turn into long-term counseling while motivational changes may halt plans for long-term counseling. Frequency of contact also is difficult to predict and should be determined by client needs and progress throughout the course of counseling.

Level of Directiveness

Counseling modalities range in level of directiveness from the client-centered (or "person-centered") model of Carl Rogers through the flexible but often educative approach of the Rational-emotive therapists to the directive style of the Behaviorists. Most counselors evolve a level of directiveness with which they are most comfortable. However, it is important for counselors to maintain some flexibility in their level of directiveness since different clients respond best to different levels.

In some publications, the terms "client-centered" and "non-directive" are used interchangeably to characterize the sort of counseling that typically encourages clients to establish the pace and agenda of the sessions. However, the term "non-directive" seems to be a misnomer in that the counselor always exerts influence on the nature of the counseling process. Consequently, the term "client-centered" appears preferable. Typically, clients who respond best to a client-centered approach are those who are highly self-motivated, who are articulate and relatively high in self-awareness, and who have some good coping skills but who are low in self-confidence and self-esteem. They also need help in exploring and expressing feelings. Since a client-centered approach may be more leisurely paced than a directive approach, any time constraints should be flexible. A client for whom client-centered counseling is recommended probably will not be experiencing an immediate crisis.

A more directive or active-interventionist approach tends to work best with a different kind of client, one who seems underorganized, overwhelmed by negative emotions, or coping at a minimal level of effectiveness. Clients who respond best to a directive approach typically are those who are not very comfortable with verbal interaction or self-disclosure, and who may have poor communication skills or limited motivation. Their primary concerns are often behavioral in nature.

While clients' preferences certainly should be taken into account when determining optimal levels of directiveness, clients sometimes incline toward the approach that is easiest for them but may not necessarily produce the most change. For example, a client with strong dependency needs may initially respond best to a directive approach. However, the counselor probably will do best to gradually reduce counselor-directiveness as a way of maximizing the client's own resources and sense of competence. Some degree of client anxiety in counseling sessions seems to promote growth and counselors should consider the variable of anxiety carefully when determining the level of directiveness.

Level of directiveness is a continuum; it is not an either-or dimension. One should not speak of a counselor as either directive or client-centered but, for example, as moderately directive or strongly client-centered. This continuum is, of course, related to the style or model of counseling embraced by the counselor. It would be difficult, for example, to be a strongly client-centered Behaviorist. However, a Behaviorist can lean in either a directive or client-centered direction, depending on the needs of a client at a particular phase in the counseling process. The level of directiveness, then, can be viewed as one of the overriding variables in the counseling process, one which should be frequently assessed in light of clients' strengths and objectives.

Supportive vs. Exploratory Counseling

Another continuum that enters into treatment planning is the continuum ranging from supportive to exploratory counseling. The intent of supportive counseling is to build on the client's existing strengths. Defenses generally are left in place and little attention is devoted to past experiences or the development of insight. Candidates for counseling with a strong supportive thrust are those who tend to be action-oriented, who may be rather fragile and limited in both internal and external supports, or who need help in coping effectively with the demands of their daily lives.

Exploratory counseling typically encourages clients to look beyond their presenting problems. Counseling may focus on antecedents of present concerns, earlier difficulties, patterns of relationships, or family dynamics. While presenting concerns certainly will not be ignored, efforts will be made to understand them as part of clients' lifelong patterns. The counseling process will seek not only to ameliorate presenting concerns but also to provide clients with greater insight into themselves and their lifestyles, to examine other salient facets of clients' lives, and to promote overall personal growth and development. Cognitive concerns will often receive particular attention. This process may entail weakening some defenses, raising clients' anxiety levels, and opening up some concerns that previously had been suppressed or denied. Clients who are suitable for exploratory counseling must have the emotional resources necessary to take a close look at their developmental concerns and life patterns.

Such clients must have the time and motivation to engage in counseling that goes beyond their presenting concerns, and they should have an interest in personal growth.

It must be emphasized that supportive and exploratory counseling are ends of a continuum. It probably is impossible for counseling to be purely supportive or entirely exploratory. The counseling process inevitably includes supportive and exploratory elements. The question the counselor must answer is where on the continuum counseling with a particular client generally should fall.

This variable, too, is one that shifts frequently during the counseling process. A client who comes to counseling in crisis, for example, may require a strong dose of supportive counseling. However, once the crisis has been resolved satisfactorily, that same client may be interested in exploring the impact of earlier family relationships on present family dynamics and so may move into a more exploratory counseling relationship. Despite the shifting nature of this variable, it is an important one for counselors to bear in mind during treatment planning.

Cognitive, Affective, or Behavioral Counseling

Another ingredient in the counseling relationship is the balance of attention paid to cognitive, affective, and behavioral areas. Here, too, the counselor is not making an either-or decision; the counseling process nearly always will attend to all three areas. However, the three areas rarely receive equal attention during counseling.

Counselors need to take account of their personal styles as well as of clients' needs when considering this three-pronged variable. A counselor who strongly believes in the overriding importance of behavioral change, for example, and views it as the key to bringing about needed cognitive and affective change will be reluctant to deviate far from that model. It is not necessary (and probably is not possible in many cases) for counselors to employ radically different counseling modalities with equal efficacy. However, counselors should retain a good measure of flexibility in their approaches to clients.

The cognitive approach focuses primarily on clients'

thoughts and seeks to ferret out, evaluate, and revise thoughts that are self-destructive or inaccurate. Such thoughts often have a dogmatic or absolute quality that provides a clue to their inaccuracy. A client might think, for example, "If only I could lose weight, my social life would be terrific and I wouldn't have any problems," while another might think, "If Joan won't marry me, it will be awful; I can't go on without her." Counselors should listen for such cognitive inaccuracies in their dialogues with clients. Pointing them out, helping clients to assess the merits or accuracy of these thoughts, and encouraging clients to replace them with more constructive thoughts can facilitate the counseling process. For example, the overweight client might be helped to see that while losing weight might well be desirable and might contribute to the improvement of his social life, it almost certainly will not solve all his problems. Also, being overweight almost certainly is not the only reason why he has not established a satisfactory social life; he might examine other ingredients of his relationships and discover ways to improve his interpersonal interaction regardless of whether he loses weight.

Some attention to the cognitive realm almost certainly is warranted with clients who manifest self-destructive thinking. However, some clients are so comfortable with the realm of thinking and intellectualization that counselors who focus heavily on the cognitive realm can stymie progress. Similarly, cognitively oriented counselors working with clients who have a limited interest in or capacity for examining ideation will achieve only limited progress. Especially in such cases, behavioral and affective foci must be integrated with the cognitive.

A behavioral focus generally is the preferred mode of treatment with clients who manifest phobias (e.g., fear of heights, fear of public places) or habit disorders (e.g., overeating, drug or alcohol abuse). The demonstrated efficacy of a behavioral approach in ameliorating such disorders probably will lead most counselors to rely heavily on behavioral techniques for clients presenting phobias or habit disorders. However, it often will be evident that there is a strong affective or cognitive component to a behavioral disorder. For example, clients might use drugs as a way of bolstering a weak self-concept (affective) or might believe that if they do not use drugs, they will be rejected by their peers (cognitive). Although some counselors adhere strictly to a behavioral approach regardless of whether the presenting problem has strong cognitive or affective elements, other counselors will treat a concern such as drug abuse with an integrated approach. The behavioral thrust might be primary since the first priority probably would be to reduce or eliminate self-destructive drug use. However, some attention probably also would be paid to improving self-image and examining the client's potentially inaccurate thoughts about social relationships. The behavioral approach also might be expanded and used to teach improved interpersonal and socialization skills and to provide assertiveness training so the client can deal more capably with peer pressure.

A strongly affective approach is most likely to be used with clients who have low self-esteem, who are suffering from debilitating anxiety or depression, or who have difficulty understanding or controlling their feelings. Counselors who rely heavily on an affective model often feel that they are facilitating more sustained personal growth than counselors who rely primarily on cognitive or behavioral models. However, the affective approach tends to be a slowly paced one and its effectiveness often can be accelerated by combining it with another approach. For example, exploration of the antecedents and nature of a client's depression in the context of a supportive and accepting counseling relationship often will succeed in alleviating the depression and providing the client with the self-confidence needed to gain greater control of his or her life. However, that process often can be speeded up if the client is simultaneously urged to plan some pleasurable activities and to take on some manageable challenges (behavioral) and is helped to focus on successes rather than dwelling on failures (cognitive).

Once again, we seem to have arrived at the conclusion that counseling is optimally an integrated approach. However, determining the balance of its ingredients is an important and often difficult decision.

Modality of Counseling

Another aspect of treatment planning is determining who will be involved in the counseling process. There are three broad categories that can be reviewed in answering this question: individual counseling, group counseling, or family counseling.

Individual counseling is the most common form of treatment. Almost any concern that is amenable to counseling can be treated through individual counseling. Sometimes it is used because it seems more likely to help the client than would group or family counseling. For example, the client may be extremely anxious and may have difficulty sharing his or her concerns in the presence of family members or other clients. Privacy and independence may be important issues. The presenting problem may be an intrapsychic or idiosyncratic one that would seem most effectively treated in individual counseling. The client should be able to handle the costs and intimacy involved in individual counseling, if individual counseling is recommended.

Individual counseling may also be the method of choice for pragmatic reasons. A particular agency may not be starting an appropriate group in the near future or the client's family may refuse to attend counseling sessions. In cases like these, counselors can use techniques that bring some of the advantages of group or family counseling into the one-to-one counseling session. Role playing or use of the empty-chair technique can help clients to deal with family or other interpersonal issues in individual counseling. Counselors can view clients through a family dynamics perspective even though family members may not be present. Homework assignments, focusing on client interaction with others, can further broaden the scope of individual counseling.

Group counseling, like individual counseling, can be employed for both therapeutic and pragmatic reasons. Some counseling agencies rely heavily on group counseling because it allows them to provide services to more clients than they could help through individual counseling. While group counseling probably is better than no counseling at all for most clients, group counseling should not be thought of as simply a more efficient approach to counseling than individual treatment. There are some concerns for which group counseling is particularly suited and some for which it is contraindicated.

On a superficial level, it seems that clients with interpersonal or socialization difficulties are most likely to benefit from group interaction and so should recieve group counseling. However, participation in a counseling group does require at least a minimal level of communication skills. It also can be a more stressful and anxiety-producing situation than individual counseling, at least until the group has developed a supportive and cohesive environment. Consequently, clients who have severe depression or anxiety, have very weak interpersonal skills, or are in crisis probably should not be placed in group counseling until their symptoms have been somewhat ameliorated. However, for the reasonably well-functioning client who could benefit from practice in communication skills and who is confident enough to benefit from peer feedback, group counseling can be very effective in improving socialization skills and helping clients become more aware of how others react to them. Group counseling is also recommended for clients who are overly intellectualized or uncomfortable with the intimacy of one-to-one counseling.

Counseling groups of peers also can help clients feel less alone and less stigmatized and can help them learn from the insights and efforts of others in similar situations. Such groups also can be very supportive to fragile or emotionally damaged clients. Peer support groups have been formed for people in marital or career transitions, for rape victims, for spouse or child abusers, and for individuals with life-threatening illnesses, to cite just a few.

Although group counseling may not be appropriate for all clients, it certainly is useful for a great many. Even if group counseling does not seem to be the primary mode of treatment, for some clients it is a valuable source of adjunct help. Such clients might be in individual and group counseling concurrently or might be referred to a counseling or support group after some progress has been made through individual counseling. Alternatively, group counseling might be recommended to deal with one aspect of a client's concerns while individual or family counseling is used for other aspects. However, the realities of the counseling situation should be considered. Many clients cannot afford the money or time required to participate in several modes of treatment simultaneously. Similarly, many agencies, especially those of a nonprofit nature, do not have the resources to supply clients with both group and individual counseling. Again, treatment planning will need to be pragmatic as well as therapeutic.

Family counseling has received increasing attention over the past 20 years and is growing in importance as a mode of treatment. Varieties of family counseling will be examined further in a later chapter. Some counselors believe that nearly all difficulties stem from family dynamics and prefer to see an entire family together for counseling whenever possible. Other counselors occasionally may see a couple together for a marital problem or see a parent and child for a behavioral concern, but feel that most concerns can be dealt with effectively through the more established methods of individual or group counseling. When planning a treatment, counselors should consider the relevance of the client's family background and circumstances to the presenting problems, the willingness of the client to involve family members, and the proximity and reported motivation of those family members (though a great deal of weight should not be placed on clients' perceptions of their family's motivation toward treatment). The cost-effectiveness of family treatment should also be considered as well as the severity of disturbance in the family and the interrelationship of members' symptoms. Interrelated symptoms indicate family treatment while the presence of a severely disturbed family member may contraindicate family counseling. If all of these considerations suggest that family counseling is warranted, counselors then should consider who should be present (spouse, children, siblings, parents, or grandparents). Type of family counseling (considered in a later chapter) also must be determined.

Family counseling, like group counseling, can be combined with other modes of treatment. A common model is for a client to be seen for a few sessions of individual counseling followed by some joint sessions with a spouse or parent and then by the eventual resumption of individual counseling once the counselor has gathered information on family dynamics and helped to improve family interaction and communication. Although family counseling may be the most effective mode of treatment in some cases, it is possible to effect changes in a family by working with an individual, especially if a counselor is adept at assuming a family dynamics perspective regardless of who is present at the counseling session.

Counselor Variables

Part of treatment planning is locating a suitable counselor for a client. Often, however, there is little choice as to who will work with a particular client. The match between counselors' and clients' schedules may be the overriding determinant of which counselor at an agency is assigned to a client. If a client contacts a counselor in private practice, there is a choice only if it is a group practice. Even if the constraints of reality do limit the process of counselor selection, the impact of counselor variables on the counseling process should be considered.

Experience probably is the most important variable and must be considered in all counseling situations. Once the mode of treatment has been determined, whether potential counselors have training or experience in that mode of treatment must be ascertained. If, for example, a client seeks marital counseling from a counselor in private practice who is not skilled in marital counseling, that counselor should refer the client to another counselor if indeed marital counseling seems warranted.

A related but perhaps more difficult issue is that of mutual comfort. Counselors may have the expertise to help clients with certain concerns but may have such strong emotional reactions to those concerns that they would prefer not to work with them. For example, a counselor whose religious beliefs lead him to believe that abortion is sinful may feel that he could not be sufficiently objective to help a client considering an abortion. A counselor who has been raped herself may fear that her anger will get in the way of her counseling a client who is a convicted rapist. A counselor with alcoholic parents may feel discomfort in working with alcoholic clients.

Although it is important for counselors to maintain a strong measure of objectivity and generally to refrain from imposing their own values on their clients, it is inevitable that counselors will have feelings toward their clients and their behaviors. These reactions often are strongly colored by the counselors' own backgrounds and experiences. When these reactions bear little relation to the reality of the clients' behaviors but are more a reflection of the counselors' inner experiences, the reactions are termed "countertransference." An example is the counselor who was severely punished for lateness as a child and becomes extremely angry with a client who is 5 minutes late for a session.

Other counselor reactions may be more grounded in objective reality. For example, many counselors would feel angry and upset when a client described an incident in which he sexually abused his nine-year-old daughter. Neither countertransference reactions nor other emotional reactions to clients are, in themselves, grounds for referral. First, counselors should attend to and seek to understand their own feelings. Strong emotional reactions to clients, especially of a countertransference nature, perhaps should prompt counselors to seek further supervision or some counseling for themselves. Especially if more than a few counseling sessions have taken place, efforts should be made to avoid referring a client due to the counselor's emotional reactions since that might well be perceived by the client as a rejection and be countertherapeutic. Only in extreme circumstances should a referral be made because the counselor's affective reactions to a client prevent the development of a positive counseling relationship.

Occasionally, counselors are aware in advance that they are likely to be emotionally uncomfortable working with a client. An example might be the religious counselor who does not wish to counsel clients considering abortions. In such cases, the counselor's supervisors can be made aware of those constraints and the clients can be channelled unobtrusively to other counselors. However, counselors rarely have the luxury of choosing their clients. In general, counselors should try to deal with their biases and work through negative reactions so that they can work with a broad range of clients.

Demographic counselor variables also should be considered during treatment planning. Age, sex, and race of the counselor are probably the most important of these, although others such as the counselor's marital status, whether he or she is a parent, or religious preference also can have an impact on the counseling process. There are few clear answers as to how clients and counselors should be matched with respect to demographic variables (Pietrofesa, Hoffman, & Splete, 1984). In assessing these variables, particular notice should be taken of:

1. Great disparities between counselor and client—a sixty-five-year-old client, adjusting to retirement, may have some difficulty trusting and accepting help from a twenty-five-year-old counselor.
2. Great similarities between counselor and client—a client who is having difficulty coping with the pressures of becoming a single parent may overidentify with or become envious of a counselor who also is a recent single parent.
3. Strong feelings on the part of the client toward particular groups—a client who has always assumed a passive role in relation to women may have difficulty engaging in a productive counseling relationship with a female counselor.

Of course, these are only hypothetical examples and very different reactions may ensue. The sixty-five-year-old retiree may find that the youthful counselor sharpens his awareness of the breadth of his life experiences, leading to increased self-confidence. The single parent may benefit from the empathy and support he receives from the counselor in similar circumstances. The client who has had difficulty relating to women as peers may learn a new way to interact with women through a female counselor. There is no precise way to predict the impact of demographic variables on the nature of the counselor-client relationship. However, counselors should still attend to such variables and draw on their insight and clinical skills to effect productive counselor-client matches and to handle the impact of such variables on the counselor-client relationship.

Pacing and Sequencing in Treatment Planning

A treatment plan typically is a multifaceted and constantly evolving entity. Although a basic treatment plan generally is developed following an intake interview, a treatment plan often has several phases or stages and must be continuously evaluated as clients' needs shift and the counselor moves from one phase of a treatment plan to the next. Discussion of this is provided in the final chapter.

Treatment plans should take account of clients' readiness for change and be paced accordingly. A gentle, gradual approach to counseling might be used with a fearful, fragile client with few support systems, while a more rapid approach to change might be adopted with a usually well-functioning client in a situational crisis. The sequence of counseling modalities is another aspect of counseling, closely linked to pacing of treatment. A fragile client may first be seen in individual counseling and then, when confidence has grown, be placed in a peer support group to learn social skills. The more stable client might be able to tolerate concurrent career and family counseling. Pacing and sequence, then, are two additional aspects of the counseling process that must be considered during treatment planning.

RELATIONSHIP OF COUNSELING TECHNIQUES TO DIAGNOSIS

The field of counseling has developed to the point that there are more than a dozen relatively discreet and major approaches to individual counseling. It has been argued that the client/counselor relationship and the skill of the counselor are more important than the nature of the treatment (Frances et al., 1984). Although there is insufficient information to answer the question of which techniques are best for which clients, most counseling modalities seem to work better with certain types of clients or concerns than they do with others. This section will consider the major approaches to individual counseling in relation to diagnosis and treatment planning. (The major approaches to group and family counseling are considered similarly in later chapters.) For purposes of this chapter, it is assumed that readers possess at least some familiarity with the salient theories of counseling. Consequently, although some review of the essential ingredients of these approaches will be provided, it is not the intent of this chapter to teach theories of counseling. Neither is it the intent to encourage counselors to become chameleonlike, and adopt a different approach to counseling for every client they see. Most counselors develop their own counseling styles that they are understandably unwilling or unable to modify radically. However, it is possible for counselors to shift their styles within broad parameters, to borrow from a variety of counseling approaches, and to develop a way of relating to and helping each client that is uniquely suited to the client's needs. It is the purpose of the remainder of this chapter to provide counselors with some guidelines for accomplishing that.

Client-Centered Counseling

Client-centered counseling, also known as self-theory, person-centered counseling, or relationship theory, is an approach to counseling originated by Carl Rogers in the 1940s. It has continued to evolve since and has consistently had a profound impact on the field of counseling, providing the basis for many more recent counseling approaches.

The overriding principle of this approach is the idea that if the counselor can provide clients with a genuine relationship in which they feel understood, accepted, and receive what Rogers called "unconditional positive regard," the clients' self-esteem will blossom and they will increasingly be able to draw on their own resources to help themselves. The client-centered model is characterized by the following qualities:

1. Present-oriented (past is deemphasized)
2. Holistic
3. Emphasis on client's experience, agenda, and goals
4. Stress on lifelong development and self-actualization (not problem-focused)
5. Empathic, accepting, genuine, and congruent counselor
6. Focus on feelings, emotions
7. Little or no use made of tests, exercises, information-giving
8. Client-counselor relationship of great importance
9. Concreteness and specificity encouraged
10. Promotion of client's self-awareness, exploration, self-esteem, and competence

Some elements of the client-centered model such as empathy, concreteness, and a focus on the present seem to pervade almost all approaches to counseling. Others, such as the emphases on emotions, self-actualization, and the counselor-client relationship characterize some approaches but not others. Clearly, one can use aspects of the client-centered model (can stress or integrate them into other approaches) without making full use of Rogers' approach. However, there are some clients for whom the client-centered model is particularly well-suited.

These clients seem to be most often diagnosed in one of the following categories:

1. Mild to moderate depression or anxiety (e.g., dysthymic disorder, anxiety state)
2. Adjustment disorders
3. Conditions not attributable to a mental disorder (e.g., uncomplicated bereavement; interpersonal, phase of life, or family circumstance problem)

While it is impossible to establish a one-to-one correspondence between diagnosis and counseling approach, to say, for example, that clients suffering from dysthymic disorders should always be treated via a client-centered model, there are certain groups of clients who seem more likely to be helped by some counseling approaches than by others.

Clients in the above diagnostic groups generally have some effective coping mechanisms, are in relatively good contact with reality, are capable of forming a communicative relationship with the counselor, are self-referred and self-motivated, and are not seriously disturbed. Such clients usually can accept the responsiblity placed on them by the client-centered model, have resources that they can develop, and are interested in engaging with the counselor in the treatment process. They can tolerate the sometimes leisurely pace of the client-centered model and can make changes in feeling and self-concept leading to changes in behavior and interpersonal relationships. The client-centered model is a supportive and positive one and so is useful with clients who are feeling fragile and unsure of themselves. It can enable clients to leave counseling with a greater sense of well-being and the ability and courage to take greater responsibility for their lives.

Behavioral Counseling

Behavioral counseling is a very different model. Originating with the work of B. F. Skinner in the late 1930s and 1940s, the behavioral model of counseling may well be as pervasive and influential as the client-centered model. Behavioral counseling is essentially the process of teaching and reinforcing positive behaviors while eliminating maladaptive ones through punishment or extinction. It is characterized by the following dimensions:

1. Generally present-oriented, though some attention is paid to symptom formation
2. Problem/symptom focused
3. Focus on behavior
4. Counselor primarily responsible for agenda of sessions
5. Concreteness and specificity encouraged
6. Unlearning and learning are the goals
7. Considerable use made of information-giving, inventories, homework assignments, varied techniques (e.g., modeling, shaping, rewarding, contracts)
8. Client self-awareness, overall growth, and emotional responses deemphasized
9. Interface between individual and environment considered
10. Goal directed

The behavioral model sometimes has been criticized for being insensitive to client's inner needs. However, this may well be a misunderstanding since most modern behaviorists view the counselor-client relationship as quite important. Empathy and acceptance of the client are communicated and time is taken to develop rapport and understand the place of clients' symptoms in their overall life patterns. The ultimate goal of behavioral counseling is, nonetheless, symptom removal and behavioral change.

Clients for whom behavioral counseling is likely to be effective are those who present disorders of behavior or habit control. Often, behavioral counseling is helpful to children or adults who may lack the motivation or verbal facility to engage in extensive self-exploration. Behavioral counseling typically is short-term and time-limited in nature and so may appeal to clients who do not have the motivation, patience, or resources to engage in a prolonged counseling experience and who are seeking circumscribed and measurable changes. Such clients are most likely to be diagnosed as follows:

1. Attention deficit disorder ⎫ Disorders usually first
2. Conduct disorder   ⎬ evident in infancy,
3. Eating disorders   ⎭ childhood, or adoles-
4. Substance use disorders   cence
5. Psychosexual dysfunction
6. Disorders of impulse control
7. Phobic disorders

It can readily be seen that a major component of treatment of the above disorders is learning new habits and behaviors and eliminating old ones. However, counselors often find that behavioral counseling techniques accelerate client growth even though another model of treatment is primary. For example, a client with low self-esteem and strong feelings of interpersonal insecurity may require the pace and support of a client-centered counselor but also may benefit considerably from the inclusion of some assertiveness training and interpersonal communication skills in the treatment plan, a marriage of behavioral and client-centered models. On the other hand, a client who presents a problem of functional vaginismus may well overcome her sexual difficulty through behavioral counseling but also may require some marital therapy and supportive counseling to help her and her spouse deal with the impact the dysfunction has had on their marriage and levels of self-esteem. Inevitably, the counselor's judgment is the essential ingredient in determining the nature of the approach to a given client and the mix and balance of techniques that will comprise the approach.

Reality Therapy

William Glasser first wrote about Reality Therapy in the middle 1960s and it has evolved and gained in popularity since. Reality Therapists generally believe that people who behave responsibly, in a socially acceptable manner, and in a way that attends to the framework of the real world will be most likely to meet their needs and develop a "success identity." This philosophy is embodied in the three R's of Reality Therapy: right, responsibility, and reality.

Reality Therapy can be characterized by the following dimensions:

1. Present and future oriented
2. Importance of counselor-client rapport
3. Focus on behavior, not emotion
4. Client self-evaluation, goal-setting, and contracting
5. Elimination of punishment and excuses; clients learn through the natural consequences of their behavior.

There are several similarities between behavioral counseling and reality therapy. However, Reality Therapists place greater emphasis on the establishment of a warm, understanding counseling relationship. Also, although Reality Therapists focus on present behavior, they are implicitly concerned with self-esteem and the clients' environments. Glasser viewed people as having strong needs to love and be loved and to feel that they are worthwhile. His therapy is designed to help people reach the point where they are able to give and receive love and perceive themselves as valuable members of society.

Glasser developed his approach while working with adolescent females who had been placed in an institution because of their delinquent behavior. These clients generally were mistrustful of counseling, had little initial motivation to change, and typically were not experienced or interested in analyzing their thoughts and emotions. Glasser developed a model that would be effective with such clients, those who have difficulty meeting their own needs without violating the rights of others, who often behave irresponsibly, and who tend to disregard or defy social norms. Diagnostically, such clients might fit into the following categories:

1. Conduct disorder (of childhood or adolescence)
2. Substance use disorders
3. Factitious disorders
4. Disorders of impulse control
5. Personality disorders
6. Adult, adolescent, or childhood antisocial behavior

Clients in these categories tend to be resistant to treatment and to have difficulties that manifest themselves behaviorally. Reality Therapy often is effective with clients who present such a combination of characteristics.

Occasionally, counselors misinterpret the nature of Reality Therapy and view it as designed for clients who are in poor contact with reality (e.g., schizophrenic clients). While Reality Therapy might well be useful in helping severely disturbed clients to mobilize themselves and to act more effectively, this is not the population for whom Reality Therapy was primarily developed. In combination with medication and other forms of supportive treatment, however, Reality Therapy can be quite effective with disoriented or otherwise confused clients.

Rational-Emotive Therapy

Rational-Emotive Therapy, known as RET, initially was developed by Albert Ellis in the 1950s. Ellis, like Glasser, became disillusioned with the psychoanalytic model and sought an approach to counseling that was more effective at ameliorating the problems that his clients were presenting. The seeds of Ellis' psychoanalytic training are evident, however, in his view of emotional difficulties as stemming from a pattern of childhood development that leads people to care too much about what others think of them and stress behaving in a way that will win favor. Such people tend to be other-directed, to have little confidence in their own skills and attributes, and to have beliefs that Ellis termed "irrational." Ellis defined eleven major irrational ideas, summarized by Hansen, Stevic, and Warner (1977) as follows:

1. It is absolutely essential for individuals to have the love or approval of all significant people in their environment.
2. Individuals must be fully competent, adequate, and achieving in all areas if they are to be viewed as worthwhile.
3. Some people are evil or bad and these people should be blamed and punished.
4. It is awful and catastrophic when things are not the way an individual wants them to be.
5. Unhappiness is a function of events outside the control of the individual.
6. If something may be dangerous or harmful, an individual should constantly be concerned about it.
7. It is easier to run away from difficulties and responsibilities than to face them.
8. People need to be dependent on others and to have someone stronger than themselves on whom they can lean.
9. Past events in a person's life determine present behavior; people, therefore, cannot change.
10. People should be very concerned and upset about the problems of others.
11. There always is a correct solution to every problem and it is terrible if it is not found (pp. 205–206).

This set of irrational ideas illustrates that RET is directed toward people who tend to "awful-ize," as Ellis has put it, to think in extremes, to feel disaster lurking around the bend, and to believe they have little control over their lives. Ellis' model views the onset of difficulties and their resolution according to a five-step sequence:

A—An *a*ctivating event occurs.

B—The individual's *b*elief system comes into play; rational or irrational thoughts emerge,—

C—in response to the *c*onsequences.

D—The counselor's role is to *d*ispute the irrational ideas, so that—

E—new *e*motional consequences can ensue.

RET can be characterized by:

1. Emphasis on the present, though past and future both receive attention.
2. Thoughts viewed as the key to changing both emotions and behavior.
3. Counselor assuming a directive and instructional role. Rapport is necessary but not sufficient.

Reality Therapy and RET have in common an emphasis on encouraging clients to value themselves and take responsibility for themselves. Both stress the importance of action through contracts and homework assignments but for Ellis cognitive change is primary, while for Glasser behavioral change leads to change in other areas. Ellis looks more at internal dynamics, while Glasser is more aware of the client's environment.

Although both RET and Reality Therapy place the counselor in a directive role and stress behavioral change, Ellis' approach seems to call for a higher degree of motivation and commitment on the client's part. Also, RET's emphasis on cognitive analysis and restructuring seems best-suited for clients who have a fair amount of verbal fluency, intellectual ability, and self-discipline. RET seems particularly appropriate for clients who are confused by dysfunctional emotions and are having difficulty bringing their thinking skills to bear on an issue. Such clients might fall into the following diagnostic categories:

1. Affective disorders
2. Anxiety disorders
3. Adjustment disorders

For the more severe of these disorders, such as bipolar disorders or major depressions, medication or other treatment modalities often are combined with RET to accelerate progress.

Both RET and Reality Therapy are characterized by their developers as serving a broad spectrum of the population. Both have been modified for use by teachers as well as by counselors and have been perceived as ways of helping troubled people as well as those who are functioning satisfactorily to think, feel, and act in healthier and happier ways. Although these modes of treatment certainly are not ideal for all clients, they do have broad application and can supplement many other approaches.

Cognitive Therapy

Cognitive therapy, a relatively new approach to counseling, was developed by Aaron Beck and his colleagues who, as did Glasser and Ellis, became disillusioned with the effectiveness of psychoanalysis. Related to and yet different from RET, cognitive therapy assumes that affect and behavior are influenced by underlying assumptions or cognitions derived from previous experiences. This is a directive, structured approach that seeks to identify and correct distorted cognitions. Although behavior and emotion receive attention in this model, more attention is paid to cognition.

Cognitive therapy differs from RET in the approach used to effect change in thinking. Cognitive therapy has been described as consisting of "highly specific learning experiences" designed to teach clients to:

1. Monitor negative automatic thoughts.
2. Recognize links between cognition, affect, and behavior.
3. Reality-test distorted automatic thoughts.
4. Substitute correct cognitions for ones based on misinterpretation.
5. Identify and change dysfunctional beliefs that lead to biased and distorted cognitions (Beck, Rush, Shaw, & Emery, 1979).

Cognitive therapy seems to be particularly effective with clients experiencing:

1. Affective disorders, especially depression
2. Anxiety disorders, especially phobias
3. Somatoform disorders
4. Adjustment disorders

Cognitive therapy is a sophisticated and complex approach that thus far has received only limited attention in the counseling literature. Its advocates recommend an extensive period of training in the model for would-be practitioners. The apparent usefulness of the model, especially with depressed and suicidal clients, makes it worthy of increased attention. It seems to be the forerunner of a group of time-limited, directive, cognitive, strategic approaches that have begun to attract attention from counselors and that seem to be establishing new direction for the field.

Gestalt Counseling

Gestalt counseling, developed by Fritz Perls, had a powerful impact on the field of counseling in the 1960s and has become one of the established approaches in the field. Gestalt counseling offers quite a different model than that of the cognitive approaches. The Gestaltists, as their name suggests, emphasize wholeness of experience. They seek to help clients gain access to neglected aspects of themselves and bring closure to unfinished experiences. Their attention to the whole picture leads them to attend to mind and body; affect, behavior, and cognition; and person and environment. However, Gestaltists believe that most people in modern western society are predisposed to neglect bodily reactions and emotions. The Gestalt approach to counseling, then, promotes reintegration of the self by increasing clients' awareness of nonverbal reactions and of their emotions.

The Gestalt approach to counseling is characterized by the following:

1. Counselor assumes a directive role, frustrates, interprets, leads, and interacts with client.

2. Awareness is emphasized, especially of affect and non-verbal responses.
3. Focus is on the present.
4. "What" and "how" are of concern, not "why."
5. Experiential techniques are stressed.
6. Dreams are viewed as an important source of information.
7. Client responsiblity is emphasized.

Because of its confrontational nature and its emphasis on making the unconscious conscious, the Gestalt model generally does not seem appropriate for clients who are severely disturbed, are in a crisis situation, or are poorly motivated toward change. The model appears useful for clients who tend to intellectualize, to have trouble clarifying their feelings, or to cut themselves off from aspects of themselves (e.g., the "workaholic"). It also might be useful with clients presenting psychosomatic or other physical symptoms that seem linked to emotional difficulties. Such clients may need help in attending to and making better use of the bodily messages that they are receiving. Diagnostically, these clients might present the following syndromes:

1. Cyclothymic disorder
2. Dysthymic disorder
3. Anxiety states
4. Somatoform disorders
5. Factitious disorders
6. Adjustment disorders
7. Psychological factors affecting physical conditions
8. Some V code diagnoses (e.g., occupational problem, phase of life problem, interpersonal problem)

The Gestalt approach, as with the cognitive approaches discussed earlier, seems uniquely suited to many of the problems resulting from the pressures of modern life. It is a rich model with a broad repertoire of techniques, many of which can be used to enhance or expand on other models of counseling even if the primary mode of treatment is not Gestalt.

Individual Psychology/Adlerian Counseling

About 70 years ago, Alfred Adler, a student of Freud's, developed an approach now known as Individual Psychology. Recently there has been a resurgence of interest in this approach, especially for working with children. Adler's approach has a strong philosophical base. The model is a phenomenological one that postulates that people are motivated by needs for both pleasure and social acceptance. Adler believed that people are born with strong feelings of inferiority that they strive to overcome by seeking achievement and mastery. He thought that each individual had his or her own lifestyle and goals formed early in development. Adlerian counseling, then, tends to focus on the child and on the parent-child interaction because Adler believed that the seeds for rewarding adult development were sown in childhood. More recent theorists such as Rudolph Dreikurs, Raymond Corsini, Donald Dinkmeyer, William McKelvie, and others elaborated and updated Adler's theory so that the approach now is used not only with children and their families, but also in adult personal counseling, career counseling, and marital counseling.

The Adlerian model of counseling is characterized by:

1. Emphasis on early childhood development and its impact on present attitudes and behavior.
2. Increasing self-awareness and behavioral change.
3. Holistic examination of person and environment.
4. Stress on counselor-client relationship.
5. Use of interpretation (sharing hunches or intuitive guesses).
6. Development of personally rewarding and socially responsible goals and modes of achieving them.

Adler and his followers have several strategies or approaches that enhance their model. They view birth order as a powerful determinant of lifestyle and personality and use it as a basis for exploration. Early recollections, too, are seen as important vehicles for gaining access to clients' self-images and lifestyles. In counseling with parents and children, parents are helped to use encouragement, understanding, clear and consistent communication, and natural consequences to promote healthy development in their children. Family councils also are perceived as promoting family communication.

The Adlerian model differs from many of the newer approaches to counseling in that it emphasizes the importance of early childhood development and seeks to foster insight and understanding. It is less symptom-focused and more oriented toward improving one's overall dealing with life. Like RET and Reality Therapy, however, it is a broad-based approach to helping others that can be used by teachers and parents as well as by counselors.

Conceptually, the Adlerian model seems to have something to contribute to almost all counseling situations. Although it is an analytical approach, the counselor tends to assume a directive role in this model and offers hunches to both verbal and silent clients. Consequently, this model does not require a client who is either motivated or communicative. However, the approach does seem best suited to clients who are neither severely disturbed nor confronting a specific problem or issue (e.g., divorce, job problem). Individual psychology seems most appropriate for clients who are experiencing emotional upset of some duration and who are having difficulty mobilizing themselves and finding a rewarding direction. This approach also can be particularly effective with children who are able to comprehend and communicate reasonably well. Clients for whom this model seems likely to be helpful might fall into the following diagnostic categories:

1. Conduct disorder of childhood or adolescence
2. Anxiety disorders of childhood or adolescence
3. Dysthymic disorder
4. Anxiety states
5. Personality disorders
6. Childhood or adolescent antisocial behavior
7. Parent-child problem

Multimodal Behavior Therapy

Arnold Lazarus, until recently a strong advocate of behavioral counseling, developed an approach to counseling that integrates and expands on many of the approaches discussed in this chapter. Lazarus' model enables counselors to take a systematic and comprehensive look at a client, determine areas of strength and weakness, and develop a treatment plan designed to have a multifaceted impact. Multimodal counselors view counseling as a holistic learning process and believe that change in one aspect of an individual will affect and be encouraged by change in other aspects of that person.

A sevenfold model for assessing the individual and planning the treatment is used. The acronym, BASIC ID, represents the model as:

B—Behavior (observable habits and activities)
A—Affect (feelings and emotions)
S—Sensation (physical concerns, sensory responses)
I—Imagery (images and fantasies)
C—Cognition (beliefs, thoughts, plans, philosophies)
I—Interpersonal relations (relationships with others)
D—Drugs/Diet (broadly defined as biological functioning)

The first six are viewed as constituting personality: all seven are assessed by the counselor.

Multimodal counseling can be characterized by:

1. Counselor assuming a directive, responsible role.
2. Limited attention paid to antecedent and precipitating factors; focus largely on the present.
3. Holistic attitude.
4. BASIC ID assessed.
5. Objective evaluation of progress.

The behavioral origins of the multimodal approach are evident. However, this approach has gone beyond behaviorism and has attempted to establish a comprehensive model that is flexible enough to be used with nearly all client concerns. Even if a client presents difficulties in only one or two of the seven areas, the BASIC ID framework enables counselors to perform a psychological checkup on clients to ensure not only that presenting or obvious problems receive attention, but that all important areas of concern receive it. This model also helps counselors define and build on clients' strengths as a way of reducing problem areas.

Because of the breadth of the multimodal approach, it is not feasible to list diagnostic categories for which the model would be most appropriate. This model, perhaps more than any of the others, has a contribution to make to almost every sort of client concern. However, it seems there are some types of clients, difficulties, and circumstances that lend themselves particularly well to this sort of an approach. Although the counselor takes primary responsiblity for assessing clients according to BASIC ID and suggesting the details of the treatment plan, this model seems most likely to work with a client who is reasonably well-motivated, in satisfactory contact with reality, and capable of at least a moderate level of planning, organizing, and self-monitoring. Clients who present a range of diverse concerns (e.g., depression, obesity, and poor social skills) might be particularly responsive to the multimodal model because it will help them develop a systematic approach to their concerns and can help relieve feelings of panic and hopelessness, common in multiproblem clients.

Eclectic and Other Models of Treatment

Approaches to counseling are constantly being developed and modified. This chapter was not intended to provide a comprehensive discussion of the relationships between existing modes of counseling and categories of client concern. Rather, its purpose was to help readers appreciate the broad range of counseling approaches and develop an ability to evaluate the suitability of counseling models for various types of client concerns.

Many counselors align themselves with one or two approaches to counseling. They may characterize themselves, for example, as Reality Therapists or client-centered counselors. Their preferred approach to counseling probably has been selected for several reasons: the counselor's exposure to that model through training and experience, the suitability of that model for their work setting or client population, the compatibility of that model with the counselors' personal style and philosophy, and their confidence in the effectiveness of that model.

Even though most counselors have preferred modes of counseling, most counselors are eclectic. That is, even if they make greater use of one approach than of others, they often modify that approach, borrowing from other modes of counseling to suit their counseling to the unique needs and concerns of each client. Saying that a counselor is eclectic, then, does not provide much information about the counseling style and attitudes of that counselor. When counselors are asked to label their preferred style of counseling, more counselors call themselves eclectic than affiliate with any one particular approach.

What does it mean, then, when counselors describe themselves as eclectic? For some, it means that they are strongly committed to individualizing their approaches to the diverse needs of their clients and that they are skilled in accomplishing that. For others, it means that they have not yet developed a preferred or thoughtful approach to working with clients and are still floundering in their orientation, using bits and pieces of various approaches in a relatively random fashion. Although the best treatment often can be provided by a counselor who is knowledgeable and flexible enough to select the most appropriate ingredients of several theories in helping their clients, the catchall term "eclectic" is almost meaningless and should generally be avoided, both in treatment planning and when counselors are describing their counseling orientation to others. Rather, counselors who are not strongly committed to a particular theoretical model should elaborate on their approach, systematically tailoring it to individual client needs. Methods for accomplishing this will be further clarified in the remainder of this chapter.

SAMPLE TREATMENT PLANS

This section will present two abbreviated counseling cases and will show how treatment plans have been developed to suit the particular needs of these clients. These examples are designed to illustrate the application of principles discussed throughout this chapter.

Nancy

A. Presenting problem

Nancy, a twenty-nine-year-old female, presented herself for counseling seeking help in deciding how to handle an unplanned pregnancy. She had become pregnant on her first date with a man she had met at a bar. She subsequently informed him of her pregnancy, but he expressed no interest in continuing their relationship and advised her to have an abortion as soon as possible.

Nancy had consulted a physician who confirmed that she was nearly 3 months pregnant. She was upset and confused, cried frequently, and seemed depressed and angry, yet she was in relatively good contact with reality. Depression since the death of her mother 3 years ago was reported.

B. History

History taking indicated that Nancy was living with her widowed father. She had completed high school and had worked as a clerk-typist for the same firm for the last 10 years. She was bored and dissatisfied with her work but had not taken steps toward change. Her social life was extremely limited. However, she did occasionally drink enough alcohol to bolster her courage and spent an evening in a bar. She occasionally dated men she met there. She had only had a few sexual experiences and assumed that her partners would take responsibility for birth control.

C. Diagnostic impression

> Axis I —V62.89 Life circumstance problem (unplanned pregnancy)
> 300.40 Dysthymic disorder
> 305.02 Alcohol abuse, episodic (provisional)
> Axis II —301.60 Dependent personality disorder (provisional)
> Axis III—Pregnancy

Axis IV—Severity of psychosocial stressors: 4. Moderate—
unplanned pregnancy

Axis V —Highest level of adaptive functioning in past
year: 5. Poor—marked impairment in social
relations

D. Treatment plan

Nancy presents a number of concerns, requiring several
modes of intervention. The following goals were established:

1. Immediate: make decision about pregnancy
2. Short-term: develop social skills and activities, increase
knowledge of and sense of responsibility for birth control
measures, reduce reliance on alcohol
3. Long-Term: assess and improve career direction and
living situation, continue to develop social skills

Goals were mutually agreed upon and defined in measureable
terms.

The following recommendations were made about the nature of counseling to be provided:

Table 5-1

Variable	Recommendations	Reasons
1. Duration	Crisis intervention followed by medium/long-term counseling	Immediate decision on the pregnancy was needed. Multiple, long-standing concerns warranted subsequent lengthy counseling involvement.
2. Level of directiveness	Relatively directive, gradually decreasing in directiveness	Nancy's confusion and crisis mandated a directive approach to mobilize her energy and promote a prompt decision. However, she needs to assume more responsibility for herself so counselor should gradually become less directive as Nancy becomes more competent.

Table 5-1. (Continued)

Variable	Recommendations	Reasons
3. Supportive or exploratory	Generally supportive	Nancy is depressed, not well motivated, and uncomfortable with analysis. She needs a supportive, present-oriented approach that will strengthen her optimism and commitment to counseling.
4. Cognitive/ behavioral/ affective	Primarily behavioral, with attention to cognitive and affective aspects	Presented and diagnosed concerns all have behavioral manifestations (e.g., pregnancy, alcoholism, poor social skills) which, if changed, seem likely to promote cognitive and affective changes. However, cognitive/affective areas must be attended to so that they do not block behavioral change and do show improvement
5. Group/ individual/ family	Initially individual. Possibly group or family later	Crisis situation and social apprehension of client warrant individual counseling. Group counseling might be used later to develop her social skills and peer relationships; family counseling might be useful to explore relationship with father.
6. Relevant counselor variables	Female counselor	Client might be more comfortable discussing her pregnancy with a female, especially in light of her difficult and charged relationships with men. Other variables do not seem relevant.
7. Pacing	Crisis counseling, followed by individual counseling to attend to short-term	Nancy has several levels of concern and only seems ready to confront the immediate crisis at present. Evaluation should be

(Continued)

Table 5-1. (Continued)

Variable	Recommendations	Reasons
	goals, followed by subsequent or additional group or family counseling. Career assessment.	ongoing to ensure that goals are met but that client is not becoming overly resistant or depressed. Diagnoses should be reevaluated since several were provisional, requiring more information.
8. Counseling approach	Primarily behavioral, relying heavily on information-giving; teaching decision-making strategies, social skills; behavioral control; contracting. May move toward affective/cognitive focus in time to further alleviate depression, promote career change.	Behavioral concerns are paramount. A multimodal approach may be conceputally useful in understanding this client but, since she is not committed to extended counseling, that model seems too broad. A behavioral approach is generally effective with clients who have trouble with impulse control and who lack skills and information. It can also provide some relief to depression.

Nancy's case is a complex one which could be approached in a number of different ways, all of which might be helpful to her. The assessment and treatment plan above is only one of those ways. The treatment plan, in this case, is likely to be modified during the counseling process in light of Nancy's ability to resolve her immediate crisis and move on to other concerns, her commitment to counseling, her facility for cognitive analysis and emotional expression, and additional information acquired.

Sam

A. Presenting problem.

Sam, a twenty-seven-year-old male, came to counseling shortly after the woman he was dating seriously for the past 7 months left him for another man. Sam is feeling some rejection and sadness, as well as anger at himself and the woman (Diane). He feels he made a self-destructive choice in Diane and berates himself for "being taken for a ride by another beautiful woman." He is seeking some help in understanding and changing his patterns of choosing and relating to women.

B. History.
Sam grew up in a financially and emotionally impoverished environment. One of eight children, born to blue-collar parents, he left home at seventeen, finished high school while in the army, and then was trained to repair computers. He has had two responsible jobs since his military discharge and has recently begun taking college courses while working full-time. Sam expresses a wish for marriage and children but, instead, has had a series of unfulfilling relationships with what he terms "gorgeous gold diggers." He is on amiable, if distant, terms with his family and has several close friends, both male and female. He functions quite well in all areas of his life except for his romantic relationships with women where he seems to have a need to prove his self-worth by pursuing very attractive, often materialistic women who show only limited interest in him.   .

C. Diagnostic impression.

Axis I —309.00 Adjustment disorder with depressed mood.

Axis II —V71.09 No diagnosis on Axis II

Axis III—None.

Axis IV—Severity of psychosocial stressors: 3- Mild—recent end of relationship.

Axis V —Highest level of adaptive functioning in past year: 4- Fair—moderate impairment in social relations.

D. Treatment plan.
Sam's concerns are far more circumscribed and less severe than were Nancy's. He also seems more motivated toward counseling and is functioning at a higher level. He is not in a crisis

despite his recent disappointments in relationships. The following goals were established: gain understanding of self-destructive patterns of socializing with women and form more rewarding and enduring relationships based on that understanding; possibly review and revise career direction and college plans. Sam has one focal goal, improving his relationships with women. Short-term counseling should give Sam the insight and tools he needs to modify his behavior. Long-term counseling, perhaps at irregular or infrequent intervals, might be used to monitor and support Sam's progress.

The following recommendations were made about the nature of counseling to be provided to Sam:

Table 5-2

Variable	Recommendations	Reasons
1. Duration	Short-term, perhaps with extended follow-up	Client functions well in most areas, seems to have thought about his concerns and is ready for change. Concerns are limited, circumscribed.
2. Level of directiveness	Relatively client-centered	Sam seems emotionally stable, motivated, and insightful enough to take charge of his own counseling. Also, he seems to need the acceptance and development of self-esteem which a client-centered model can offer. Counselor will become more directive as needed to keep Sam focused.
3. Supportive or exploratory	Combination	Sam seems able and eager to gain insight into the origins of his dysfunctional patterns. Such insight may be useful in effecting change. Current strengths as well as self-esteem will also be supported and encouraged.
4. Cognitive/ behavioral/	Cognitive will be emphasized with at-	Sam seems to view involvement with a beautiful woman as vali-

Table 5-2. (Continued)

Variable	Recommendations	Reasons
affective	ttention paid to affect and behavior	dation of his own worth. Assumptions behind this need to be examined and modified. Feelings of sadness and low self-esteem as well as interpersonal interactions and socialization patterns will also be considered in counseling.
5. Group/ individual/ family	Group or individual	Either could help Sam. Ideally, he might begin to develop self-esteem and insight in individual counseling and then shift to a group to receive feedback on how he relates to others and to have an opportunity to try out new patterns of interacting.
6. Relevant counselor variables	None	There are pros and cons to Sam having a female counselor. He might mistrust her and try to win her favor, but that would present a firsthand opportunity for him to examine his feelings. Other variables do not seem important.
7. Pacing	Steady and fairly rapid	Client seems to have relatively good ego-strength and to be ready to tackle the problem he presents. Movement will probably be from the cognitive-affective realm to the cognitive-behavioral.
8. Counseling approach	Cognitive-behavioral with counselor being more client-centered than usual	Sam needs to examine and modify cognitions so that behavioral change can be made. Low self-esteem is an important factor, suggesting that counse-

(Continued)

Table 5-2. (Continued)

Variable	Recommendations	Reasons
		lor should be less directive than usual in this model to promote client's sense of competence and ability to take control of his own life.

Sam's case does not present the complexity of Nancy's and seems amenable to treatment via short-term counseling. However, even in a relatively straightforward case like this one, unanticipated issues may arise as client-counselor rapport builds and with Sam, as with Nancy, the counselor should constantly evaluate the effectiveness of the treatment plan.

SUMMARY

This chapter focused on the development of suitable treatment plans for clients. It provided guidelines for determining the suitability of clients for counseling and for determining the appropriateness of a particular agency as a source of treatment for clients. The nature and process of goal setting was described. The significant parameters of the counseling process (e.g., level of directiveness, modality of treatment, counselor variables, and others) were discussed and readers were given direction in selecting the most helpful parameters for their clients. The relationships between eight major approaches to individual counseling and the diagnostic categories were presented. Finally, two case studies were provided, offering an overview of the process of treatment planning. Readers might try to develop treatment plans for the clients described at the end of chapter 2.

Chapter 6

ADJUNCT SERVICES AS PART OF TREATMENT PLANS

NEED FOR ADJUNCT SERVICES

Individual counseling has thus far been the focus of treatment planning as presented in this book. While individual counseling is typically the most important or core element of clients' treatment plans, there are some clients for whom other modes of counseling (e.g., group, couples, or family counseling) are most appropriate. There also are many clients for whom some adjunct modes of treatment are indicated. This chapter will discuss the nature and provision of adjunct modes of treatment while the following two chapters will consider group and family counseling as important elements of treatment plans.

Information derived from intake interviews, assessment procedures, and clients' records often indicate that clients have needs that cannot easily be met exclusively through counseling. Such needs might include medical treatment, educational services, or the development of specialized interpersonal skills, to cite just a few. When such needs are noted, services that supplement general counseling should be built into the clients' treatment plans and the intake worker, counselor, or case manager should take steps to ensure that clients do receive those needed services.

INTEGRATION INTO TREATMENT PLAN

When they are indicated, adjunct services should become an integral part of treatment plans. It is not enough for counselors to simply state that a client should be referred for a medical consultation or for job placement. Rather, the treatment plan should answer the following questions:

1. *When* should the adjunct services be provided? Should they be concurrent and integrated with general counseling? Should they be utilized only after some progress has been made (e.g., when the client's depression has begun to lift)? Should the referral be made immediately? (A referral for medication, for example, might be urgent, preceding the inception of counseling.) The immediacy of the clients' need for the services, the clients' readiness to benefit from the services, and the availability of the services will determine the answers to these questions.

2. *What adjunct services* should be recommended? Typically, the counselor will suggest not only the nature of the adjunct services that are needed but also sources (individuals or agencies) that can provide the client with appropriate services of good quality. Again, need and availability of services must be considered. (The referral process will be discussed further in this chapter.)

3. *What connection* will be maintained between the primary treatment provider (e.g., the counselor) and the provider of the adjunct services? Will the counselor simply give the client the name of an agency or service provider without follow-up? Will the counselor follow up at a distance by occasionally inquiring about the client's involvement with and reactions to the adjunct services? Or will the counselor contact directly the providers of adjunct services so that they can work as partners in implementing the client's treatment plan? These options, too, will be discussed later. However, the answers to these questions will be determined primarily by the client's ability to follow up independently on a referral and the link between the counseling process and the nature of the adjunct service. Clients who are fearful, fragile, confused, or in poor control of their impulses typically will require more support, supervision, and direction of their efforts to obtain adjunct services. There also is likely to be a closer connection between a counselor and the provider of adjunct ser-

vices if the services are variations on the counseling process (e.g., career counseling, assertiveness training) rather than being provided by other disciplines (e.g., tutoring, speech therapy).

4. *Who* will oversee the treatment plan? One of the pitfalls of a multifaceted treatment plan is the lack of clarity surrounding the question of who will oversee, coordinate, and take responsibility for the implementation of that treatment plan. If the treatment plan includes individual or family counseling, provided on a regular basis, then the mental health professional conducting the counseling sessions generally will take charge of the plan. If, however, the primary mode of treatment is group counseling, medication, or a combination of adjunct services, the choice of case manager may not be self-evident. Designation of a primary counselor or case manager, then, should be done soon after an intake interview is completed.

5. What will be the *sequence* of the components of a treatment plan? Sometimes several adjunct services will be recommended as part of a treatment plan. To be most effective, the plan should specify whether the services should be provided in a particular sequence (e.g., communication skills training should precede client's involvement in a social organization), whether the services should be concurrent (e.g., exercise class and a weight control program), or whether the sequence of services is unimportant and can be determined by client preference and availability of services.

Approaches to Utilization of Adjunct Services

Adjunct services can be divided into six broad categories. Their categorization depends on their nature, their role in the treatment process, their integration with counseling that might be taking place, and the nature of the communication between the primary counselor and the provider of adjunct services.

Referral

Referral is the process of utilizing adjunct services in which there is the least amount of contact or communication between the counselor who makes the referral and the agency to which the client is referred. The counselor may simply supply the client with the names of a few well-respected agencies or individuals providing the recommended services, and the client is expected to assume the responsibility of following up on the referral. A referral is common under two conditions.

Under the first condition, the referring counselor has decided not to provide the basic services needed by the client. Those services might not be available through the counselor's agency, might be outside of the counselor's area of expertise, or might not include counseling. Consequently, the counselor transfers the major responsibility for the client's treatment to another agency or individual.

Of course, it is important to make such referrals with sensitivity to the client's needs. It might have been difficult for the client to take the first step in seeking counseling. Being told that services must be sought elsewhere might feel like a rejection to the client or might so diminish the client's determination to seek counseling that the client might procrastinate and fail to follow up on the referral. The counselor, then, must use judgment in making a referral. With a fragile or apprehensive client, the counselor might want to work with the client temporarily until the case can be transferred to a more suitable treatment person, or the counselor might want to contact the referral source directly to introduce the client and perhaps schedule an appointment, thereby easing the transition for the client. Counselors also should make clear to clients why a referral is indicated so it will not be perceived as a rejection or a sign that the client is too troubled to be helped by counseling alone. A discussion of what is likely to happen when the client contacts the referral agency and of what services are available there can further reduce client anxiety.

The second condition under which a referral often is made occurs when clients need services that seem likely to contribute to their development but that generally are not viewed as mental health services. An example of this is an overweight client who consults a counselor for help in dealing with social and interpersonal concerns. The counselor might refer the client to a weight control clinic, an exercise facility, or a social organization for overweight people. At the same time, the counselor will work with the client in individual counseling, focusing on such areas as communication skills, self-image, and dependency needs. Discussion of the client's progress in weight control and socialization almost certainly would occur during the counseling sessions but it would be unusual, for example, for there to be direct contact between the counselor and the client's fitness instructor.

When making a referral, it is customary to provide clients with a choice of places to obtain the recommended services. This enables clients to have more independence and control over the referral process and maximizes their chances of finding a place that is comfortable and appropriate to their needs. This process also communicates to the client that the counselor is not omniscient and may not know exactly which outside agency is most likely to suit the client. This can reinforce the importance of working together to build a sound counseling relationship. From ethical and legal standpoints as well, the counselor who suggests several places for clients to obtain services seems to be on safer ground than the counselor who offers only one source of adjunct services when many are available.

Of course, there are exceptions. If the counselor knows a particular source to be superior to others that are available or if the client is too fragile or apprehensive to investigate options, then a referral to a single source of services might be preferable.

Linkage

Linkage is a second approach to using adjunct services to ameliorate emotional difficulties. In the linkage process, the counselor plays the role of an intermediary, reaching out to clients to help them identify their needs and then matching them to appropriate services. Lewis and Lewis (1977) described four approaches to the linkage process:

1. *Outreach*—The counselor uses telephone calls or home visits to detect client concerns, links clients to appropriate services, and follows up with clients to be sure that services have been obtained.
2. *Broker*—Counselor expedites clients' efforts to obtain services by helping them to get to and make use of appropriate services. The counselor might arrange trans-

portation for the client and might even accompany the client to a service-delivery agency if communication, bureaucratic, or other difficulties are anticipated.

3. *Advocate*—The counselor seeks services for which clients do not immediately seem to be eligible. This may involve the counselor negotiating with the service-delivery agency or working with clients to help them ascertain and prove their eligibility for needed services (e.g., aid to dependent children).

4. *Interpreter*—In this role, the counselor serves as a conduit of information between clients and service-delivery agencies, helping both sides to understand each other's needs and values and to establish a positive working relationship.

The primary difference between referral and linkage is that referral involves a transfer of full or partial responsibility for the client whereas linkage involves the counselor remaining in charge, overseeing and monitoring the services provided to the client, intervening with both client and service-delivery agency as needed to ensure expeditious and appropriate delivery of services. Linkage is particularly useful for helping clients from non-English speaking or lower socioeconomic backgrounds, clients with little formal education, minority clients, and older clients. Such clients often are uncomfortable dealing with administrative and bureaucratic procedures and may feel mistrustful of social service agencies or may feel embarrassed and ashamed of their need for such services. These feelings can prevent them from obtaining needed services for themselves and their families and can exacerbate emotional and physical concerns (e.g., isolation, depression, malnutrition).

Services that often call for a linkage approach are those that involve the clients' dealing with extensive administrative procedures, with a number of agencies or service providers, or with eligibility standards. Such services might include legal aid, food stamps, Social Security payments, aid to dependent children, foster care, low-income housing, and related social services.

Collaboration

In collaboration, responsibility for clients' treatment is shared between two or more mental health professionals. Each generally will be in charge of an important aspect of the clients' treatment plans. The collaboration might be between a family counselor, working with the client and his spouse and children, and a general counselor, seeing the client for individual sessions. It might be among a psychiatrist who is prescribing and monitoring a client's medication, the resident counselor in the halfway house where the client is living, and the rehabilitation counselor who is helping the client to establish career goals and to obtain training and employment.

Clearly, collaboration can take many forms and might involve the entire spectrum of helping professionals. It has advantages in that more than one person is available to pay attention to clients and to provide needed services. However, there also are pitfalls in the collaborating process. Power issues may arise between the collaborating professionals, each feeling that his or her mode of treatment is more important or more appropriate and his or her relationship with the client stronger and more productive. An opposite difficulty also can occur, especially if the service providers feel overworked or uncommitted to their fields. They may shirk their responsibility to the client and assume that the other person working with the client will fill in any gaps. Of course, that could be an erroneous assumption, leading to neglect of the client.

Manipulative, dependent, or resistant clients can make collaboration particularly difficult. They may disrupt their treatment by playing the collaborators against each other, telling each how valuable his or her help is and how unfeeling and unskilled the other treatment provider is. Resistant clients may avoid or minimize their treatment by telling each collaborator that all their needs are being met by the other helper.

Clearly, it is important that collaborators have a shared understanding of the nature of a client's concerns, the services required by the client, and how the responsiblity for those services will be divided. Collaborating mental health professionals also should arrange to confer regularly on the client's progress to ensure appropriate delivery of services.

Cooperation

Cooperation describes an approach to treatment in which one mental health professional is clearly in charge of a client's treatment and probably also provides the most essential services to the client (e.g., individual or family counseling). However, another individual is brought in to work directly with the client on a particular aspect of the treatment. Typically, the other worker will be another mental health professional with expertise in a particular aspect of human services or a particular approach to counseling such as sex therapy, assertiveness training, or career counseling. The primary treatment provider may seek the services of the adjunct treatment provider because the primary counselor lacks skills in a particular area or because that counselor wants to be able to concentrate on other concerns in working with the client.

In the process of cooperation, communication between service providers is important, as it is in collaboration. Although competition or client neglect may occur during cooperation, as it can during collaboration, it is less likely because the case manager or person responsible for the client's treatment is clearly designated.

Consultation

In consultation, an outside expert is called in by the primary counselor or treatment team to assist them in providing appropriate services to the client. Although the consultant may interview, observe, or test the client, the consultant interacts primarily with those responsible for treating the client. The consultant focuses on the needs of the treatment providers and, although the consultant's goal is to improve the quality of the help being offered to the client, the consultant is only indirectly concerned with the client's needs.

Caplan (1963) described four types of mental health consultation:

1. Client-centered case consultation.   The consultant assesses the client's concerns through interviews, testing, or other methods and then advises the treatment providers on the most effective approach to helping that client.

2. Consultee-centered case consultation.   In this approach, the consultant focuses on the consultee's difficulties in working with one or more clients. These difficulties might be gaps in the treatment provider's areas of expertise, countertransference issues, or a poor working relationship among the members of a treatment team. Once the nature of the problem has been identified, the consultant works directly with the mental health professionals to help them perform more effectively. This might involve the consultant providing or recommending skill development programs or serving as a facilitator and expert in group process for the treatment team.

3. Program-centered case consultation.   Here, the consultant would be engaged to assess the nature of services provided to ensure that an agency is appropriately and efficiently meeting clients' needs. This variety of consultation might be used when it is felt that an agency is not adequately helping many of its clients, perhaps because of inadequate outreach, inappropriate services, unskilled staff, or inefficient distribution of services.

4. Consultee-centered administrative consultation.   In an approach related to program-centered case consultation, the consultant works with an agency, treatment team, or mental health professional to identify difficulties that inhibit consultees' efforts to institute program changes. These might include administrative barriers, resistance to change, adherence to dated and inappropriate models or confusion over the mission of the agency. The consultant's focus will be on the consultees and the administrative structure of their agency rather than on the specific programs or services provided.

Lewis and Lewis (1977) cited five characteristics of the consulting process:

1. The consultee (e.g., the treatment provider) is the one who requests help from the consultant.

2. The consultant serves in an advisory capacity and has no direct power or control over the consultee's actions.
3. The consulting process involves education and information-giving.
4. The concentration of the consulting process is on the consultee as a service provider.
5. The ultimate goal is to provide better help to a third party (e.g., individual client, family, or community).

In order to accomplish this process effectively, consultants (often themselves mental health professionals) should have a clear understanding of who their client is (e.g., the treatment provider), what service or information is sought, and what that client's environment or work system is like. Consultants also need good interpersonal and communication skills as well as mastery of whatever body of technical skills or information is required by their clients.

Perhaps the most common use of a consultant in mental health treatment involves the primary counselor asking a psychiatrist, physician, or psychologist to assess a client and provide the counselor with information on aspects of the client's physical, emotional, or intellectual functioning. However, consultants can be used in many ways during treatment and can be particularly useful when counselors feel blocked or stymied in their efforts.

Outreach

Outreach is a final approach to the use of adjunct services, presenting a somewhat different slant on the process. Often, a client presents concerns that are intertwined with the attitudes and behaviors of significant others in the client's life. Helping the client, then, may be very difficult without the involvement and cooperation of those significant others. For example, an anxious woman, low in self-esteem, might report that she has an alcoholic and abusive husband. Clients also might describe others' concerns that are not strongly connected to the clients' own concerns but that warrant counseling intervention. Examples may include a client whose child seems extremely anxious and withdrawn at school and a client whose eighty-year-old father seems severely depressed.

In cases such as these, the counselor often will want to make help available to the client's significant others. Ideally, this should be done through the client. For example, the client might ask her spouse to come in for couples counseling or might encourage her father to contact the counselor for an appointment. Sometimes, however, the client is apprehensive about suggesting counseling and so may prefer the counselor to make a direct contact. This is appropriate, as long as it is done in a way that maintains open communication between client and counselor and, at the same time, maintains the confidentiality of both present and prospective clients.

CATEGORIES OF ADJUNCT SERVICES

The six approaches to using adjunct services suggest many ways in which counselors can elaborate on a treatment plan and take a holistic and comprehensive approach to meeting client needs. Another way of looking at adjunct services is by reviewing some of the important categories of such services. There is no one-to-one correspondence between a type of service and the way in which it is incorporated into a client's treatment plan, although some services seem particularly well suited to one or two of the six approaches. However, the needs of the client, the philosophy of counseling and preferred style of the counselor, and the parameters of the agency where treatment is being provided all determine the choice of adjunct services that are most likely to be helpful to the client and how they are used.

The following is a broad (but not all-inclusive) list of adjunct services that might become part of a mental health treatment plan.

I. *Skill-development*

    A. Tutoring and academic remediation
    B. Study skills
    C. Training in effective parenting
    D. Relaxation
    E. Preparation for standardized tests (e.g., high school equivalency, Scholastic Aptitude Test, Graduate Records Examination)

    F. College courses
    G. Specific vocational preparation
    H. Adult education courses to develop interests (e.g., a foreign language, decorating)
    I. Job-seeking skills (e.g., resume writing, interviewing)

II. *Focused counseling*

    A. Career counseling
    B. Sex therapy
    C. Art therapy (drawing, music, poetry)
    D. Hypnotherapy
    E. Biofeedback training
    F. Group counseling
    G. Couples or family counseling
    H. Premarital counseling

III. *Personal growth*

    A. Assertiveness training
    B. Communications training
    C. Values clarification
    D. Image-building workshops
    E. Training in decision making and problem solving
    F. Relationship enhancement

IV. *Peer support groups*

    A. Alcoholics Anonymous
    B. Gamblers Anonymous
    C. Vietnam veterans
    D. Spouse abusers and abused spouses
    E. Families of individuals with severe illnesses or disabilities
    F. Men's or women's support groups

V. *Alternate care or living arrangements*

    A. Halfway houses for previous substance abusers, psychiatric patients, ex-offenders

   B.   Group homes for troubled adolescents, mentally re-
        tarded or physically disabled clients
   C.   Low-income housing for the elderly or disabled
   D.   Day treatment centers for the elderly or for clients with
        severe mental disorders
   E.   Foster homes for children, pregnant adolescents, dis-
        abled or aged clients
   F.   Shelters for abused women and their children, clients
        without homes
   G.   Homemaking services

VI. *Medical and psychological services*

   A.   Physical examinations
   B.   Evaluation of sexual dysfunction
   C.   Chemotherapy
   D.   Intelligence testing
   E.   Psychological assessment
   F.   Hospitalization

VII. *Other health-related services*

   A.   Weight-control
   B.   Exercise or aerobics classes
   C.   Physical rehabilitation
   D.   Meditation, yoga

VIII. *Organizations for socialization and leisure activity*

   A.   Dating or social clubs
   B.   Organized sports activities (e.g., ski club, volleyball team)
   C.   Special-interest groups (e.g., bridge clubs, gardening
        clubs)
   D.   Cultural societies or groups
   E.   Religious organizations
   F.   Nature-oriented activities (e.g., Sierra Club, Wilderness
        Society)
   G.   Parents Without Partners
   H.   Relevant professional associations (e.g., American Fed-
        eration of Teachers)

IX. *Other professional services*

    A. Legal assistance
    B. Financial planning
    C. Divorce mediation
    D. Speech therapy
    E. Employment services
    F. Information on starting a business

X. *Social and governmental services*

    A. Aid to dependent children
    B. Food stamps
    C. Social Security
    D. Unemployment compensation

The nature of most of the preceding services is self-evident. Counselors will encounter additional services through experience. Knowledge of the community in which they work and the typical needs and resources of clients in that community should enable counselors to seek out and select appropriate adjunct services for their clients.

MEDICATION

One important resource does, however, seem to require further clarification. Many clients enter counseling already receiving some form of chemotherapy or medication. Medication often is prescribed to clients in counseling to help them overcome debilitating anxiety, depression, mood swings, or panic attacks, or to reduce a psychotic process. Although counselors are not qualified to prescribe medication, there are several reasons why it is important that they have some knowledge of the types and effects of drugs that are commonly used to treat emotional disorders:

1. Clients may state, during an initial interview, that they are taking prescribed medication. Knowledge of that medication can provide the counselor with important information about the

client's condition and can enable the counselor to have a better idea of how the client functioned before being given medication and what the client might be like without it.

2. By knowing what medication can and cannot do for clients, counselors are better able to judge when to refer a client to a psychiatrist for medication.

3. Counselors often see clients on a more frequent or more regular basis than does a collaborating psychiatrist who prescribes medication for counselors' clients. Consequently, the counselors are in a better position to monitor treatment compliance and the effectiveness of the medication and to suggest another visit to the psychiatrist if the medication does not seem to be helping.

4. Similarly, counselors are likely to learn before a consulting psychiatrist of a change in the client's medical condition, such as a pregnancy or the diagnosis of a physical illness. Such information should prompt a strong recommendation from the counselor that the client taking medication should contact the psychiatrist quickly.

5. Medication brings many benefits but also can cause a wide range of sometimes serious and occasionally lethal side effects. The following is a catalogue of common side effects:

1. Anxiety
2. Appetite changes
3. Bowel changes
4. Breast enlargement
5. Breathing difficulty
6. Confusion
7. Depression
8. Dizziness
9. Drowsiness
10. Faintness
11. Gastrointestinal upset
12. Hair loss
13. Headaches
14. Heartbeat irregularities
15. Impaired coordination
16. Impotence
17. Jaundice

18. Libidinal changes
19. Light sensitivity
20. Menstrual irregularities
21. Mouth dryness
22. Muscle spasms, tremors
23. Nausea
24. Nightmares
25. Pains—body, chest, joints
26. Panic
27. Rashes
28. Restlessness
29. Ringing in ears
30. Sleep disturbances
31. Speech slurred
32. Sweating
33. Swelling
34. Tingling sensations
35. Tongue changes
36. Urinary changes
37. Visual abnormalities
38. Weakness
39. Weight changes

When clients take medication, it often is difficult for counselors to determine whether the above symptoms are caused by emotional factors or whether they are by-products of the clients' medication. These side effects also can be confusing to clients. Some side effects such as impotence, hair loss, libidinal changes, and weight changes, can have an adverse impact on clients' self-images and their interpersonal relationships, while others such as confusion, heartbeat irregularities, and pains can be frightening. Counselors should be aware of the potential side effects of commonly prescribed medications and should consult with clients' physicians when possible side effects are reported.

6. Another reason why counselors should have at least a limited knowledge of medication is that clients may not be as open with a psychiatrist, seen for brief monthly medication sessions, as they are with a counselor whom they see for weekly 50-minute sessions. For example, a client who is abusing alcohol may not

disclose the abuse to the psychiatrist, but may share this information with the counselor. Some drugs, such as the minor tranquilizers, can be fatal if combined with alcohol. The well-informed counselor can warn the client of any dangers associated with the medication being taken and can ensure that the psychiatrist has full information on the client's condition.

A brief overview of the major categories of psychotropic medication is presented here to give readers some familiarity with relevant medication. Additional information can be obtained from the annual compendium of pharmaceuticals and biologicals, the *Physicians Desk Reference,* available at nearly every medical facility in the United States. Briefer references, such as *The Pill Book* (Silverman & Simon, 1979) and *The Medicine Show* (Editors of Consumer Reports Books, 1980), also can be useful and convenient references.

Categories of Commonly Used Psychotropic Medication

1. Anxiolytics (minor tranquilizers).   These include the benzodiazepines such as Librium, Valium, and Serax and the substituted diols such as Miltown and Equanil (Abrams, 1976). These are prescribed to reduce anxiety and insomnia and also serve as muscle relaxants. Widely prescribed until recent years, especially as a palliative for anxiety and dissatisfaction experienced by homemakers, these drugs have addictive properties and can be lethal when combined, in excess, with alcohol. More judicious use is being made of these medications, but they are still frequently prescribed.

2. Lithium.   Lithium is highly effective in the treatment of bipolar (manic-depressive) disorders (Bowden, 1981). It seems to act by controlling the acute manic episodes and reducing the severity of the depression. Although 80 to 90 percent of those with bipolar disorders show significant improvement in response to Lithium, they may need to be maintained on the drug for many years and require regular monitoring of their blood levels.

3. Tricyclic antidepressants.   Well-known examples of this category of medication include Elavil, Tofranil, Sinequan, Norpramine, and Vivactil. They are particularly useful for clients experiencing major depressive disorders (especially those accompanied by melancholia) and panic disorders. The onset of the effect of these drugs typically requires 10 to 14 days. Four to 6 weeks may be needed for the full impact of the drug to be felt, so rapid improvement should not be anticipated. Weight gain and several other side effects frequently are associated with this category of medication. An overdose of tricyclic antidepressents can be fatal, so they should be prescribed cautiously for clients experiencing confusion or suicidal ideation. Nevertheless, they seem to have less significant side effects than MAOIs (see below) and their use has been increasing (Meyer, 1983).

4. *Monoamine Oxidase Inhibitors (MAOIs).* A second category of antidepressant medication, MAOIs, includes Marplan, Nardil, and Parnate. They, too, take several weeks to take effect and are used in the treatment of such disorders as depression, panic disorders, anxiety, phobias, obsessional thinking, hypochondriasis, and depersonalization (Bowden, 1981). They seem to be particularly effective in the treatment of depression accompanied by one or more of the above symptoms (Abrams, 1976). The ingestion of certain foods (e.g., ripened cheese, beer, wine, and yeast) in combination with these drugs can cause an adverse reaction.

5. *Neuroleptics (major tranquilizers).* This category is subdivided into:

    a. *Tricyclics*
        (1). Phenothiazines (e.g., Thorazine, Prolixin, Stelazine, Mellaril)
        (2). Thioxanthenes (e.g., Navane)
    b. *Butyrophenones* (e.g., Haldol, Seranace)

The major tranquilizers can control psychotic disturbances and eliminate, within 2 to 6 weeks, accompanying symptoms such as delusions, hallucinations, paranoia, agitation, and confusion. This category of drugs has greatly reduced the need for long-term hospitalization of psychotic individuals and has enabled many clients with a history of psychotic episodes to lead rewarding and productive lives. However, these drugs, too, can cause a number of unwanted side effects such as trembling, uneasiness, and postural rigidity and are not effective in reducing anxiety (Frances, et al., 1984).

6. *Barbiturates.*   Exemplified by Amytal, Nembutal, Seconal, and Tuinal, these produce prompt and sustained sedation. They often are given to patients to relax them prior to surgery and are effective in reducing insomnia and anxiety. However, the use of these drugs is limited because they are readily addictive, have a number of side effects, and can be lethal if an overdose is taken. They also can cause drowsiness and may interfere with driving.

Nonbarbiturate sedatives also are available such as Dalmane, Placidyl, and Quaalude. Both their effects and their dangers are similar to those of barbiturates.

7. *Amphetamines.*   Amphetamine risks, too, are becoming well-known and their authorized use is diminishing as a result. Amphetamines can be addictive and can lead to the appearance of psychotic symptoms. However, amphetamines, notably Ritalin, are still used to modify the behavior of children who manifest hyperactivity. In adults, amphetamines can reduce depression and apathy but can produce anxiety and excessive weight loss.

Although not a form of medication, electroconvulsive therapy (ECT)is mentioned here because it, too, is prescribed by physicians and often is used as an alternative to chemotherapy. ECT has received a great deal of negative publicity and some counselors are surprised to learn that it is still being used. However, ECT works quickly and is at least as effective as antidepressant medication in relieving acute depressions, especially those of an endogenous variety (Bowden, 1981). However, it can cause temporary or permanent memory impairment, is more costly and less convenient than medication, and often results in only short-lived improvement (Frances, et al., 1984). Consequently, ECT should almost always be accompanied by other forms of treatment.

Research has found that a blend of counseling and medication is often superior to either alone (Frances, et al., 1984). This finding, as well as the dangers inherent in medication, suggests that psychotropic medication should almost always be prescribed in the context of a therapeutic relationship.

SUMMARY

This chapter has presented a broad array of adjunct services available to counselors and their clients. Although such services will not always be warranted as part of client treatment plans, many mental health professionals have found that a holistic approach, attending to a broad range of concerns, can be particularly effective in helping clients. As Lewis and Lewis (1977) have stated, "A multifaceted approach is more efficient than a single service approach" (p. 5).

Chapter 7

DIAGNOSIS AND TREATMENT PLANNING FOR COUPLES AND FAMILIES

Family counseling has been growing in use and influence over the past 50 years. Some mental health professionals believe that it is the preferred mode of treatment for nearly all clients, while others rarely, if ever, use family counseling. Most clinicians take a middle position, making frequent but not exclusive use of family interventions. Research indicates that marital and family counseling is more effective than individual counseling in the treatment of family concerns (Frances et al., 1984). Family counseling theory not only offers a variety of approaches for helping families, but also provides a framework for understanding individuals in a family context. In a way, then, family counseling is a point of view, useful in the diagnosis and treatment of individuals, couples, and families.

It is not the purpose of this chapter to teach family counseling. It is assumed that readers have some prior knowledge of the field or, at least, that they will acquire further learning in the area if they intend to practice family counseling. This chapter does seek to provide counselors with a framework for analyzing and diagnosing family difficulties and to review the nature and appropriateness of the major approaches to family counseling so that counselors can make family counseling part of their treatment plans.

Overview of Historical Development

As early as the 1920s, Alfred Adler, Rudolph Dreikurs, and others recognized the impact of the family on children's development, and mothers usually were interviewed when their children were brought in for treatment. The 1930s saw the beginning of marriage counseling, initiating a pattern of seeing family members together. Several researchers gave great impetus to family counseling in the 1950s. Murray Bowen, on the East Coast, and the Palo Alto group (Jay Haley, Gregory Bateson, John Weakland, Don Jackson, and others), on the West Coast, were exploring the interaction between the schizophrenic behavior of one family member and the behavior of the rest of the family. Bateson and his colleagues emphasized the importance of the double-bind, a form of communication in which incompatible messages are transmitted simultaneously. For example, a parent might verbally encourage affection but then be cold and unresponsive when the child becomes affectionate. Both the double-bind and the "schizophrenogenic mother," a "domineering, aggressive, rejecting, and insecure woman," were believed to contribute to the devlopment of schizophrenia in families (Nichols, 1984, p. 19). In the next decade, Virginia Satir's *Conjoint Family Therapy* (1967) focused attention on less disturbed families and on the importance of family communication and the family unit. Salvador Minuchin (1974) made an important contribution to the family counseling movement during the 1970s by focusing attention on family structure and ways in which it could be modified to improve family functioning. Innovative approaches to family counseling in the 1980s generally have advocated a brief, directive, and problem-focused approach to treatment, exemplified by Strategic Family Therapy (Madanes, 1981).

This provides only a cursory overview of the development of the field of family counseling. However, it does offer readers a context in which to consider current approaches and methods of treatment. More information on the major approaches cited in this section will be provided later.

Diagnosis of Family Functioning

There is no taxonomy comparable to the *DSM-III* that can be used for the diagnosis of family functioning. However, a list of categories or dimensions for analyzing families has been drawn from the relevant literature and it provides the framework offered here for diagnosing families.

1. Presenting Problem

Family counseling begins with an exploration of the presenting problem that led the family to seek help and of the kinds of changes the family would like. With families, as with individuals, presenting concerns may not represent the fundamental issues troubling the family. Satir (1967) observed that often families seek help for a child with a behavioral problem. Satir dubbed this child the Identified Patient (IP) and found that the IP often is the healthiest family member, acting out in order to obtain help for the family. The attribution of a family concern to an individual member can make determination of the family's difficulties a challenging task. This task can be further complicated if family members have divergent views of the family problems. Nevertheless, the family's presenting concerns must be understood and evaluated as part of diagnosis of the family.

2. Intergenerational Family History

Bowen (1974b) believed that families can best be helped if they are viewed from a longitudinal perspective. This facilitates understanding of what Bowen termed the "intergenerational transmission process" in which patterns and traits are passed on from one generation to the next. Bowen uses a genogram (diagram of generations) to elucidate this process. The following is a brief description of a family that will be used to illustrate many points made throughout this chapter. A partial genogram of the family also is provided.

David Strauss, fifty-two, and Sandra Strauss, fifty-one, have been married for 19 years. They have three children: Lori, sixteen; Karen, eleven; and Robert, seven. The presenting problem is that Karen, until recently viewed as the family member who is always cheerful and never causes any trouble, has been presenting school-related behavioral problems (cutting classes, talking out of turn, failing to do homework assignments, and eating in class). Lori is described as the achiever of the family, gifted with strong intellectual and artistic abilities, although she also is reported to have what the family calls an artistic temperament and to be moody and somewhat unpredictable. Robert was born with mongolism; he is mildly mentally retarded and reportedly requires quite a bit of extra care and attention. David is a fairly successful accountant and Sandra, formerly a nurse, has been a homemaker since Lori's birth. David and Sandra were thirty-one and thirty, respectively, when they met, and married after 18 months of courtship. Neither had married before and Sandra was still living at home with her parents at the time. David reportedly had been so involved in putting himself through college and establishing his career, that he had had little time for dating.

David and Sandra came from Eastern European Jewish backgrounds. They were born in the United States a few years after their parents immigrated to this country. Sandra was the youngest in her family, with two older brothers, while David was the oldest, with two younger brothers.

The following genogram represents the family. In the genogram, females are represented by circles; males, by squares. An X indicates a deceased family member. Siblings are listed in order of birth, from left to right. The husband's family is placed on the left; the wife's on the right.

Sandra and David came from traditional families; their fathers worked in the business/sales area and their mothers were homemakers. Sandra was particularly close to her father; he reportedly was delighted with the birth of his daughter and pampered her until his death. David's home environment was a cold and difficult one; his father had been an alcoholic who occasionally was abusive to his wife and children. David assumed considerable responsibility for the family and often was at odds with his father and brothers.

Sandra's and David's siblings' families are not indicated on the partial genogram but would be included on a full one. Sandra's brother Robert died at age eight when his bicycle was hit by a car. Her brother Fred is divorced and has one child. Both

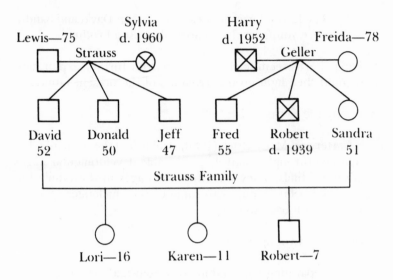

Genogram of Strauss Family

of David's brothers are wealthy businessmen and are married with children. Jeff seems to rely heavily on alcohol.

Although more exploration would be needed to determine the nature of the intergenerational transmission process in these families, the following patterns can be noted:

1. Substance abuse (Lewis, Jeff)
2. Traditional spouse roles in all families

Other patterns of importance that might have an impact on the present family:

1. David and Sandra both had important roles in their families of origin and were favored by the opposite-sex parent.
2. Abuse occurred in David's family of origin.
3. Neither David nor Sandra had sisters; both had brothers.

4. The favored parent of each died when David and Sandra were young adults. Sandra also lost a brother.

Other patterns seem likely to emerge with further exploration and could shed light on the dynamics of the present family.

3. Family Life Cycle

Carter and McGoldrick (1980) established the principle that families go through relatively predictable developmental stages as do individuals. They identified six stages in the family life cycle, listed below, along with some of the challenges typically associated with each stage.

I. Unattached young adult

    A. Separating from family of origin and achieving independence
    B. Forming relationships and chosing a mate
    C. Establishing and acting on career and personal goals

II. The newly married couple

    A. Establishing a compatible lifestyle
    B. Maintaining separateness and intimacy
    C. Redefining relationships with parents, defining relationships with in-laws
    D. Clarifying roles as marriage partners, future parents

III. The family with young children

    A. Making space for children
    B. Maintaining the spouse relationship
    C. Clarifying interactions with the new grandparents
    D. Coping with role changes, new demands on time and finances
    E. Establishing comfortable and compatible styles of parenting

IV. The family with adolescents

    A.   Increasing boundary flexibility to accommodate adolescents' need for separation, yet maintaining supervision

    B.   Coping with possible stagnation, mid-life crises, and accompanying value shifts

    C.   Dealing with own aging and that of grandparents

V. Launching children and moving on

    A.   Handling increased financial burdens; children may be in college and grandparents may need help

    B.   Reinvesting in and redefining the marriage

    C.   Expanding roles—often wives resume careers and husbands become more interested in interpersonal areas

VI. The family in later life

    A.   Continuing sexual, relationship, and role changes

    B.   Coping with aging, illness, and death

    C.   Establishing grandparenting (and maybe great-grandparenting) roles

In general, families have the most difficulty dealing with events the first time they happen (e.g., birth of the first child), events that are unanticipated and unwanted (e.g., miscarriage, the sudden loss of a job), and events that occur at ages that differ from the norm (e.g., the birth of a child to forty-five-year-old parents). Haley (1980) believed that the process of children leaving home was a particularly difficult stage or transition. Of course, each family has its unique reactions to important events and its individual patterns of development.

The Strauss family's developmental stage is that of the family with adolescents. Predictably, the family is coping with behavioral problems presented by the early-adolescent daughter. David and Sandra married later than average and so are older than most parents with children as young as seven. Their difficulties with their children may be sharpened when they look at their peers, most of whose children are in college. David and Sandra also have to cope with their aging and widowed parents. One unexpected or paranormative event that had an impact on this family was the birth of their mentally retarded son.

4. Family Structure

A number of factors determine the structure of a family. These can include:

a. Birth order, sex, and ages of children
b. Who interacts and communicates with whom and under what circumstances
c. Who has power in the family
d. Structure of family of origin

A common dysfunctional structure in a family is a triangle in which two individuals in a family, often the parents, communicate with each other through a third family member, usually a child, using that family member as a buffer or pawn.

The structure of the Strauss family can be diagramed as follows:

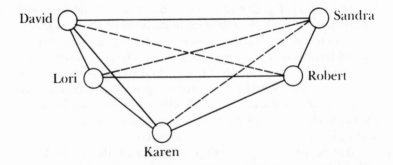

David is closest to Lori who is furthering his values through her academic achievement. He is in communication with both Sandra and Karen but tends to hold them at arm's length. Robert, his

only son, is a disappointment to him and he involves himself
little with Robert's care. Sandra finds considerable fulfillment in
her care of Robert who needs her unambiguously. Her communication with her daughters is sparse and superficial. The
sibling subsystem is fairly solid, with Lori the undisputed leader
and Karen working hard to win her favor. Both Lori and Robert
are often triangled into the parents' relationship, with Karen receiving only limited parental attention.

Birth order provides additional information on the structure
of this family. Lori, the oldest, fits the typical pattern of a first-
born by being a reasonably compliant achiever. Karen, as second-
born, could not compete effectively with Lori in the academic
arena, so she seemed to be seeking her own area in which to
stand out, the social arena. Robert, the baby of the family, was
pampered not only because of his intellectual deficits but also
because of his role as the ingratiating and charming last born.

5. Communication and Interaction Styles

Many frameworks are available for categorizing styles of
communication in family members. One of the most useful was
developed by Satir. She postulated the existence of five modes
of communication:

a. Placating—the self is viewed negatively and the individ-
    ual almost always agrees with others.
b. Blaming—the self dominates, and other people and the
    context of the situation are ignored.
c. Super-reasonable—only the context matters to this in-
    tellectualizing self; people and their feelings are ignored.
d. Irrelevant—this individual's communications generally
    ignore both people and context.
e. Congruent—this person takes account of the self, of
    others, and of the context (Seligman, 1981a).

While nearly everyone tends to shift styles, depending on the
situation, most people do have a pervasive style of communi-
cating.

David Strauss used both the blamer and super-reasonable modes. Generally an intellectualizer, under stress his defenses weaken and he can become verbally abusive. Sandra typically assumes a placater role, especially when her husband becomes a blamer. Karen, too, often assumes a placater mode while Lori tends to adopt her father's communication styles.

Generally, interaction in this family is limited to family business and an occasional family dinner. Different schedules prevent most meals from being eaten together and family outings have diminished because of Lori's and Karen's school activities and David's late work hours. Sandra and Robert often go to the park or play together and the girls, too, often play with Robert who is the only recipient of openly expressed affection in the family.

6. Family Rules, Roles, and Values

All families have rules that are stated or expressed and norms or values that may or may not be clearly stated. Rules often are very specific such as curfews and assignment of chores. Norms and values tend to be less clear than rules and might include such messages as, "The girls are expected to do well in school and to go to college," or "Don't talk about your mentally retarded brother's condition outside of the immediate family." These are norms in the Strauss household.

All family members also have roles, determined by a combination of their official status in the family (e.g., father, youngest child) and by the needs of the family and the functioning of each individual. Lori, for example, the oldest and most capable child, assumes the role of parental child, assisting her mother with Robert's care and assuming considerable responsibility for Karen's care. Sandra's role is that of care giver. David, who is more emotionally open and dependable than Sandra despite his harshness, became the family confidante. Karen's role has been to cover up family problems and present a happy facade while Robert became the focus of the family, their purpose. As in the Strauss family, rules and roles are important sources of information about family functioning.

7. Ethnic and Socioeconomic Background

Ethnic and socioeconomic patterns play a significant role in determining family functioning (McGoldrick, Pearce, & Giordano, 1982). Although interpretation of background data presents risks of stereotyping and overgeneralizing, a cautious exploration of ethnic and socioeconomic data can provide valuable understanding of the dynamics of a family's structure.

The Strauss family is middle-class; both parents are college educated. They are of eastern European Jewish origin and were the first generation of their families to be born in the United States. This background suggests a value system stressing educational achievement, family unity, and some community involvement. In families from this background, roles tend to be fairly traditional and children very important. All of these values are characteristic of the Strauss family.

8. Differentiation of Self

Bowen (1974a) postulated a differentiation of self scale, with scores ranging from a low of zero to a high of 100. He used this scale as a measure of how individualized and separated individuals were from their families. Those at the low end (0–25) of the scale tend to have symbiotic relationships with their families and tend to be narcissistic and dominated by emotion. Schizophrenics fall low on the scale. People who fall above the midpoint on the scale tend to be more inner-directed, rational, and secure, to respect others, and to have fairly well-defined opinions, beliefs, and values. Although individuals within a family can differ considerably in their degree of differentiation, some families promote differentiation while others inhibit it. Individuals tend to pick spouses and to have children with levels of differentiation comparable to their own. Bowen saw differentiation of self as a key ingredient in family health and one of the primary goals of his therapy is to increase client self-differentiation.

Levels of differentiation of the members of the Strauss family tend to fall in the middle range (25–75), with Karen, Sandra, and Robert somewhat below the midline and David and Lori above the midline. This family is not what Bowen has called an undifferentiated family ego mass; however, there is pressure on family members to conform to family and societal values rather than to think through their own value systems.

9. Significant Physical Conditions

When an individual in a family is afflicted with a significant illness, disease, or physical disorder, it inevitably has an impact on that person's family. The impact can take many forms. The affected family member can become the focus of the family's energy, at least temporarily bonding the family. This is the case in the Strauss family. It also can happen that the affected family member is viewed as a source of shame and embarrassment; efforts are made to deny the disorder and to exclude the affected member from the inner circle of the family, leading to fragmentation and resentment.

A severe or long-standing disability in a family also affects how that family interacts with the outside world. In some families, the ailment causes the family to withdraw and exclude outsiders who may intrude on the family grief or exacerbate their shame. In other families, the affliction becomes a conduit for communication as the family members expand their outside contacts in an effort to find medical treatment, information, and support to help them handle the problem condition.

Looking at the ways in which families handle physical illness can provide information on the nature and level of their coping abilities and attitudes toward family cohesiveness and community involvement.

10. External Sources of Stress and Support

External sources of stress and support can have a considerable impact on a family's homeostasis. Some families have a strong and extensive support system, perhaps extended family, neighbors, or fellow members of religious or leisure organizations. Such families typically are more able to handle stress and change than isolated nuclear families. Helping families to build support systems can be an important counseling strategy.

Families also have to cope with stress coming from outside sources. The company where a family member is employed may suddenly close, a child may be mistreated by schoolmates, or a fire may destroy family possessions and impose an unanticipated financial burden.

The Strauss family tends to be a relatively closed system with few sources of outside support, at least for the family unit and the adults. Lori and Karen are sociable and well-liked by their peers and Lori has a boyfriend. The girls, then, have some peer support. Contact with extended family is fairly limited since Sandra and David have no siblings living nearby. Sandra's mother and David's father, both in their seventies, are the only extended family with whom close contact is maintained. Sandra's mother is in a nursing home about 50 miles away and Sandra visits her weekly. David has less contact with his more self-sufficient father. Their relationship is a tense and uneasy one; the two keep track of each other but rarely visit. Some stress is imposed by the declining health of Sandra's mother, which gives the already overburdened Sandra another source of concern.

11. Anxieties and Defenses

Families, like individuals, have recurrent or pervasive anxieties as well as defenses or ways in which they fend off anxiety. These are more difficult to catalogue than are individual defenses (see chapter 3), but provide another perspective on family dynamics.

Sources of anxiety in the Strauss family include Robert's limited intelligence, David's overinvestment in his inconsistent business, his and Lori's verbal outbursts, and the family's tendency to live beyond its means. Karen's behavioral and attitudinal changes are a current source of stress.

Several defensive behaviors characterize this family. Displacement probably is the most prominent, with a range of conflicts and dissatisfactions being shifted from their original source to Robert's mongolism and its impact on the family. Inhibition and reaction formation also are employed, especially by Karen and Sandra, thereby containing unacceptable impulses and transforming them into opposite feelings. For example, anger and resentment of Robert are changed into feelings of extreme love and devotion toward him.

12. Dynamics of Symptom Maintenance

Symptoms of dysfunction serve a purpose in a family and are almost always intertwined with the overall dynamics of the family. It often is important for the counselor to understand the role of the symptom in order to effect its change or elimination. Behavioral sequences, leading to the emergence or manifestation of the symptom, provide one clue to comprehending the nature of the symptom. Other clues are provided by an examination of the family structure and the needs of individual members.

According to her parents, Karen has been presenting increasing behavioral problems for the past year. Several other family events occurred during that time. Robert was enrolled in a special school and for the first time spent part of each day away from home. Lori, who has been dating for the previous 2 years, developed a close relationship with a young man and began spending a great deal of time with him. She also took a part-time job. Lori consequently was rarely home. David's business also expanded at about that time and he became even more involved in his work than previously. A closer examination of a number of Karen's transgressions, notably cutting class, reveals that quite a few of them occurred immediately after a family crisis in which she was not involved, such as when Sandra's mother became ill and when Lori had a minor automobile accident.

Several factors, then, seem to come together to motivate Karen's behavioral changes. Long playing the role of the good child who never needed attention, Karen seems to feel that with both Robert and Lori getting more outside attention, it finally is her turn to get attention. The Strauss family tends to reward problem behavior with attention and takes good behavior for granted so Karen chooses some fairly mild acting-out behaviors that violate the family emphasis on academic achievement and social conformity as her way of getting attention. Her misbehavior increases when other family crises deflect attention onto another family member; this reminds the family that she still needs them.

It is possible that Sandra implicitly encourages Karen's behavioral changes. Less needed by Lori, Robert, and David, the family-focused care giver in Sandra needs someone to nurture. Karen's acting-out behavior enhances the importance of Sandra's role as mother and gives her another focus for her energies.

13. Special Circumstances

In addition to exploring the 12 preceding aspects of families to arrive at an understanding of their functioning, counselors also should take account of any special concerns or circumstances that might be present in the family. These might include the impact of divorce, death, or blending of families; adoption; interracial marriage; or the presence in the home of individuals outside the nuclear family. These circumstances, too, should be explored and considered in the process of family diagnosis.

INVENTORIED ASSESSMENT OF FAMILIES AND COUPLES

Although interviews are the primary vehicle for gathering information on families, many inventories have been developed or adapted for use with families. These can help counselors to gain insight into families and also can be useful in promoting increased self-awareness and mutual understanding within families. A sampling of these inventories is presented here to give readers some idea of the types of inventories that are available.

1. Family Environment Scale.   Rudolf H. Moos and Bernice S. Moos (Consulting Psychologists Press)—This scale measures 10 dimensions of family environments: cohesion, expressiveness, conflict, independence, achievement orientation, intellectual-cultural orientation, active-recreational orientation, moral-religious emphasis, organization, and control.

2. Family Pre-Counseling Inventory Program.   Richard B. Stuart and Freida Stuart (Research Press)—Offering booklets for mother, father, and adolescent, this inventory measures such factors as positive behaviors of family members, changes desired, family assets and goals, shared activities, decision-making styles, communication, and attitudes. This inventory takes a positive and behavioral approach to effecting change in families with adolescents.

3. Taylor-Johnson Temperament Analysis. Robert M. Taylor and Lucille P. Morrison (Psychological Publications, Inc.)—This is a comprehensive personality inventory, designed for use with individuals and couples. Cross-testing allows questions to be answered about self as well as spouse, thereby providing information on the couple's perceptions of themselves and each other.

4. Caring Relationship Inventory (CRI). Everett L. Shostrom (Educational and Industrial Testing Service)—The CRI measures the nature of love and caring in a couple's relationship.

TREATMENT OF FAMILIES

Once an assessment has been made of the family, the counselor is ready to formulate a treatment plan. Chapter 5 provided an overview of the aspects that must be considered in formulating treatment plans for individual clients. With slight variation (indicated below), these dimensions are considered when planning the treatment of a family. Because these dimensions were explored in depth in chapter 5, they are presented only briefly here, with emphasis given to their application to family counseling in general and to the Strauss family in particular.

1. Suitability of family for counseling. Should this be a family counseling case or should one or more individuals in the family be seen outside of the family context? Is the family able to make a commitment to counseling or does the process seem likely to be sabotaged by the destructive participation or absence of one or more family members? The Strauss family seems suitable for family counseling because the presenting problem, Karen's undesirable behavior, seems to result from and to have an impact on family dynamics. Family members are concerned about Karen and their functioning as a family, so they are prepared to make a commitment to counseling.

2. *Appropriateness of agency.*   Is there a qualified family counselor on the staff who can meet with the family at a mutually agreeable time?

3. *Goal setting.*   What short- and long-term goals will be established with the family and how will progress toward goal attainment be measured? The Strauss family's short-term goal is to restore Karen's former level of responsible and cooperative behavior. This can be measured by attendance and performance reports from her teachers. Other goals include strengthening David and Sandra's relationship, strengthening Sandra's relationships with her daughters, increasing David's involvement in the family, and improving the overall level of family communication.

4. *Length of counseling.*   Neither short-term crisis intervention nor long-term psychotherapy seems warranted for the Strauss family. Counseling of medium duration probably is indicated, the exact length of the counseling to be determined by the approach used and the progress made.

5. *Directiveness.*   On a continuum ranging from directive to client-centered, where should counseling with this family fall? The Strausses are a verbal and expressive family, eager for change. Those traits permit the effective use of a client-centered model. However, family members seem likely to have difficulty shifting their focus off Karen and onto the whole family. Also, David seems impatient and skeptical of the process. These characteristics suggest that the counselor probably should assume a middle position on the continuum.

6. *Supportiveness.*   Is this a fragile family with few strengths and insights, which requires a great deal of support, or is this a relatively cohesive and motivated family, ready to examine past influences and underlying dynamics? Again, the Strauss family falls somewhere in the middle of the continuum. They are a relatively stable family that has dealt effectively with some crises. However, family members have avoided looking at some long-standing family patterns and difficulties and might be overwhelmed by and frightened of taking a close look at their concerns.

7. Cognitive, affective, or behavioral.   Most families present a combination of cognitive, affective, and behavioral concerns. Setting priorities can facilitate treatment.

8. Communications, structural, or symptomatic.   A related question, relevant to family treatment planning, is whether the family difficulties focus on communication deficits, structural issues, or presenting symptoms. The Strauss family presents a symptom that is behavioral in nature. However, underlying concerns reflect difficulties in communication and family structure (e.g., parental child, dominating father). Feelings and cognitions, in this family, also warrant attention.

9. Couples, family, family subsystem or couples group counseling.   Although some family counseling theorists advocate working with the entire family during all counseling sessions, others will determine who should be seen in a particular session, based on the issues at hand. In counseling the Strauss family, for example, several sessions certainly will be held with the entire nuclear family. However, the counselor also might want to focus on the couple's relationship by meeting with David and Sandra; to focus on the mother-daughter subsystem by meeting with Sandra, Lori, and Karen; and to have a few sessions alone with Karen to explore her concerns. The grandparents also might be included in a session or two.

Couples or family group counseling involves several couples or families meeting together for group counseling. By sharing their concerns and giving each other feedback with the counselor's help, progress can be effected. A couples group might help David and Sandra to assess the nature of their relationship and make some rewarding changes.

10. Counselor variables.   Family counseling often is done by a pair of mental health professionals, typically a male and a female working together. The counseling couple then can model male and female behavior and can demonstrate respect and good communication skills through their own interaction. In determining who will work with a family, consideration should be given to whether there should be one or two counselors involved as well as to the possible importance of such counselor variables as age, sex, background, and experience. A complex family unit like the Strauss family, with spouse and communication difficulties, probably would benefit from counseling by a male and female pair. Other counselor variables do not seem to need consideration in this case.

MODE OF TREATMENT

Despite the newness of the family counseling field, many well-established approaches are available. Several of the most important approaches will be reviewed here. Guidelines are provided to help the reader understand the kinds of families or situations for which each approach is particularly useful. This chapter is not designed to teach theories of family counseling but rather to enable counselors to integrate these approaches into their treatment plans in an effective way.

SYSTEMS FAMILY THERAPY

Murray Bowen, director of the Family Center of Georgetown University, developed Systems Family Therapy as a result of the research he conducted on schizophrenic clients and their families. Bowen viewed the family as a system. He believed that individuals within that system did not function independently and that change in an individual would affect the system just as change in the system would have an impact on all family members.

The following concepts, many of which have been discussed earlier, are integral to systems family therapy:

1. Differentiation of self
2. Intergenerational (or multigenerational) transmission process
3. Birth order and sibling position
4. Family triangles
5. Nuclear family emotional system—This includes the focus and intensity of emotion in the nuclear family, the

nature of the marital relationship, and the functioning of individual family members.

6. Family projection process—In this process, one member of the family projects his or her own uncomfortable or unacceptable feelings onto other family members.

7. Emotional cutoff—A family member, often a young adult, establishes physical and emotional distance from the family in order to achieve some independence. This often characterizes the efforts of poorly differentiated individuals to separate themselves from enmeshed families.

In working with families, Bowen assumed the role of coach or consultant. His style and those of most of his followers seems to be cognitive and unemotional, leading clients on a slowly paced journey toward gathering information and understanding of their families and differentiating themselves via genograms, family interviews, and exploration. Clients often need 3 to 5 years to complete counseling with a systems-oriented family therapist.

Because he believed that an individual could have an impact on a system and vice versa, Bowen would work with an individual, a couple, or a family. This approach, then, can be useful regardless of whether an entire family is present for counseling. In its purest form, however, Systems Family Therapy seems suitable for only a select group of clients—those who are not in an immediate crisis and who have the time, energy, finances, and inclination to undertake a lengthy and often analytical exploration of their families. Specialized training in Systems Family Therapy is available and would probably be necessary for counselors to become skilled practitioners of this approach.

Despite the demands this approach makes on clients and counselors, it provides both a way of conceptualizing family functioning and many useful techniques that have broad application. An abbreviated genogram, for example, can promote understanding in families where the multigenerational transmission process has had a major influence on current functioning. The Strauss family members might not be willing to engage in an extended examination of their family background, so they might not be good candidates for the systems approach practiced by Bowen and his colleagues. However, the genogram and several other concepts associated with this approach do have relevance to the Strauss family situation, as discussed earlier, so they might well be incorporated into their counseling.

COMMUNICATIONS FAMILY THERAPY

Virginia Satir, who developed Conjoint Family Therapy, is the leading proponent of an approach that focuses on family communication. Satir believed that although requests for counseling often are prompted by the apparent dysfunction of one family member, the identified patient or IP often is the healthiest member of the family and is simply reacting to the overall dysfunction in the family (Satir, 1983). Satir's goal, then, was to shift the focus of the counseling from the IP to the family, especially to the couple, and to help the family reestablish caring, cohesiveness, and communication.

The following concepts are important in this model:

1. The marital relationship is integral to the health and functioning of the whole family.
2. A review of the history of the family, beginning with the spouses' families of origin and focusing on the development of the spouse relationship, is important in reestablishing positive family feelings.
3. Low self-esteem in family members is a frequent cause of difficulties.
4. Clear and congruent communication is essential to healthy family functioning.
5. Conflicting styles of communication or perception (e.g., visual versus kinesthetic) can lead to conflict.
6. It is important for families to allow separateness and individuation of their members.
7. Process usually is more important than content; counseling should explore the process of family communication.

8.   Family rules, norms, and secrets exert a powerful influence on family dynamics.

Satir's approach, with its echoes of Carl Rogers, probably is more familiar to most counselors than are the other models presented in this chapter. Satir also assumed a role that is compatible with the underlying philosophy of counseling. She viewed herself as a role model and resource person, teaching families new ways to interact and supporting their efforts to change. Her focus was largely on the present and she emphasized strength rather than pathology.

Satir's model requires involvement of the entire nuclear family in the counseling process, even though she may not meet with all family members in all sessions. Her model is particularly suitable for families where the spouse relationship has weakened and become dysfunctional and where family communication is confusing, incongruent, and limited. Satir's communications approach seems to require clients who are not in an immediate crisis and who have at least a moderate degree of motivation and verbal ability. Of course, nearly all families seeking counseling have some difficulty with communication. Consequently, as does Bowen, Satir has a great deal to offer almost all families seeking counseling.

In many ways, the communications model is well suited to treatment of the Strauss family. Karen, the IP, does seem to be manifesting symptoms in reaction to family dysfunction, symptoms that are designed to restore a more equitable balance of attention in the family. The spouses no longer have the sense of unity and closeness that led them to marry; rather, their strongest bonds are with the children of the opposite sex, a pattern that Satir has characterized as a frequent sign of dysfunction and spouse dissatisfaction. Family members communicate in limited and ambiguous ways and there is little open dialogue. Sandra and Karen seem to have low self-esteem. The members of this family are motivated to seek help and, with the possible exception of Robert, seem capable of learning to communicate clearly and directly. Satir's model also provides a mix of supportiveness and directiveness, likely to be appreciated by this family.

STRUCTURAL FAMILY THERAPY

Salvador Minuchin is viewed as the primary developer of Structural Family Therapy. Minuchin advocated taking an active approach to family counseling, becoming a part of the family system himself, if necessary, in order to challenge and change the family structure and views of the world.

The following concepts are important in structural family therapy:

1. *Family structure*—This includes patterns of transaction, styles of communication, alliances, and boundaries. In healthy families, boundaries are clear yet semipermeable. Parents are allies and are in charge of the system but are free to act childlike at times. Children have secure and clear roles, yet can occasionally and appropriately assume parental functions.
2. *Subsystems*—Subsystems are essential to carrying out family functioning. These include the spouse subsystem, sibling subsystems, and various combinations of parent-child subsystems (e.g., the female family members' subsystem). In well-functioning families, subsystems are flexible and respond to the situation at hand.
3. *Subsystem boundaries*—Families need well-defined lines of responsibility and authority. At the same time, boundaries should be flexible and clear rather than rigid and diffuse. Clear boundaries facilitate independence at the same time they protect the family.
4. *Adaptation to stress*—The manner in which families handle and adapt to stress provides information on the family structure and sources of both strength and weakness.

Minuchin uses a broad range of techniques to join the family, to evaluate their functioning, and then to restructure the family, perhaps by escalating stress or using a family member as a sort of co-counselor. Structural family therapy is an active and creative approach that often seems to be effective in overcoming resistance and engaging even difficult families in the therapeutic process. It also is a valuable approach to helping families with boundary issues, weak parental subsystems, excluded or en-meshed family members, and related concerns.

There are some noteworthy structural issues in the Strauss family. Sandra and David are reasonably effective parents, but do not have a strong spouse subsystem. Boundaries between parents and children are not always clear and the mother-son subsystem may be too isolated and close-knit. Sandra seems to have too little power in the family and needs to strengthen her alliances with her husband and her daughters. However, al-though a structural approach to working with this family might well be effective, the family structure is not severely dysfunc-tional. Attention to structural issues might, therefore, best be accomplished in the context of another approach such as the communications model.

STRATEGIC FAMILY THERAPY

Strategic Family Therapy, developed by Jay Haley and Cloé Madanes, draws heavily on the work of Milton Erickson. This theory views symptoms as a metaphor for the family difficulty and advocates an active approach to removing the symptom and simultaneously improving the overall family functioning.

Principles important in this theory include:

1. Family structure and hierarchy are both important; the parents must be clearly in charge of the family.
2. Transitions often precipitate family dysfunction. The departure of the children from the home is a particularly stressful transition.
3. The counselor is responsible for finding a way to alle-viate the symptoms and help the family. If one approach doesn't work quickly, another approach should be tried until the goal is accomplished.
4. The counseling focuses on actions; thoughts, feelings, and insights are secondary.

Strategic Family Therapy is a directive, action-oriented ap-proach, with the counselor in charge. A wide range of techniques is used. However, paradoxical interventions are a particularly important ingredient of this approach. These involve a reversal of the client's perceptions or expectations. For example, a setback may be predicted for a family that is making good progress, and a couple that seeks help because of constant fighting might be told to plan to argue on a regular schedule. These interventions serve to jostle the family's dysfunctional patterns and reduce the power of the symptom. This often will lead to a modification in family dynamics and the elimination of the symptom. The family then should be receptive to learning new skills and behavioral patterns.

Haley and Madanes believed that this approach could be helpful to all families, regardless of the nature of their concerns (Madanes, 1981). This approach seems likely to be particularly effective with resistant or passive families, families with limited verbal or analytical abilities, families experiencing stressful transitions, families in crisis, and families with dysfunctional hierarchies. Its action-oriented approach also might make it helpful to families with severely disturbed members.

A strategic approach might be effective in reducing Karen's symptoms and improving family functioning. In order to do this, the counselor might tell the family that Karen is misbehaving because she is apprehensive about her impending womanhood and is trying to hold onto childish habits. The family would be advised that Karen needs help in appreciating her increasing femininity and sexual development. This should be done by Sandra and Lori talking with Karen about their enjoyment of their roles as women, the three of them going on shopping trips to buy Karen some more sophisticated clothes, and Lori and Sandra providing Karen instruction in wearing makeup. Sandra is put in charge of the process. David is instructed to spend time playing with Robert while this is happening, so that Robert will not get in the women's way. This directive should both reduce the symptoms and improve family functioning because Karen will get the attention she wants, Sandra will gain power and a sense of competence and purpose, the three women will become closer, and David and Robert also should develop their relationship. Subsequent interventions might strengthen the bond between Sandra and David.

BEHAVIORAL FAMILY COUNSELING

Behavioral family counseling, another active, directive, and symptom-focused approach, is similar to behavioral counseling with individual clients. It is particularly useful for dealing with couples or parent-child issues where a behavioral change is desired. Behavioral counseling typically begins with an assessment of the current family situation, the nature and level of the undesirable behavior, and its secondary gains. A contract might be developed next, with both spouses or the parents and children agreeing to make specific behavioral changes. Any rewards or punishments are then specified. A range of techniques (e.g., modeling, shaping, rehearsal, sex therapy) might be used to facilitate the change. Follow-up sessions evaluate progress and, if necessary, modify the contract or the treatment plan. Necessary skills such as problem solving, communication, and decision making might be taught. The goals of behavioral counseling include not only modifying behavior but also decreasing coercion and negative control (Nichols, 1984).

The behavioral model can be effective when family concerns are fairly specific and circumscribed and when the underlying relationships are basically sound. For example, it can help parents develop techniques for managing their children's behavior and can help couples find a comfortable way to share household chores. Often, however, counseling that begins in a behavioral mode will unearth structural or communication difficulties, necessitating an alternate or combined mode of counseling.

It is possible that Karen's behavior could be improved through this approach. Her parents could be helped to establish clear behavioral guidelines for Karen, with rewards given if they are followed and, possibly, punishments dispensed if they are violated. Basically a child who is compliant and eager to please, Karen might well accept the rules and return to her former style of behavior. However, the structural and communication problems in the family might still remain, perhaps leading to future concerns.

ADLERIAN FAMILY COUNSELING

Alfred Adler and his colleague Rudolf Dreikurs were the leading proponents of what is now known as Adlerian counseling or Individual Psychology. This approach focuses primarily on the parent-child interaction and seeks to help parents to facilitate the healthy development of their children.

The following ideas are important to this theory:

1. Children feel inferior and so strive to compensate for those feelings through gaining power and mastery.
2. Birth order is instrumental in determining children's attitudes, values, and behaviors.
3. Pampered or neglected children and children with physical or intellectual deficits are particularly likely to present problems.
4. Natural consequences, encouragement, respect, and realistic expectations help parents to shape children's behavior in positive ways.
5. Family conferences and democratic family structures contribute to the development of strong and healthy family constellations.

Adlerian counselors typically work with parents and children, together and individually. Teachers also might be included in family counseling sessions. Counselors following this approach tend to be directive, interpretive, and present-oriented. They are concrete and combine supportive and educational approaches.

The Adlerian approach recently has been receiving a great deal of attention and has been expanded and modified so that it can be used with couples as well as with parents and children. Its focus on encouragement and health rather than on pathology makes it useful with a broad range of families, but it seems best suited for working with families where there is conflict between parents and young children.

Aspects of the Adlerian approach seem useful in helping to conceptualize and treat the difficulties of the Strauss family. The family council might be a helpful stimulus to family communication and might promote cohesiveness in the family. Viewing Karen as a child who has feelings of inferiority and who is striving for power in self-destructive and socially unacceptable ways can lead to the development of effective approaches to helping her. However, the Adlerian model does not address directly the concerns of the Strauss family constellation and so probably would not be the best method for helping them.

SUMMARY

This chapter has included only a few of the most important approaches to working with families and couples. All of the approaches discussed here had something to offer the Strauss family, although some seemed more useful than others. Treatment planning for families, then, even more than for individuals, is a flexible process that involves assessing family dynamics, determining the most appropriate mode of treatment, and integrating data with the skills and preferences of the counselor to determine an effective approach to working with a family.

Chapter 8

DIAGNOSIS AND TREATMENT PLANNING FOR GROUPS AND ORGANIZATIONS

Although the focus of this book primarily is on diagnosis and treatment planning with individual clients, counselors sometimes are presented with a group or aggregate of individuals who are the client unit. Counselors then assume the task of clarifying the concerns of these groups and developing ways of helping to ameliorate their difficulties and to promote their development. As with families, there is no standard format for the diagnosis of group concerns, although there are some standard treatment modalities. This chapter will suggest a framework for assessing the dynamics of client groups and for providing group treatment.

DIAGNOSING THE NEEDS OF GROUPS

Counselors can obtain a comprehensive picture of the nature of a group by looking at a number of aspects of that group. The aspects are:

1. Group Composition

Groups with which counselors work take many forms. In their most traditional form, the group is composed of eight to twelve individuals seeking counseling for somewhat similar concerns (e.g., career confusion, interpersonal difficulties). These individuals also might have been formed into a group because they shared a common stressful experience (e.g., rape, abuse, debilitating illness, natural disaster).

In recent years, however, counselors as consultants and community organizers have gotten involved with groups that are, at least initially, more amorphorus and ill-defined, and less motivated toward treatment. This type of group might be exemplified by single parents living in a community mental health center's catchment area, middle-level managers in a corporation, or learning-disabled children in a school. In working with such groups, the counselor must clarify the parameters that define the group, possibly publicize the availability of group treatment or experiences, and determine which of those eligible for participation actually will be involved in treatment. (Terms such as treatment and group experience are used loosely here to include a broad range of counseling and counseling-related modalities, to be discussed later.)

In determining the composition of a group, counselors first establish criteria for membership such as place of residence and experience with a particular event or concern. They then look at the following variables in eligible members:

a.   Number of members
b.   Relevant demographic characteristics—sex, age, race, ethnic background, socioeconomic level, marital status, or any others that seem germane
c.   Nature and history of concerns, including assessment of group's homogeneity with respect to the focal concern
d.   Relevant personal characteristics—abilities, attitudes, strengths and weaknesses
e.   Financial circumstances, if there will be a fee for the group experience
f.   Other relevant data (e.g., time constraints)

The use of an example may clarify the nature and importance of some of these variables. Counselors at one community mental health center recognized that divorced fathers were playing an increasing role in the care of their children. The counselors decided to develop some programs and group experiences to aid these men. Wanda Herbert, a mental health counselor, was put in charge of the project because of her extensive experience in working with divorced clients.

Wanda first established criteria for membership: eligible participants had to be male; separated, divorced, or widowed; single; have joint or full custody of at least one child under eighteen; and live in the center's catchment area. Wanda estimated that there were approximately 75 men who met these criteria. She then proceeded to gather more specific data on eligible and interested participants through a notice and accompanying questionnaire that was distributed through area singles organizations and church, social, and community groups. The planned group also was announced in the local newspaper, and notices were posted in supermarkets, with a telephone number to be called by interested persons.

Wanda received replies from 46 men, 40 of whom indicated an interest in participating in programs or group experiences to help them cope more effectively with single fatherhood. The men ranged in age from twenty-five to fifty-four. Nearly all were Caucasian and employed full-time in skilled trades or managerial or professional positions. The number of children the men had at home ranged from one to four and the children's ages ranged from two years to over eighteen years. The men varied considerably, too, in terms of how long they had been single. Primary concerns expressed by the men included dealing with grief and loss, a need for parenting and home management skills, sharing parenting with their ex-wives, finding time for their own leisure and social needs without hurting the children, and the need to learn to cope with stress and the many demands on their time. The more recently divorced men expressed more affective concerns (grief, anger, and guilt) while those who had been divorced for a few years were more interested in skill development (e.g., parenting, time management) and developing their own social lives. Nearly all of the men had severe time constraints and many were in difficult fianancial situations. All expressed a concern for their children and the desire to be effective parents.

2. Interest in Treatment

Although members of an identified group may share a common concern, all may not have an interest in treatment. Even among those who are motivated to accept help, individuals may be interested in different amounts or kinds of help. The question of motivation is particularly important when participation in a group experience is not voluntary. For example, clients charged with driving while intoxicated may be required to participate in counseling and educational experiences in order to regain their driver's license. Managers in a corporation may be required to participate in a group to develop their self-awareness and communication skills. Counselors should try to obtain an accurate reading of clients' interests in treatment before counseling is begun so treatment planning can take account of likely sources of resistance.

Wanda's client group consisted of 40 men who had, at least initially, indicated interest in receiving help. However, constraints on their time and finances could interfere with their level of motivation, and planning was needed to take account of those dimensions.

3. Group Development

Often, a counselor will begin to work with a client group that has a history of interacting as a group. This may be a counseling group that already has received some treatment but that is now being reevaluated or assigned to a new counselor, a peer support group being assessed for professional intervention, or a group that had been formed in another setting (e.g., a work group or a classroom group), now referred for counseling. In assessing such a group, the counselor should explore the following:

a. Cohesiveness of group—How close-knit, committed, and involved are the group members?
b. Level of trust (in counselor and each other).
c. Nature and degree of communication—How openly do

members communicate? Who communicates with whom? What styles of communication characterize individual members and the group as a whole? For example, do the group members communicate well in cognitive areas but have difficulty sharing their emotions?

d. Group decision-making style—Is it democratic or authoritarian, efficient or laborious?

e. Formal and informal roles assumed by members—This includes styles of participation typical of the group members, the structure or hierarchy of the group, patterns of influence exerted by group members, and leadership roles and functions assumed by members.

f. Rules and norms accepted by the group—What expressed and implicit policies and procedures guide the operation of the group? Most groups have norms that influence when members arrive for meetings, the regularity of attendance, the amount of self-disclosure and confrontation that occurs, the power given to the designated leader, and the topics considered in group meetings.

g. History of treatment—What counseling interventions have been made previously with this group? What impact have they had on the group?

In the example, the client group of single fathers had no prior history as a group. However, some of the individuals in the group had become acquainted through Parents Without Partners and other local social organizations. Several of the individuals also had received prior treatment related to their presenting concerns. This included divorce mediation, marital counseling, and individual counseling subsequent to the end of their marriages. Knowing this information helped Wanda to better anticipate her clients' needs and their patterns of interaction in a group experience. Two of the men currently were in individual counseling and, with their permission, Wanda contacted their individual therapists to establish communication and to be sure that they endorsed their clients' participation in the single fathers' program.

4. Environment

Consideration of the group's environment includes an exploration of the members' home base, be it a community, work setting, or school, and the environment in which treatment will be provided. Of particular importance is an examination of those factors that might promote or inhibit the success of the group.

Wanda's clients came from a middle-class suburb, the catchment area of the community mental health center. The community offered many resources for children, including after-school child care and special schools and classes to help the fathers provide appropriate care for their children. However, the services in the community were oriented more toward couples engaged in parenting than toward single parents. Few social organizations for singles were available and it was anticipated that the fathers might feel out of place and disoriented now that they were no longer married. Educational sessions as well as group meetings generally were held for the fathers in a local school. That increased availability, provided adequate space for the men and supervised play areas for their children, and increased the connection the men felt to their community.

PROGRAM DEVELOPMENT

Once the needs and dimensions of the group have been assessed through interviews, questionnaires, research, observation, or other means, the counselor is ready to plan the treatment.

1. Defining the Membership of the Group

The first step is determining exactly who will be the focus of treatment. Initially, the counselor may have had a broad description of the group membership. Assessment may have led to redefinition of membership; some potential participants may not have been interested in any treatment while others who did not fit the original definition may have been included in the group.

Wanda, for example, began with a hypothetical group of approximately 75 men. Somewhat fewer men responded to her announcements and 40 of those indicated an interest in help. However, Wanda also was contacted by two men who had never been married but who had adopted children. They shared many of the concerns of the original group and asked to be included. Although they did not share some of the affective concerns of the target group, the adoptive fathers did seem to have enough in common with the group to warrant their inclusion. Wanda's client group then consisted of 42 single men with at least half-time custody of one or more minor children.

2. Goal Setting

As with individual clients, goals should be established before treatment is planned. It may not be possible for counselors and clients in a group to reach a consensus on goals as is ideally done in individual counseling. Counselors working with groups may need to assume a greater role in goal setting, inferring appropriate goals from information provided during the assessment process. If direct contact with the client group was limited during assessment, goals may need to be based on information on comparable groups discussed in the literature. This approach might be used, for example, if the counselor were presenting goals in a grant proposal designed to obtain funds for providing counseling services to a special client group.

Wanda had sent questionnaires to all of her participants and had telephoned most of them to obtain more information. These sources of data enabled her to establish the following goals:

a. Reduction of undesirable emotional responses (e.g., depression, guilt, grief, and anger)
b. Development of effective parenting skills
c. Development of effective home and time management skills
d. Development of stress management skills
e. Effective integration of work, home, and leisure aspects of life

These goals included both the affective and the pragmatic concerns expressed by the men and could be achieved in a relatively short period (months, rather than years). The next step in treatment planning, evaluation, follows logically from the development of goals.

3. Evaluation

Accountability increasingly is being stressed for counselors. Because available funds for mental health services generally are less than needed, those who disburse such funds want to make sure the money is well spent. Mental health service delivery agencies and charitable and governmental funding agencies consequently are requiring evaluation of programs to determine whether they have met their goals and whether continued funding is indicated. To receive grants and other funds for services, counselors must demonstrate that they are accomplishing something worthwhile.

There are several approaches to evaluating the impact of group programs. An overview of some of these will be provided here. However, counselors will need some knowledge of research methodology or a research consultant when planning their evaluation procedures, to be sure they are valid. Evaluation is facilitated if goals are stated in such a way as to be specific and measurable.

Sometimes a control group is available to compare with the treatment group. This might occur if treatment could not be provided to all of the potential members of a group experience. Pre- and posttreatment evaluation could then be done of both groups to determine whether the group that received help made more positive changes than the group that was kept on the waiting list. Wanda hoped to provide rapid assistance to all 42 of the men in her eligible group, so that sort of control group was not available to her. She might have surveyed the men who chose not to participate in a counseling experience. However, in order for a comparison of changes made by two groups of individuals to be meaningful, they must have started out at approximately the same level. It seems likely that the fathers who refused treatment were adjusting differently to their situations than were the men who were interested in counseling, so a comparison of those two groups probably would not have been useful in the evaluation process. It might, however, have shed light on how to meet more effectively the needs of such men.

With or without a control group, the most common method of evaluating program effectiveness involves the administration of inventories or questionnaires before and shortly after the group experience. A third administration of the instruments might occur in a follow-up, some months later, to provide information on the development or persistence of any changes over time.

Standardized tests and inventories, those that previously have been ascertained to be reliable and valid and that have norms based on groups similar to the one receiving treatment, typically provide the most trustworthy information. Sources discussed in chapter 3 can help counselors select such appropriate instruments. Often, however, the counselor also is interested in more subjective reactions and wants to ask questions geared specifically to the particular group and the interventions they received. In such cases, a questionnaire may be used, as long as it is recognized that its validity and reliability have not yet been demonstrated.

Wanda chose a combination of questionnaires that she developed and standardized inventories. Standardized instruments were used to measure daily mood levels and degree of stress experienced by the participants. In addition, Wanda administered a quiz on parenting interventions and a self-report inventory, asking for information on clients' progress in time management and home management as well as on their overall reactions to treatment. Participants were asked to complete these inventories (with the exception of the mood questionnaire) 1 week prior to beginning their group experience, 2 days after the experience was completed, and 6 months later. The mood schedule was completed daily.

Evaluation data also can be gathered by looking at the perceptions significant others have of the impact of the group experience on the participants. For example, the children of the fathers in Wanda's group might have been surveyed, both before and after treatment, on their evaluations of their relationships with their fathers and their perceptions of their fathers' parenting and home management skills.

Yet another approach to evaluation involves obtaining data on demonstrated behavioral changes. While the importance of the treatment in producing these changes is difficult to determine without the availability of a control group, such data can be strongly suggestive of the value of the group. For example, Wanda might have gathered data on the number of social activities the fathers participated in each week, the number of arguments they had with their children each week, the number of fathers who showed clear signs of advancement in their work during the 6 months following treatment, or the number of fathers who formed rewarding dating relationships during that time.

Evaluation is particularly important if similar group experiences are planned in the future or if similar client groups need services. Evaluation than can be used not only to evaluate the effectiveness of a particular program of intervention but also to guide the development of future programs.

4. Program Development

Programs designed to meet the needs of client groups can take many forms. McCollum (1981), describing the role of the mental health educator, listed eleven: colloquium, demonstration, open discussion with resource personnel, peer-support groups, small group discussions, workshops, interviews conducted in front of an audience, panel discussions, role playing, seminars, and lectures. McCollum also listed several approaches to promoting group involvement in some of these didactic experiences. They included audience-reaction teams, buzz sessions, and brainstorming or question-and-answer sessions. Less educationally oriented approaches include various types of counseling groups, some of which will be discussed later.

Counselors should take account of the following program variables in order to determine how best to meet the goals of their groups:

a. *Nature of programs.* Should the program be primarily educational or primarily therapeutic? In other words, do the clients need to learn specific skills and acquire information or are they more in need of help in exploring, understanding, and managing their feelings?

   b. Modality of treatment.   There are many ways to facilitate learning and personal change. Learning might come through didactic presentations, sharing of experiences, role playing, or brainstorming sessions. Many theories and techniques of group counseling have been developed to promote personal change. (These will be discussed further later.) Often, a combination of treatment modalities will seem best suited to accomplishing the group's goals. Ideally, counselors should have a rationale for the approaches to treatment that are used and the sequence of those treatment modalities.

   c. Timing.   Determining timing involves deciding on the urgency of the group's need for help and finding a schedule of treatments that seems likely to be effective and takes account of the demands already placed on the group members' time.

   The single fathers seemed to need a combination of educational and therapeutic modes of treatment. Personal concerns included development of self-esteem and self-confidence as well as modification of dysfunctional emotions and cognitions. Wanda's approach to counseling was, therefore, grounded in a client-centered model designed to help participants develop and appreciate their own resources and to provide a supportive environment. However, Wanda assumed a more active role than does the typical client-centered group leader, drawing on many aspects of Rational-Emotive Therapy in an effort to help the men modify their thoughts and, consequently, improve their emotional adjustment. Homework assignments also were suggested to develop the men's self-confidence and coping mechanisms as well as to relieve their depression and mobilize their own resources.

   The fathers' educational needs were met through a combination of didactic presentations and shared experiences. They needed information in such areas as time management, household maintenance, parenting, and social skills. Guest speakers who specialized in those areas were invited to share their expertise with the group. Application of the didactic material that had been presented was facilitated through relevant homework assignments (e.g., tasks, activities, readings) and group members' discussions of their own successes and difficulties in these areas.

Because several of the men were showing symptoms of significant depression and anxiety while several others seemed nearly overwhelmed by the demands of running a home and caring for children, the group experience was begun as soon as possible. From a treatment perspective, it might have been ideal to meet with these men twice a week for several months. However, Wanda recognized that a compromise had to be made in light of the fathers' limited free time. Meetings also had to be scheduled so that conflicts with the fathers' work and home commitments would be avoided. Consequently, the group was scheduled to meet one early evening a week for 8 weeks. Child care was provided. The time-limited format provided structure and organization to the group and encouraged the men's commitment to the group. Each session was 2 hours long, with a speaker or presentation occupying the first 45 minutes. The last 75 minutes were devoted to more traditional counseling, sharing of experiences, and processing of the information provided in the first part of the session. This format, then, was designed to take account of a broad range of needs: emotional, educational, and temporal. All participants met together for the educational aspect of the group. They were then divided into four subgroups of approximately 10 members each for counseling and discussion.

d. Location.   The location selected for the group experience should be one that is likely to maximize attendance and promote a sense of comfort and belonging. It also should have facilities that are appropriate to the group including a room that is large enough to accommodate the members, but affords privacy and freedom from distractions. If counselors think that a particular client group will feel uncomfortable, stigmatized, or inconvenienced by meeting at a mental health facility, group meetings might be scheduled at area churches, libraries, or community centers or at the homes, schools, or work places of group members.

The single-fathers group held its meetings in the community room of a neighborhood school. That location was more convenient for most of the men than was the mental health center.

It also served to emphasize the educational and growth-promoting nature of the group and offered play facilities for the children.

e. *Staffing.*   For a group experience, staffing involves identifying the areas of expertise that are needed, which members of the agency staff have that expertise and the time available to work with the group, and what outside resources are available to supplement the services that will be provided by the agency staff. Using resources from the clients' own environment can be an effective way of developing their support systems and helping them to feel accepted and appreciated. Group members might even be involved in the process of recruiting speakers from the community or surveying community resources that seem likely to be helpful to them. This process can help group members develop their sense of independence and competence and familiarize them with additional sources of help.

Wanda, a mental health counselor, served as coordinator of the groups, screening the participants, planning the sessions, recruiting staff and speakers, conducting the evaluation process, and generally ensuring the smooth functioning of the experience. Guest speakers, most of whom donated their services to the group, were recruited from the community. Four mental health professionals (two counselors, one social worker, and one psychologist), employed by the community mental health center, became the group leaders, working closely with each other and with Wanda to ensure some consistency of goals and methods.

f. *Budgeting.*   Although budgeting is the last item to be considered under program development, it should not be the last item considered by counselors who are planning group treatments. Budget exerts a powerful influence over all aspects of program development and must be taken into account throughout the planning process.

Budget planning is particularly important for counselors who are tryng to secure grants to fund their programs or for counselors who are working on a contractual or consultant basis. In these situations, the costs of the program often will have to be projected well in advance of the actual experience. A budget that is unrealistic or excessive can cause the loss of grants or the awarding of contracts to other service providers. Grant or contract budgets are likely to have little flexibility, so counselors must be sure that they can implement their program within the boundaries of the budgets that they have requested. Generally, the budget for a group program or experience will encompass the following items, as indicated in the budget that Wanda developed for her group:

Budget for Single Fathers Program

1.	Publicity, recruitment—includes flyers, posters, postage, cost of radio/newspaper advertisements	$350
2.	Staffing	
	a. Secretary—average of 3 hours per week for 20 weeks at $5 per hour	$300
	b. Coordinator—average of 5 hours per week for 20 weeks at $30 per hour	$3,000
	c. Group leaders—4 helping professionals at 3 hours per week for 10 weeks at $25 per hour	$3,000
	d. Honoraria for guest speakers—6 stipends of $50	$300
	e. Child care—3 hours per week for 8 weeks at $4 per hour	$96
3.	Evaluation—tests, duplication of materials, postage for follow-up	$250
4.	Duplicating costs	$100
5.	Facilities—rental of 5 rooms in local school for educational sessions, small group meetings, child care	(Donated)
6.	Data analysis—computer time and services of data entry clerk and programmer	$250
	Total:	$7,646

Part of the budgeting process is determining potential sources of program funds. Typical sources include participant fees; funds, often in the form of space and staff time, from the mental health agency; grants from the federal government, the United Way, and other funding agencies; donations of money, facilities, or services by local community and charitable groups; and third-party payments from insurance companies.

Wanda decided to charge all participants a small fee in order to help defray the cost of the program and to solidify members' commitments to the group. However, she realized that many of the participants were in difficult financial situations so she decided to seek supplementary sources of funding rather than having the entire cost of the program borne by the participants. Wanda anticipated the following sources of funding:

1. Participants—$50 each from 35 participants $1,750
    (fees might be waived or not paid by several
    participants)
2. United Way funds $4,000
3. Donations from local singles and charitable $500
    organizations
4. Community mental health center—donation of $1,396
    services

                                                       ———————
                                                       $7,646

For counselors whose training has focused primarily on mastering the theories and techniques of counseling, it may be surprising and dismaying to discover the diverse and often pragmatic skills that are required of the counselor involved in program development. However, for counselors to deal effectively with the broad range of client needs, the growing demand for accountability, and the tightening funds available for mental health services, they must have a mastery of a plethora of therapeutic, educational, and practical techniques.

APPROACHES TO GROUP COUNSELING

Approaches to group counseling include models that have been developed for individual counseling and then adapted to group settings, those that have been developed for both individual and group counseling, and those that have been developed primarily or exclusively for group settings. This chapter focuses particularly on those approaches to group counseling that are better suited for group counseling settings than for individual counseling.

Chapter 5 reviewed several theories of individual counseling. All of them, especially Client-centered Counseling, behavioral counseling, Reality Therapy, Rational-emotive Therapy, and Gestalt Therapy also have been discussed in the literature as approaches to group treatment. Although some adaptation of those models occurs when they are used with groups, the approaches remain basically the same. Consequently, the application of those approaches to group settings will be discussed only briefly here. Readers are referred to chapter 5 for additional information on the nature and application of those models. Further understanding of those approaches as applied to groups can be obtained from almost any comprehensive textbook on group counseling. As has been stated elsewhere in this book, it is assumed that the reader already has some familiarity with models of group counseling. This section will not seek to teach these approaches to the reader but, rather, to review the salient characteristics of the models and discuss their application to the process of diagnosis and treatment planning.

MODELS COMMONLY USED IN BOTH INDIVIDUAL AND GROUP COUNSELING

1. Client-Centered Counseling

Although this approach has been developed more for use in individual counseling than for use in group counseling, it is a model that seems to lend itself well to a group setting. Clients in groups following this model can receive acceptance and develop genuine and congruent relationships not only with their counselors, but also with the other members of the group. A safe climate and models of open and honest communication are provided. Feelings of alienation and differentness can be ameliorated in such a situation (Corey, 1981). This seems likely to accelerate the development of self-confidence and individual resources. Play therapy, often grounded in a client-centered framework, is a variation on group counseling using this approach.

2. Rational-Emotive Therapy (RET)

RET has been widely used for both group and individual counseling. Albert Ellis, its originator, also has espoused RET as a method of fostering personal growth and a positive atmosphere in a classroom setting. RET has been used in marathon group sessions as well as in weekly counseling groups where it seems to be an effective approach to helping members give each other feedback on their cognitions and behaviors. In a group counseling context, RET tends to be a leader-centered technique with the group generally focusing on the concerns of one member at a time.

3. Reality Therapy

Reality Therapy, too, has been applied by its developer, Wiliam Glasser, to a school setting and has been viewed as a way to promote self-esteem (a success identity) in young people and to help them learn realistic and responsible ways of meeting their needs. Reality Therapy, as an approach to counseling, has been used more in individual than in group settings and the literature on Reality Therapy as a model of group counseling is fairly limited. However, it does seem to be a viable approach to working with groups, especially in such settings as prisons and treatment facilities for substance abusers where resistance and self-destructive behavior are common and where group members can promote goal achievement.

4. Behavioral Counseling

Behavioral counseling frequently is used in group settings. The presence of other members provides additional sources of feedback and reinforcement while the microcosim of the group environment gives clients a safe arena for trying out new behaviors. Typically, behavioral counseling groups will be composed of clients with similar concerns (e.g., alcohol abuse or poor social skills) so that opportunities for behavorial rehearsal, modeling, group support, and social rewards and punishment are provided.

5. Gestalt Counseling

The Gestalt model is widely used in both group and individual counseling. Even in groups, however, the focus of Gestalt counseling tends to be on individual members. Little concern is paid to facilitating member interaction. The presence of other group members can, however, promote self-awareness and vicarious learning. Often, the significance of a member's statement or behavior will be emphasized by having that member "make the rounds," go up to all of the group members and announce or demonstrate an important insight or piece of behavior. The presence of others sometimes can increase the threat posed by Gestalt counseling, an approach that often involves pressure and confrontation. However, the threat also can be diminished by the support of the group and the freedom it affords members to chose their levels of participation in the group experience. Resistant members and those who engage in excessive intellectualization and rationalization are particularly likely to benefit from feedback provided in Gestalt counseling as well as from seeing aspects of themselves in other members.

MODELS USED PRIMARILY IN GROUP SETTINGS

Transactional Analysis

Transactional Analysis (TA) was developed by Eric Berne in the 1950s and nearly always is conducted as a group experience. The approach hypothesizes that personality is formed through a combination of innate and acquired psychological and physiological needs (Hansen, Warner, & Smith, 1980). According to TA, each person identifies with one of the following positions: "I'm OK; you're OK," "I'm not OK; you are OK," "I'm OK; you're not OK," or "I'm not OK; you're not OK." The second position is thought to be the most common. TA theorists also believe that there are three primary ego states: parent, adult, and child. The child embodies creativity, joy, and spontaneity; the parent includes the conscience as well as long-standing traditions, beliefs, and values needed to guide daily functioning; and the adult is the assimilator, the rational evaluator and decision maker. All of us have and need all three ego states. However, difficulties can develop when there is an imbalance among the three or when one or more of the ego states tends to come into play at inappropriate or self-destructive moments. TA also pays particular attention to transactions between individuals (especially between group members and group leaders), to structural analysis (analysis of ego states), to group members' games (repetitive, self-destructive, often dishonest patterns of behavior), and to scripts or blueprints for life.

TA groups are designed to help participants have positive access to their ego states and to develop productive life scripts as well as to make desired individual changes. The groups tend to be leader-centered, to make considerable use of instruction and exercises, to emphasize long-term treatment, and to focus on one client at a time. Although TA has been used with a broad and heterogeneous client group, its use has been discouraged with clients suffering from manic states, hysteria, phobias, or obsessions (Rosenbaum, 1976). This approach also does not seem well-suited to clients with personality disorders characterized by limited motivation for treatment, with schizophrenic clients who may be too confused to participate effectively in such groups, and with clients in crisis or with specific, circumscribed concerns. In practice, TA seems best suited to clients who are very verbal and highly motivated and who seem likely to benefit from a structured, leader-centered experience. Such clients might be experiencing long-standing depression or anxiety.

Psychodrama

Psychodrama was introduced in the United States in the 1920s by Jacob L. Moreno and has been developed by his followers. The approach emphasizes action and interaction, present behavior and emotion, spontaneity, creativity, and reality-testing (Corey, 1981). It encourages participants to act out difficult areas of their lives, to try out new methods of behavior, to receive feedback from others, to release inhibiting and dysfunctional feelings, and to assume greater responsibility for their lives.

Psychodrama may be used as the predominant mode of

therapy in a small counseling group, as an occasional alternate mode of treatment, or as a technique for short-term counseling or demonstrations with a large group. Five instruments are used in this approach: 1) a stage, often with several levels, where the life experiences of the client are represented; 2) the subject or protagonist who describes and participates in the scene to be acted; 3) the psychodrama director or group leader who keeps the action going, maintains the involvement of the audience, makes use of a broad range of techniques, and integrates interpretations made by participants and audience; 4) the auxiliary egos who promote the director's therapeutic goals by representing ideals, absent people, or protagonist aspects that are important; and 5) the audience, which serves as a sounding board and source of feedback for the protagonist and whose members are assumed to benefit vicariously from the drama by relating it to their own concerns (Rosenbaum, 1976).

Because the nature of the drama can be geared to the needs of an individual client, it is suitable for use with a wide range of clients and would only be contraindicated for clients who are so confused, depressed, or anxious that they could not function as participants in the drama. This approach seems particularly useful for:

1. Clients with mild to moderate levels of depression or anxiety.
2. Clients with a combination of physical and emotional concerns who are having difficulty specifying their concerns and mobilizing their resources.
3. Clients with readily definable concerns (e.g., those with adjustment disorders or V code conditions).
4. Clients who manifest some resistance to treatment. They may be experiencing personality disorders or disorders of impulse control.

Training Groups (or T-Groups)

T-groups generally are designed for fairly well-functioning individuals who are seeking personal growth, greater understanding of self and others, insight into group functioning, and improved interpersonal relationships. These groups tend to be short-term and time-limited, often following a marathon week-end format.

T-groups have been termed an educational training labo-ratory (Hansen, Warner, & Smith, 1980). Exemplified by groups offered by the National Training Laboratory (NTL), T-groups emphasize inquiry and experimentation. Group participants are encouraged to take responsibility for their own learning. Al-though group leaders may suggest exercises or learning oppor-tunities, they rarely take control of the group and provide less structure than do most counselors working in group settings. T-groups tend to focus on present interactions among members and encourage feedback, interpretation, analysis of group process and member-member and member-leader interaction. Although group support is facilitated, the groups often are ambiguous and stressful. These qualities, combined with the short-term nature of the groups, make them well suited only to clients who are free of serious emotional difficulties. Such groups can play an im-portant role in preventive counseling and might be used as an adjunct form of treatment for a client who has a mild disorder and is concurrently in individual counseling.

Tavistock Groups

Tavistock Groups were initiated in England by Wilfred Bion and subsequently were developed by A. K. Rice and Margaret Rioch. Tavistock groups are similar to T-groups in that they are designed to promote the personal and professional growth of individuals who are not suffering from significant emotional dis-orders. However, the structure of Tavistock groups and the leadership model they follow are quite different from those of T-groups. The Tavistock approach typically is implemented at a weekend or week-long institute or conference consisting of several types of groups, both large and small, with the small study group the most central.

The primary task of such a group is to study its own be-havior. The leader or consultant plays the role of observer and interpreter, with analyses often grounded in a psychoanalytic framework. This frequently leads the group members to become initially demanding and dissatisfied with the consultant. However, as the group becomes more able to use its own resources and develops insight into the group process, members' frustrations tend to lessen and they develop appreciation of the open and accepting qualities of the group environment (Shaffer & Galinsky, 1974).

Like T-groups, Tavistock groups are designed to develop insight, improved work behavior and interpersonal relationships, and knowledge of group functioning. However, Tavistock groups focus more on authority concerns, group process, and task performance than do T-groups, while T-groups place more emphasis on the development of individual resources and interpersonal interactions. Both have a place in preventive counseling, especially in work settings, but are not for clients who are functioning very poorly or who are severely troubled.

Theme-Centered Interactional Method (Theme Groups)

Theme-centered counseling was developed primarily by Ruth C. Cohn. Typically conducted as time-limited, relatively short-term group experiences (1 to 15 sessions), theme-centered workshops have a predetermined theme that is announced and briefly described by the group leader at the start of each session. Issues of autonomy and interdependence are particularly important to this approach as members explore their own thoughts and feelings and react to the theme and the input of the other members (the "I-We-It" triangle).

Theme-centered groups are moderately well-structured by the leader (and by the existence of a theme) and take a positive and personal approach. Leaders tend to be genuine and empathic and draw heavily on client-centered techniques. Silence is used strategically by the leader to promote member self-exploration. Although the leader keeps the group working productively and appropriately focused on the theme, members are encouraged to take responsibility for their own participation and learning during the sessions (self-chairmanship) (Shaffer & Galinsky, 1974). Deflections from the theme are accepted if they are important to members and relevant to group goals; rigid adherence to the theme is not necessary.

Although the theme-centered approach to group counseling has not yet gained the widespread use and attention enjoyed by the other models discussed in this section, it is included here because it seems to be an extremely flexible technique that offers a balance of structure and support. These qualities make this approach appropriate for use with a broad range of clients, including severely disturbed clients who are not appropriate for treatment in most group settings. Theme groups that emphasize present-oriented and pragmatic concerns have been used in conjunction with other modes of treatment in day-treatment centers and psychiatric facilities to promote interaction, symptom abatement, and development of clients' coping mechanisms.

Overview

With some exceptions, group counseling, especially as the primary or sole method of treatment, is most suitable for clients who are in reasonably good contact with reality; who have cognitive, behavioral, or emotional concerns rather than specific situational problems; who are not severely anxious or deficient in interpersonal skills; and who seem capable of benefiting from overall personal development. Group counseling can help clients develop trust in others, increase self-awareness, become more sensitive to the needs and feelings of others, experiment with new behaviors, increase self-confidence and a sense of identity, develop responsibility and the ability to engage in effective reality testing, have a sense of belonging and acceptance, improve social and communication skills, modify troubling thoughts and feelings, and work on individual issues. Although group counseling is not a viable form of treatment for all clients and should not be viewed as simply a more efficient and economical variation on individual counseling, it plays an important role in the treatment of many clients and can be particularly useful as an adjunct or supplementary approach to treatment.

CASES FOR STUDY

The following brief cases are presented to give readers an opportunity to diagnose the needs of groups and develop a program designed to meet those needs. Readers should feel free to fill in the gaps in these cases by adding information that seems necessary to the process of diagnosis and treatment planning.

Case 1

You are a counselor in a community mental health center in a medium-sized city in the Northeast. You are aware that in the center's catchment area there are many Vietnam veterans who are still experiencing emotional and behavioral difficulties as a result of their military service. Describe the anticipated needs and characteristics of this group and develop a program to help them. In planning your program, consider goal setting, a definition of the target population, evaluation, staffing, the nature and location of the group experience you will provide, and the budget you will need to implement your plan.

Case 2

You are a counselor at a coeducational college with approximately 3,000 graduate and undergraduate students. Eating disorders (bulimia, anorexia) seem to be troubling a significant number of students. Consider how you will assess the students' need for help with this problem and how you will involve students in a program designed to ameliorate such disorders. Develop hypotheses to describe the nature of your group and plan a program that combines educational and therapeutic interventions and is aimed toward students with eating disorders. Assume that you will be writing a grant proposal to obtain funding for your program, so be sure that all plans are specific and well-justified to maximize your chances of receiving funding.

Case 3

In your private practice, you have been counseling eight women who have been married more than 10 years each, who have remained at home with children for most of that time, and who are now feeling unhappy and confused about their future goals. Provide further information about this group of women and then plan a 10-week group counseling experience to help them. Pay particular attention to the nature of the experience, the treatment approach that you will use, and how the group experience will be integrated with the individual counseling that the women are now receiving.

Chapter 9

PROGRESS NOTES, INTERIM REPORTS, MID-TREATMENT CASE CONFERENCES, AND CLOSING REPORTS

Thus far, this book has focused on the process of diagnosis and treatment planning that takes place during the initial phase of the counselor-client interaction. However, a number of events can happen to require a reevaluation of the original treatment plans:

1. As the initial counseling goals are achieved, the client may present other concerns that warrant attention.
2. The client may show little progress or may even deteriorate over several months of counseling.
3. New areas of importance may come to light as counselor and client develop rapport and the client becomes less guarded and defensive.
4. The client may express dissatisfaction with the treatment being provided.
5. Client's life circumstances may change, thereby warranting a change in treatment plan. For example, a client who presented a career concern may develop marital difficulties as he becomes more invested in his career and less involved with his family.
6. The insurance company providing third-party payments may request a report reviewing the treatment

to determine whether continued mental health services are needed for a client.

7. The counselor may feel stuck or confused by the dynamics of a client and refer the client for a psychiatric or psychological evaluation.

8. The counselor working with a client may relocate or resign, requiring the assignment of a new treatment provider to the client.

9. The client's family may express concern about the progress that is being made.

10. Termination of the counseling relationship may seem indicated.

All are circumstances that can occur during counseling relationships that call for a structured evaluation of progress and perhaps a reconceptualization of a client's diagnosis and treatment plan.

Ideally, evaluation should be a continuous part of every counseling relationship, with the counselor reviewing the progress demonstrated at every session and counselor and client frequently discussing the client's growth. Such a process of informal evaluation is important to ensure that client and counselor are working together effectively and that the client is making satisfactory progress toward achieving established goals. Informal evaluations can facilitate the process of more formal interim evaluations.

This chapter will consider both formal and informal, continuous and time-limited approaches to evaluating the client's progress once an initial diagnosis and treatment plan have been formulated and counseling has begun. Guidelines for conducting such evaluations and examples of them will be provided.

COUNSELOR-CLIENT COLLABORATIVE EVALUATIONS

A collaborative discussion of progress, built into a counseling session, can be a useful way to reinforce progress, to clarify goals and objectives, and to make changes in a nonproductive counseling relationship. Some counselors conduct such evaluations on a regular schedule, perhaps every 3 months, while others are more spontaneous, waiting for appropriate times in the client's development or for significant calendar times. Such times might be a clear sign of progress (e.g., separated client's first social event as a single person), a setback (e.g., a perceptible increase in the client's level of anxiety), a noteworthy life event (e.g., the client's first day at college), calendar times such as the client's birthday, the start of a new year, the first anniversary of the client's divorce or when the client expresses unusually positive or negative feelings about the counseling process.

One way to approach such an evaluation is to make lists of accomplishments, goals, and strategies for goal achievement. Counselor and client can then work together to generate items for each list. This process seems to be most effective if the client takes the lead in developing the lists, with the counselor writing the items and helping the client to propose and clarify ideas. Items should be as specific and concrete as possible and should be written in such a way as to make the list a meaningful point of reference the next time such an evaluation is done.

The following is an example of such lists, developed with a twenty-four-year-old single female client, Carrie Carter:

Accomplishments

> Finally ended relationship with George
> Lost 7 pounds in last month
> Spending more time with women friends
> Revised resume
> Generally feel more self-confident and optimistic

Goals

> Begin to date again
> Lose 10 more pounds
> Begin to look for a new job
> Reestablish contact with sister
> Continue to build self-confidence

Strategies	Time
Attend dances and parties	At least once a week
Continue present diet	Until I weigh 120 lbs
Sign up for an aerobics class	By September 1
Read the want ads	Every Sunday
Telephone sister, suggest a meeting	By August 15
Continue to focus on accomplishments, try new experiences	Ongoing, keep a list

Such lists can help both client and counselor to see that progress has indeed been made, can clarify areas where change is still needed, and can provide the client with some encouragement to make those changes. Client and counselor should each retain a copy of the lists so they can be used as the basis for future discussion.

PROGRESS NOTES

In many mental health agencies, especially those where short-term, in-patient services are provided, counselors are required to maintain progress notes. Typically, progress notes are entries made in the client's chart each time the counselor has a session or other significant interaction with a client.

Progress notes are particularly useful in settings where several mental health professionals are working with an individual client. In a psychiatric hospital, for example, a nurse, a family counselor, a psychiatrist, and a case aide all may have contact with a particular client in a single day. Different schedules and other commitments often make it impossible for the four helping professionals to meet daily to share their perceptions of the client's development. Progress notes provide the vehicle for that sort of communication.

While counselors in private practice and in many outpatient mental health agencies may not be required to maintain progress notes, such notes may be a useful way for counselors to gauge client progress and plan the session-by-session direction of treatment. Consequently, many counselors, especially those with a large caseload who see their clients on an irregular schedule, elect to keep progress notes as an aid to counseling.

Often, progress notes are simply unstructured comments written into the client's chart after each session. However, having a framework for writing progress notes can facilitate that process and make the notes more useful. Many formats are available for maintaining progress notes. Moracco and Wilmarth (1981) have suggested a method that seems useful. The acronym SOAP is used to identify four categories that should be covered in the progress notes:

> Subjective—In this section, counselors briefly summarize their subjective reactions to a session, perhaps considering the degree of progress made in the session, the client's mood level, the client-counselor interaction, and the pace of the session.
>
> Objective—This includes specific and factual information on the client's progress and behavior, and on the nature of the session itself.
>
> Analysis—Next, counselors analyze the implications of the subjective and objective material provided earlier. Particularly important would be comments on the relationship of the session to overall treatment goals.
>
> Plans—Finally, counselors focus on the future and list any tasks that clients have agreed to undertake, anything the counselor needs to do to prepare for the next meeting with the client, and areas to be explored or considered in the next session. Long-range plans also may be included in this section.

The following is an example of a progress note, written according to the SOAP format:

5/18—Fifth individual counseling session held with Carrie Carter. (S) Carrie seemed more animated and talkative than she had in previous sessions. She was more comfortable discussing her weight and her relationship with George, but she still seemed afraid to talk about her family relationships. (O) For the first time, Carrie arrived on time for our appointment. She reported that she had revised her resume and had begun a diet. She stated that she was feeling more cheerful but still felt stuck in her relationship with her boyfriend. (A) The supportive approach to treatment, with some behavioral interventions, seems to be working. Carrie is mobilizing her own resources and is beginning to take constructive action. Homework assignments (e.g., rewriting her resume) seem particularly useful. (P) Progress should be reinforced and continued in career and physical-fitness areas, with homework assignments suggested. Client also may be ready to role-play a discussion with George of some of her concerns. However, she is making good progress and should be allowed to move at her own pace.

Progress notes tend to be fairly brief, often shorter than the example presented here. Counselors with limited time may become perfunctory in their approach to such notes and may view them as burdensome. Such attitudes may be spotted in notes that look like the following: "Ms. Carter was seen for counseling today. Session dealt with career and interpersonal issues." While such notes may satisfy an agency requirement, they are not helpful to either the counselor or others working with a client. Brief progress notes can be written that are informative. Whenever possible, counselors should use progress notes as an opportunity to reflect on a session and refine treatment planning.

One caution must be raised about progress notes and other client reports. Such records may be subpoenaed by the courts and may be subject to review by the client. Counselors should bear this in mind; they should avoid labeling or judging the client and should avoid using terminology that may be stigmatizing or unprofessional.

INTERIM REPORTS

Sometimes, a formal evaluation of a client's progress seems indicated, although the client has not yet reached initial treatment goals. Such an evaluation may be requested by the client's insurance company, may be part of the agency's procedure for monitoring treatment effectiveness, may be indicated by the client's deterioration or failure to progress, or may result from a transfer of the client from one counselor to another.

In writing interim reports, counselors can usually assume that their readers have some knowledge of the intake report completed when the client entered treatment. While data on that report may be summarized, then, it need not be repeated. Typically, interim reports are fairly brief (longer than progress notes but shorter than intake reports). Primarily, they will be intended to evaluate the client's progress in light of treatment goals and to make recommendations for further treatment, if indicated. A combination of the intake report, the progress notes, and the interim report should provide a new counselor with all the information needed to begin working productively with a client.

If an interim report is being prepared according to agency policy or in response to a request from an insurance company, a format for writing such a report probably will be provided. The following example, however, illustrates a typical format.

TRANSFER SUMMARY

Client: Terry Martin   Date of report: 8/21/85
Date of birth: 8/6/61   Counselor: Doris Santiago,
                                        M.Ed., N.C.C.

Presenting Problems

Mr. Terry Martin, a twenty-four-year-old white male, sought treatment from this agency in February, 1985, complaining of severe depression and isolation. He was living with his parents and had no social contacts. He was not performing well in his secretarial job and disliked his work. Sleeping and eating habits were poor.

Diagnosis and Treatment Plan

Mr. Martin was diagnosed as suffering from a dysthymic disorder and was referred to this counselor for individual career and personal counseling. A psychiatric consultation also was recommended.

Nature of Treatment

The client has been seen for weekly individual counseling for the past 5 months. He has attended sessions regularly and cooperated fully with his treatment. Antidepressent medication was prescribed for the client but that has been discontinued recently at the request of the client.

When the client entered treatment, he seemed confused and mistrustful and was having difficulty taking any control of his life. Although he was dependent on his parents, he seemed apprehensive about contact with any authority figure, including this counselor. Treatment modality was Reality Therapy, with a gradual pace and considerable support. This eventually led to the development of a good working relationship between counselor and client. Trust was satisfactory and contracts were established in order to relieve depression and promote the client's assumption of control over his life.

Progress

A number of changes have been observed in Mr. Martin. His depression has lifted enough so that he no longer seems to need medication. However, situational factors such as a fight with his mother can still send him back into depression. Although these feelings often are accompanied by expressions of hopelessness, the periods of severe depression now tend to be short-lived.

Mr. Martin has gained more confidence in himself and his abilities and is beginning to participate in some groups. He has joined a chess club and has been attending church regularly. He still sees himself as different from most people and has difficulty finding friends with whom he feels comfortable. However, he is beginning to appreciate his own sensitivity and high intelligence. He has met several people at church and has even gone to dinner with a young woman.

After two unsuccessful attempts, he has separated himself, at least physically, from his parents and is living at the YMCA. Although his relationship with his parents has not changed much, Mr. Martin seems more accepting of their way of life and less dependent on them.

Sleeping and eating habits have returned to normal. Some appropriate weight gain has been reported.

Mr. Martin also changed his work schedule from full-time to 2/3 time and has enrolled in a college course. He continues to be dissatisfied with his work but is optimistic that his return to college eventually will enable him to change careers.

Recommendations

This client seems to have responded well to treatment and has made significant progress. However, he needs continued help in clarifying his career goals and implementing his plans. His fear of failure is so great that it often prevents him from attempting new activities, and he becomes discouraged easily. He also can be unrealistic and sets overly high standards for himself. At the same time, he has been a motivated and responsible client who has attended sessions regularly, welcomed small homework assignments, and followed up on suggestions. He seems to need a great deal of support and generally uses it well, but may become too dependent on his counselor.

Continued individual counseling is recommended to help this client deal further with his depression, improve his interpersonal skills, and clarify his career goals. It is anticipated that in a few months he may be ready for participation in a counseling group where he can receive feedback and encouragement from his peers and practice his communication skills. The client thus far has not been receptive to family counseling. However, he remains quite enmeshed with his family and family counseling might be considered when the case is next evaluated.

Mr. Martin is transferred to Arlene Davidson for individual counseling because this counselor is leaving the agency.

The report provided here was designed to help a new counselor continue the treatment of a client who already has been in individual counseling for 5 months. It provides an overview of the client's treatment history, focusing on progress as well as continuing concerns, and provides information on how to work effectively with this client based on his reactions to his first 5 months of treatment. Although some transition time probably will be needed for the client to develop trust and rapport with the new counselor and to work through any feelings of anger and grief connected with the departure of the first counselor, the report should reduce the difficulties inherent in such a transition and pave the way for the establishment of a good counseling relationship.

Test Reports

Another kind of report that counselors frequently write and receive is a report on the testing or psychometric evaluation of clients. Often, a psychometric evaluation involves the writing of two reports. One will be written to the psychometrician by the client's primary therapist or caseworker. The other, written by the psychometrician, will provide an analysis of the test results and respond to the therapist's questions.

Referring for Testing

Sometimes a counselor may feel stymied by clients' lack of progress, confused about the nature of their difficulties, uncertain of the degree of pathology present, or simply in need of more information than the clients are providing. At such times, the counselor might refer clients to a psychologist or psychometrician for testing and evaluation. (See chapter 3.)

Generally, counselors prepare a brief written referral report to provide the psychometrician some background information on the client to be tested, the reason for the referral, and the information that is sought from the assessment. This helps the psychometrician develop some rapport with the client, select those tests and inventories that are most likely to yield the needed information, and provide answers to the counselor's questions.

The following items typically are included in a referral report:

1. Identifying information (counselor, client, client's date of birth)
2. Presenting problems
3. Reason for referral (referral questions)

4. Brief overview of background (development, health, family situation, educational/occupational history)
5. Treatment history
6. Summary of previous psychological and psychiatric tests
7. Client's attitude toward the assessment process

The following report exemplifies the information often provided prior to a psychometric evaluation. The next section includes the test report that was prepared in response to this referral.

MERRIWEATHER FOSTER HOME AND ADOPTION SERVICE
PSYCHOLOGICAL REFERRAL

Client: Jon Roberts   Counselor: Pearl Jones
Date of birth: 10/5/68   Date of Assessment: 2/5/85

Presenting Problems

Jon Roberts, a sixteen-year-old black male, has been in foster care since he was four years of age. His emotional and behavioral adjustment seemed satisfactory until this year. Jon has begun to treat his foster parents in a negative and rejecting way and has begun to search for his biological mother. He stated that soon he will go to college to become a successful engineer and no longer will need Mr. and Mrs. Hermes, his foster parents. Jon's thinking sometimes seems grandiose, confused, and unrealistic. He seems to be having difficulty accepting his foster sister's recent departure for college.

Reason for Referral

Referral is requested for the following reasons:

1. To provide information on the nature of Jon's behavioral changes
2. To determine the degree of pathology that is present
3. To assess the appropriateness of Jon's current career goals

Background

Jon resided with his biological mother until he was four years of age. At that time, his mother was incarcerated for possession of narcotics and Jon was placed in foster care with the Hermes family. The whereabouts of his biological mother and father are unknown.

Jon's development seems to have been satisfactory and until recently he has gotten along well with Mr. and Mrs. Hermes and their daughter Lisa, age eighteen.

Jon is in the eleventh grade at Conrad High School. He has been passing all his courses with C's. Both his foster parents and his teachers have reported that he studies little and does not seem to be working up to his potential. Mr. and Mrs. Hermes seem to be warm and caring but set very high standards and sometimes are too stern and controlling. Although Jon participates in sports and goes to parties, he rarely forms close friendships and has not begun to date.

Treatment History

Jon has had no previous individual counseling. For the past 3 months, he has been in an adolescent counseling group intended to promote his socialization. His progress since he was placed in foster care has been monitored by caseworkers. He generally has had a comfortable relationship with his workers but has not spoken freely about himself or his family situation.

Previous Test Results

Jon was last tested on 8/21/81, a routine evaluation. Testing placed him in the average range of intelligence (91 IQ). Test report described him as "an anxious boy who has difficulty forming interpersonal relationships." No problems were noted in the family situation at that time.

Attitude Toward Assessment

Jon has a quiet and serious manner and deals fairly well with new situations. Consequently, it is anticipated that he will cooperate with the testing.

PSYCHOMETRIC REPORT

The psychometrician or individual conducting the assessment process generally will be a masters or doctoral level psychologist. However, counselors are increasingly conducting assessments, especially in cases where information is needed on the client's career development, disability, or rehabilitation. Although most counselors are not qualified to administer projective tests and many are not trained in the use of individual intelligence tests, a battery of tests still can be compiled, consisting entirely of tests that can be used by counselors, which can provide a comprehensive picture of clients' overall functioning and can answer most referral questions. However, the focus of this section will be on referrals made to psychologists for assessment. Assessment by counselors was discussed in chapter 3.

Although it is possible for psychometricians to test without a referral report or any guidance from the client's mental health worker, that would be unusual. In such cases a comprehensive test battery, assessing the following areas, might be administered.

1.   Intellectual functioning—The Stanford-Binet Intelligence Scale or one of the Wechsler Intelligence Scales most often are used.
2.   Personality—This is commonly measured through a combination of the Rorschach Test, the Thematic Apperception Test, and the House-Tree-Person or other drawings. A sentence-completion inventory and the Minnesota Multiphasic Personality Inventory also are commonly used in addition to or instead of some of the other instruments. Numerous other objective measures of personality also are available.
3.   Perception and organicity—The Bender Gestalt is frequently used to provide this information as well as supplementary data on the client's personality dynamics and intellectual functioning.

Measurement of career-related interests, aptitudes, and level of achievement typically is not done as part of a comprehensive assessment unless such information was requested beforehand by the client's mental health worker or unless the psychometrician

realized that such information would be particularly important to the referring agency (e.g., a rehabilitation counseling
agency).

The referral report for Jon indicated that information was
needed in four areas of functioning: personality, interests, intelligence, and abilities. Data would be needed to provide insight
into Jon's current behavioral and attitudinal changes and to determine the appropriateness of his current occupational goal,
engineering. The psychometrician who tested Jon used the following tests and inventories:

Personality—Rorschach Test, House-Tree-Person, Sentence
Completion

Intelligence—Wechsler Intelligence Scale for Children-re-
vised

Personality, intelligence, cognitive functioning—Bender
Gestalt

Interests—Kuder Occupational Interest Survey—form DD

Abilities—Wide Range Achievement Test to measure overall readiness for college, the Mechanical Reasoning Subtest of the Differential Aptitude Test to indicate aptitude
for engineerng.

In addition, psychometrists generally conduct a brief interview with the client and observe the client's attitude toward the
testing process. The test report is based not only on the test data
but also on observations and inferences drawn during the interview.

Test reports tend to be more analytical and interpretive than
reports based on intake interviews. This is acceptable because
the tests have been studied extensively and their interpretation
generally justified by research. As much as possible, however,
psychometricians should make their reports clear, free of jargon,
and useful to the practitioner. The report should respond to the
referral questions and enable the mental health professional to
help the client more effectively.

A report of the psychological evaluation of Jon Roberts follows. It is organized according to a typical framework.

Merriweather Foster Home and Adoption Service
Psychological Assessment

Client: Jon Roberts   Psychologist: Dr. Stuart Kelly
Date of birth: 10/5/68   Dates of assessment: 2/5/85 and 2/6/85

Tests administered:
   Bender Gestalt
   Wechsler Intelligence Scale for Children—revised
   Wide Range Achievement Test
   Modified Sentence Completion
   RorschachTest
   House-Tree-Person
   Kuder Occupational Interest Survey—form DD
   Mechanical Reasoning Subtest—Differential Aptitude Test

Reason for Evaluation

Jon Roberts, a sixteen-year-old black male, in foster care for 12 years, was referred for a psychological evaluation due to recent behavioral problems. Foster parents reported that Jon has become disobedient since his sister began college. Testing was requested to facilitate development of Jon's career plans. A high school junior receiving C's, he reportedly is an underachiever. He is planning to attend college to become an engineer.

Impression of Client

Jon arrived on schedule for his appointments. He is a tall, slender, good-looking young man who was appropriately, though casually, dressed. Although he initially appeared somewhat shy and a slight hesitancy was noted in his speech, a rapport was easily established. Jon had a pleasant, warm, and open manner and a good sense of humor. Although he said little about his biological and foster families, he spoke quite openly about his "fooling around" and his resolve to behave more appropriately. Throughout the evaluation, he was cooperative and eager to please.

Test-Taking Behavior

Jon's work habits generally were quite good. He worked at a satisfactory speed and approached the tasks in a systematic fashion. He was able to make good use of trial-and-error behavior. He was not easily frustrated and was able to work hard for long periods. He was motivated and interested and seemed to derive some gratification from the evaluation process.

Jon performed best on tasks that maximized interaction between him and this examiner. When he was left to work on his own, his motivation waned and his effort declined markedly. He also sometimes overreacted to praise and became overconfident and careless following a task on which he was told he had performed particularly well.

Jon seemed to have such a great investment in making a good impression, that this sometimes impaired his judgment. Rather than admit he did not know the answer to a question, he often chose to make a wild guess.

Intellectual Functioning

On the Wechsler Intelligence Scale for Children, Jon achieved a Verbal IQ of 87, a Performance IQ of 90, and a Full Scale IQ of 87, placing him in the low average range of intelligence. This intelligence score does not differ markedly from his performance on a previous intelligence test on which he achieved an IQ of 91. His performance was consistent and reflected little interference by emotional factors. There were few indications of a higher intellectual potential and Jon's current performance seems to be a reliable indication of his intellectual abilities. Jon had the greatest difficulty with subtests related to academic knowledge (arithmetic and information). His memory and learning ability were average.

Achievement

On the Wide Range Achievement Test, Jon achieved a reading grade equivalent of 11.3; a spelling grade equivalent of 7.8; and an arithmetic grade equivalent of 6.1. At the time of the evaluation, Jon was sixteen years, four months of age and in the eleventh grade. His reading score was, therefore, average for his age while his spelling and arithmetic scores were in the low average range. Jon's achievement level was in line with his inventoried intelligence, so that while some improvement in math and spelling probably could be obtained through tutoring or increased studying, Jon seemed to be working close to his capacity.

It was reported that Jon plans to become an engineer. In light of his inventoried intelligence and his below-average mathematical ability, his chances of completing an engineering curriculum do not seem good.

Aptitude

On the Mechanical Reasoning subtest of the Differential Aptitude Test, Jon scored in the low average range. This is another indication that he may not possess the abilities required for an engineering career. Although Jon spoke of his interest in engineering, he seems to have little understanding of the field and expressed a dislike for the sort of work typically associated with engineering. Jon enjoys working with his hands and stated that he prefers to work by himself. He has had some experience as a plumber's assistant and found that sort of work very enjoyable. Jon's interests and abilities, then, lie more in technical than academic fields.

Interests

The Kuder Occupational Interest Survey indicated that Jon's occupational interests are not yet well developed and he has no strong occupational interests at present. Most of his interests lie in technical, blue-collar fields and include such occupations as truck driver, printer, welder, and house painter. Jon also manifested an interest in sales, especially when combined with his technical interests, as in the position of automobile salesman. An additional interest is in the field of art; the inventory reflected the likelihood of Jon's enjoying such occupations as photographer and interior decorator. The college majors he seemed most likely to enjoy were art and art education.

Jon expressed an interest in applying to a Navy ROTC program in which he could acquire the technical skills required to work on ships. Since a 4-year college program cannot be recommended for Jon at the present time, ROTC may not be a realistic alternative. However, the military might well offer Jon the technical training he wishes and the sort of structure that seems helpful to him. Enlistment might be considered. Another appropriate alternative would be enrollment in an apprenticeship program or a 1- or 2-year training program aimed at development of technical skills. If some improvement in Jon's arithmetic can be effected, he could have a good chance of completing a two-year technically oriented college program. In the meantime, it is important to clarify Jon's misunderstanding of the field of engineering and begin to explore related technical fields with him.

Personality

Although Jon has some emotional and interpersonal difficulties, he seems to have made satisfactory progress since he was last evaluated (8/81) and is relatively well-adjusted. He has established an appropriate masculine identity and seems able to use his foster father as a role model. He continues to have some difficulty relating to his peers but is making progress in that area.

Although Jon finds his foster home confining and has expressed the wish that he could be permitted more freedom at home, he views his foster parents as warm and approachable. He also seems to have accepted his lack of contact with his biological mother. There is some indication that he feels his foster parents expect too much of him but he is working hard to cope with this difficulty. Jon feels particularly close to his sister and although he has acknowledged some rivalry between them, she seems to be his closest confidante.

On the other hand, Jon is sometimes depressed and tends to see the world as a discouraging place. He feels that he has not fully developed and he seems to be hiding quite a bit. Although he is not unusually mistrustful, he is wary and may appear defensive and secretive. He can be immature and obstructionistic, but generally has control over his behavior. He feels uneasy in his peer relationships and sometimes may behave in an attention-getting fashion in an effort to force others to accept him. He wants to appear manly and may tend to overemphasize the external attributes of masculinity. He is unsure of his ability to live up to the standard of masculinity set by his foster father and is still troubled by an image of himself as a small child who used to wet his bed. He is somewhat egocentric and may seem insensitive to the feelings of others. He has a confused view of his abilities and vacillates between seeing himself as a failure and seeing himself as an undiscovered genius. As a result, his judgment may falter and his common sense may be poor.

Jon benefits from structure and direction. He works hard to control his angry and impulsive feelings and, although he usually is successful, he does not have adequate releases. He is cautious and requires support and reassurance. Although he has some difficulty handling pressure, he makes a good impression and can deal satisfactorily with most situations.

Summary

At the time of the evaluation, Jon was sixteen years, four months of age and in the eleventh grade. He achieved an IQ of 87, placing him in the low average range of intelligence. His reading score was at grade level but his spelling and arithmetic scores were in the low average range. Despite Jon's expressed interest in engineering, his pattern of abilities and inventoried interests point to a technical career as a more realistic and rewarding choice. Jon is moderately depressed, insecure, and egocentric. He requires support and has difficulty relating to his peers.

Diagnostic Impression: Adjustment disorder with depressed mood.

Recommendations

1. Continued participation in teenage group to develop interpersonal skills and relationships.

2. Career planning, probably focusing on a technical career.
3. Individual counseling of a supportive and structured nature to help Jon deal with his depression and current adjustment difficulties.

Clearly, the information provided in this report can facilitate treatment planning for Jon. It is useful not only in providing understanding of the dynamics and severity of his current behavioral difficulties, but also in helping the counselor to promote realistic career planning.

CASE CONFERENCES

Referring a client for a psychological assessment is one strategy for dealing with an impasse in a counseling relationship. Another approach is to present the client at a case conference in order to obtain help from other staff members. Some agencies have regularly scheduled case conferences in which staff members take turns at presenting cases. These are not necessarily problem cases but may be a client with an unusual or interesting history or concern.

Case conferences generally are intended to be learning experiences for the presenter as well as for the other staff members attending the conference, although they may be intimidating or anxiety-providing for the presenter. Case conferences should not be a place for mental health professionals to belittle each other's work or flaunt their own accomplishments. Rather, it should be a place where colleagues work together to help each other provide more effective client treatment.

The counselor responsible for making a presentation at a case conference need not feel obligated to have all the answers about a client. In fact, the conference probably will be more interesting and productive if the counselor has some questions about the dynamics, diagnosis, or treatment of the client to be presented.

Case conferences vary, depending on the nature of the

mental health facility, the client being presented, and the style of the presenter. Some conferences involve the staff in observing the client and counselor in a session, while at others the client may attend part of the conference and speak directly to the participants about his or her concerns. Another approach to such conferences involves the counselor presenting an audiotape or videotape of part of a counseling session. Regardless of the particular format of a case conference, the presenting counselor generally should plan to cover the following areas in the information provided to the group:

I. *Identifying information*—client's name, age, education, occupation, family constellation, and other important demographic data.

II. *Presenting concerns*

III. *Brief overview of background*—physical and emotional adjustment, family history, educational and occupational history, relevant leisure activities, social relationships, significant events.

IV. *Treatment history*—previous treatment, duration and nature of present treatment, client attitude toward treatment, progress made.

V. *Counselor's concerns/questions*—diagnostic questions, confusing dynamics, treatment impasses, client resistance, or questions about treatment planning.

Readers probably have noticed that there is considerable similarity between a test referral report and the sort of presentation counselors might make at case conferences. That is because both have the same purpose: providing others with enough information on a client so they can help the counselor answer questions about the client's development, diagnosis, and treatment plan. In both the written report and the oral presentation, counselors should be concise and should not undertake the impossible task of giving a full picture of a client's background and treatment. Only material that is crucial to understanding either the client or the concerns of the counselor should be included. That process of selectivity should maximize counselors' chances of receiving the help they need with a case.

CLOSING REPORTS

A last report to be reviewed here is the closing or termination report. These are prepared when a client discontinues counseling, regardless of whether the termination is a decision reached jointly by client and counselor or is a unilateral decision. Closing reports generally become part of clients' files at the mental health agency where they have been treated so that if they return for treatment, information will be available on the clients' difficulties, the nature of the treatment, and its impact on the clients. With the client's written permission, this information also can be released to medical or mental health personnel outside of the agency, should the client decide to continue treatment elsewhere. Some counselors also prepare abbreviated versions of their closing reports to give to clients when they finish counseling. These may even be prepared in conjunction with clients and can serve as a means of reminding clients of the gains that have been made, reinforcing progress, and setting forth some future goals and plans for the clients.

Closing reports typically are fairly brief, one to two pages at most. Although they usualy include a short review of the client's history and develpment, these reports focus primarily on the current treatment, considering what worked, what didn't work, and what still needs to be done to facilitate resuming treatment with the client, if that should occur. Closing reports also provide quantifiable information for the agency on the nature of the clients who are being treated, the type and length of treatment provided, and the progress made.

An example of a closing report follows. Its organization provides a structure that counselors may wish to adopt in writing their own closing reports.

CLOSING REPORT

Client: Nora Homer   Counselor: Howard Fox, L.P.C.
Dates of counseling: Date of report: 8/30/85
   3/10/85–8/27/85

Presenting Concerns

Nora Homer, a forty-two-year-old white female, sought counseling to help her cope with anxiety and depression surrounding her separation from her second husband. She was suffering from low self-esteem and isolation and was having trouble dealing with her two children and her finanacial circumstances. She was diagnosed as suffering from an adjustment disorder with mixed emotional features.

Background

Ms. Homer was the youngest of six children in a lower middle-class family. Her father was often intoxicated and abusive. Nora married at seventeen to escape her home situation. However, her husband was also a heavy drinker who was abusive toward the client. When she was thirty-two, she met the man who was to become her second husband. She left her first husband a year later in order to marry Lyle Homer and brought her two children with her. Lyle has been in frequent trouble with the law (fighting, speeding, driving while intoxicated) and, over the past year, began openly seeing other women. After much hesitation, Nora took her children, now fifteen and thirteen, and moved in with her widowed mother.

Treatment History

Nora was in a crisis when she began counseling. She saw herself as a failure because she had ended two marriages and was overwhelmed by her responsibilities. She is a reasonably intelligent woman who relates fairly well to others in a shy and gentle way and is willing to work hard to help herself and her children. However, she tends to be dependent and can be debilitated by depression and anxiety. The client was seen for weekly individual counseling for 5 months. Only two appointments were missed. A crisis counseling model was used to build on the client's strengths and prevent further dependency. Counseling was supportive and structured in nature, promoting both expression of feelings and behavioral change. Goals included reducing dysfunctional emotions and helping the client to take more control over her life.

Outcomes

Ms. Homer responded extremely well to treatment. Depression abated quickly as she began to take steps to improve her situation. She obtained employment as a factory worker and recently has been accepted into an apprenticeship training program. She has obtained low-cost legal assistance in order to pursue divorce proceedings and obtain child support payments. She has joined Parents Without Partners and has begun to make some new friends. She hopes to move into her own apartment in the next few months. She is interacting fairly well with her children.

Recommendations

Despite the notable progress made by this client, it will take time for her to build self-confidence and an independent lifestyle. Another crisis or disappointing relationship may reactivate her dependency and depression and necessitate further counseling. She also may need help in developing more effective parenting skills.

These concerns were discussed with the client. However, she felt that counseling had enabled her to meet her immediate goals and she was not motivated toward continued counseling. Should she resume counseling, however, a structured, behavioral approach is recommended. Such an approach should allow for client self-expression but should not encourage extensive discussion of negative feelings or past difficulties.

From this report, another counselor working with Nora Homer has some direction, some knowledge of the client's strengths and weaknesses, and information on the sort of counselng that is likely to be effective in helping her. Such information can ease the client's return to counseling and can facilitate the counseling process for both client and counselor.

Follow-Up

A final procedure to be mentioned in this chapter on papers and procedures is the follow-up. Follow-up involves contacting clients by mail or telephone some time after they have completed counseling in order to ascertain whether the gains made during counseling have been sustained (and perhaps even continued). Follow-up provides a way for counselors and agencies to monitor their level of effectiveness and is a vehicle for offering continued help to former clients who may be experiencing difficulties but who are reluctant to reestablish contact with their counselors.

Counselors who choose to conduct follow-ups of their clients are taking a risk. The counselors may learn that they have not helped clients as much as they thought they had. They may find that more work still needs to be done with clients who seemed to be doing well a few months earlier. Counselors who make follow-up contact should be prepared to offer further assistance to their clients. Another risk is that clients may misinterpret the contact and may try to transform a professional relationship into a social one.

On the other hand, learning that a client is doing well can be very rewarding to the counselor. The follow-up process also can be reassuring to clients, whether or not further counseling is indicated, and can make it easier for them to seek help if it is needed in the future.

Some agencies use written questionnaires for follow-up contact. These questionnaires are sent to clients at predetermined intervals after they have completed treatment. Other agencies have no policy on follow-up contact and leave it to the discretion and preference of the counselors. Therefore, it is difficult to recommend a particular approach to follow-up. It should occur long enough after counseling to reflect persistence of change but not so long after that it seems out of place or overdue. A 3-month interval between termination and follow-up is common but both longer and shorter intervals are appropriate, depending on the nature of the client-counselor relationship, the client's concerns, and the guidelines of the mental health agency. Informing the client at termination that a follow-up contact will be done can pave the way for that contact as well as encourage the client's progress. No format need be used for follow-up contact: an unstructured telephone call by the counselor is sufficient. However, some counselors and agencies use follow-up contacts as a vehicle for data gathering in order to demonstrate accountability. In such cases, a written questionnaire or structured interview might be preferable. Regardless of the format used, the follow-up contact can be an excellent way for counselors to show that they are genuinely concerned about and committed to helping their clients and are, indeed, advocates of the lifelong process of personal growth and development.

REFERENCES

Abrams, R. 1976. Psychopharmacology and convulsive therapy. In B.B. Wolman (Ed.), *The therapist's handbook.* New York: Van Nostrand Reinhold Co.

Adams, R.L., and Jenkins, R.L. 1981. Basic principles of the neuropsychological examination. In C.E.Walker (Ed.), *Clinical practice of psychology.* New York: Pergamon Press.

Adler, A. 1927. *The practice and theory of individual psychology.* New York: Harcourt, Brace.

Aiken, R.L. 1976. *Psychological testing and assessment.* Boston: Allyn & Bacon, Inc.

American Mental Health Counselors Association. 1978. Report of AMHCA Certification Committee. Washington, DC: AMHCA.

Atkinson, D.R., Morten, G., & Sue, D.W. 1983. *Counseling American minorities.* Dubuque: William C. Brown Company.

Bandura, A. 1969. *Principles of behavior modification.* New York: Holt, Rinehart & Winston.

Beck, A.T. 1976. *Cognitive therapy and the emotional disorders.* New York: International Universities Press.

Beck, A.T., Rush, A.J., Shaw, B.F., & Emery, G. 1979. *Cognitive therapy of depression.* New York: Guilford Press.

Beck, S.J. 1961. *Rorschach's test: I. Basic Processes.* New York: Grune & Stratton.

Bender, L. 1938. *A visual motor gestalt test and its clinical use.* New York: American Orthopsychiatric Association.

Benjamin, A. 1974. *The helping interview.* Boston: Houghton-Mifflin.

Blocher, D.H., & Biggs, D.A. 1983. *Counseling psychology in community settings.* New York: Springer.

Bloom, B.L. 1983/1977. *Community mental health: A general introduction.* Monterey, CA: Brooks/Cole.

Bowden, C. 1981. Biological treatment of emotional disturbances. In C.E. Walker (Ed.), *Clinical practice of psychology.* New York: Pergamon Press.

Bowen, M. 1974a. Toward the differentiation of self in one's family of origin. In F. Andres & J. Lorio (Eds.), *Georgetown family symposia (Vol. 1).* Washington, DC: Georgetown University Medical Center.

Bowen, M. 1974b. Theory in the practice of psychotherapy. In P.J. Guerin, Jr. (Ed.), *Family therapy: Theory and practice.* New York: Gardner Press.

Brill, A.A. (Ed.) 1938. *The basic writings of Sigmund Freud.* New York: Modern Library.

Bry, A. (Ed.) 1972. *Inside psychotherapy.* New York: Basic Books.

Caplan, G. 1963. Types of mental health consultation. *American Journal of Orthopsychiatry, 33,* 470–481.

Carter, E., & McGoldrick, M. (Eds.) 1980. *The family life cycle: A framework for family therapy.* New York: Gardner Press.

Cautela, J.R., & Upper, D. 1976. The behavioral inventory battery: The use of self-report measures in behavioral analyses and therapy. In M. Hersen & A.S. Bellack (Eds.), *Behavioral assessment: A practical handbook.* New York: Pergamon Press.

Corey, G. 1981. *Theory and practice of group counseling.* Monterey, CA: Brooks/Cole.

Corsini, R.J. (Ed.) 1973. *Current psychotherapies.* Itasca, IL: F.E. Peacock.

Corsini, R.J. (Ed.) 1977. *Current personality theories.* Itasca, IL: F.E. Peacock.

Davis, J. 1979. Why must I be "sick" before my insurance pays? *AMHCA News,* June 1979, p. 1.

DeRidder, L.M., Stephens, T.A., English, J.T., & Watkins, C.E., Jr. 1983. The development of graduate programs in community counseling: One approach. *AMHCA Journal, 5,* 61–68.

Diagnostic and statistical manual of mental disorders (3rd ed.) (DSM-III) 1980. Washington, DC: American Psychiatric Association.

Dreikurs, R. 1967. *Psychodynamics, psychotherapy and counseling.* Chicago: Alfred Adler Institute.

Dyer, W.W. & Vriend, J. 1975. *Counseling techniques that work.* Washington, DC: APGA.

Editors of Consumer Reports Books. 1980. *The medicine show.* Mt. Vernon, NY: Consumers Union.

Eisenberg, S. & Delancy, D.J. 1977. *The counseling process.* Chicago: Rand McNally.

Ellis, A. 1962. *Reason and emotion in psychotherapy.* New York: Lyle Stuart.

Ellis, A. 1973. *Humanistic psychotherapy.* New York: McGraw-Hill.

Erikson, E.H. 1983. *Childhood and society.* New York: W.W. Norton.

Evans, R.I. 1975. *Carl Rogers: A man and his ideas.* New York: E.P. Dutton.

Fagen, J. & Shepherd, I.L. (Eds.) 1970. *Gestalt therapy now.* Palo Alto, CA: Science and Behavior.

Fields, C.M. 1984. "Extinction" of psychiatry seen as possible with fewer doctors choosing to specialize. *The Chronicle of Higher Education, 28*(12), 16.

Forster, J. 1978. Counseling credentialing revisited. *Personnel and Guidance Journal, 56,* 593–598.

Fraiberg, S. 1959. *The magic years.* New York: Charles Scribner's Sons.

Frances, A., Clarkin, J., & Perry, S. 1984. *Differential therapeutics in psychiatry.* New York: Brunner/Mazel.

Ginzberg, E. 1972. Towards a theory of occupational choice: A restatement. *Vocational Guidance Quarterly, 20,* 169–176.

Glasser, W. 1965. *Reality therapy.* New York: Harper & Row.

Gottman, J.M., & Leiblum, S.R. 1974. *How to do psychotherapy and how to evaluate it: A manual for beginners.* New York: Holt, Rinehart, & Winston.

Gough, H.G. 1969. *Manual for the California Personality Inventory.* Palo Alto, CA: Consulting Psychologists Press.

Greist, J.H., Jefferson, J.W., & Spitzer, R.L. (Eds.) 1982. *Treatment of mental disorders.* New York: Oxford University Press.

Haley, J. 1980. *Leaving home.* New York: McGraw Hill.

Hansen, J.C., Stevic, R.R., & Warner, R.W., Jr. 1977. *Counseling theory and process.* Boston: Allyn & Bacon.

Hansen, J.C., Warner, R.W., & Smith, E.J. 1980. *Group counseling: Theory and process.* Chicago: Rand McNally.

Harold, M. 1984. Credentialing bodies develop exams, standards. *Guidepost, 26*(10), 1.

Havighurst, R.J. 1972. *Developmental tasks and education.* New York: David McKay, Co.

Herson, M., & Bellack, A.S. (Eds.) 1976. *Behavioral assessment: A practical handbook.* New York: Pergamon Press.

Hipple, J., & Cimbolic, P. 1979. *The counselor and suicidal crisis.* Springfield, IL: C.C. Thomas.

Jastak, J.F., & Jastak, S. 1978. *WRAT manual.* Wilmington, DE: Jastak Associates.

Jones, L.K. 1976. A national survey of the program and enrollment characteristics of counselor education programs. *Counselor Education and Supervision, 15,* 166–176.

Kaplan, H.I., & Sadock, B.J. 1981. *Modern synopsis of psychiatry III.* Baltimore: Williams & Wilkins.

Kaplan, H.S. 1974. *The new sex therapy.* New York: Brunner/Mazel.

Kline, P. 1975. *Psychology of vocational guidance.* New York: John Wiley & Sons.

Krumboltz, J.D., & Thoresen, C.E. 1969. *Behavioral counseling: Cases and techniques.* New York: Holt, Rinehart, & Winston.

Law, J., Moracco, J., & Wilmarth, R.R. 1981. A problem oriented record system for counselors. *AMHCA Journal, 3,* 7–16.

Lazarus, A.A. 1971. *Behavior therapy and beyond.* New York: McGraw-Hill.

Lazarus, A.A. (Ed.) 1976. *Multimodal behavior therapy.* New York: Springer.

Lazarus, A.A. 1977. *Multimodal life history questionnaire.* Kingston, NJ: Multimodal Therapy Institute.

Lewis, J.A., & Lewis, M.D. 1977. *Community counseling: A human services approach.* New York: John Wiley & Sons.

Litman, R.E., Farbarow, N.L., Wold, C.I., & Brown, T.R. 1974. Prediction models of suicidal behaviors. In A.T. Beck, H.L.P. Resnik, & D.J. Lettieri (Eds.), *The prediction of suicide.* Bowie, MD: Charles Press.

Madanes, C. 1981. *Strategic family therapy.* San Francisco: Jossey-Bass.

Magoon, T.M., Golan, S.E., & Freeman, R.W. 1969. *Mental health counselors at work.* New York: Pergamon Press.

Manual of international statistical classification of diseases, injuries and causes of death. 1977. Geneva: World Health Organization.

McCollum, M.G. 1981. Recasting a role for mental health educators. *AMHCA Journal, 3*, 37–47.

McGoldrick, M., Pearce, R., & Giordano, J. 1982. *Ethnicity and family therapy.* New York: Guilford Press.

Messina, J.J. 1979. Why establish a certification system for professional counselors? A rationale. *AMHCA Journal, 1*, 9–22.

Meyer, R.G. 1983. *The clinician's handbook.* Boston: Allyn & Bacon.

Millman, H.L., Huber, J.T., & Diggins, D.R. 1982. *Therapy for adults.* San Francisco: Jossey-Bass.

Minuchin, S. 1974. *Families and family therapy.* Cambridge: Harvard University Press.

Minuchin, S. 1977. *The middle years of childhood.* Monterey, CA: Brooks-Cole.

Mooney, R.L., & Gordon, L.V. 1950. *The Mooney problem check list manual.* New York: Psychological Corporation.

Morgan, C.D., & Murray, H.A. 1935. A method for investigating fantasies: The Thematic Apperception Test. *Archives of Neurology and Psychiatry, 34*, 289–306.

Neugarten, B.L. (Ed.) 1968. *Middle age and aging.* Chicago: University of Chicago Press.

Nichols, M. 1984. *Family therapy.* New York: Gardner Press.

Okun, B.F. 1976. *Effective helping: Interviewing & counseling techniques.* North Scituate, MA: Duxbury Press.

Perle, F., Hefferline, R., & Goodman, P. 1951. *Gestalt therapy: Excitement and growth in the human personality.* New York: Julian Press.

Piaget, J. 1948. *The moral development of the child.* Glencoe, IL: The Free Press.

Piaget, J. & Inhelder, B. 1969. *The psychology of the child.* New York: Basic Books.

Pietrofesa, J.J., Hoffman, A., & Splete, H.H. 1984. *Counseling: An introduction.* Boston: Houghton Mifflin.

Quick reference to diagnostic criteria from DSM-III. 1980. Washington, DC: American Psychiatric Association.

Randolph, D.L. 1979. CMHC requisites for employment of master's level psychologists/counselors. *AMHCA Journal, 1*, 54–58.

Reid, W.H. 1983. *Treatment of the DSM III psychiatric disorders.* New York: Brunner/Mazel.

Ritter, K.Y. 1979. The present and future of the profession: View from a counselor-education program. *Personnel and Guidance Journal, 8,* 279–284.

Rogers, C.R. 1942. *Counseling and psychotherapy.* Boston: Houghton Mifflin.

Rogers, C.R. 1951. *Client-centered therapy: Its current practice, implications and theory.* Boston: Houghton-Mifflin.

Rosenbaum, M. 1976. Group psychotherapies. In B.B. Wolman (Ed.), *The therapist's handbook,* pp. 163–183. New York: Van Nostrand Reinhold Co.

Rotter, J.B. 1946. The incomplete sentences as a method in studying personality. *American Psychologist, 1,* 286.

Sahakian, W.S. (Ed.) 1976. *Psychotherapy and counseling: Techniques in intervention.* Chicago: Rand McNally.

Sahakian, W.S. 1979. *Psychopathology today.* Itasca, IL: F.E. Peacock.

Satir, V. 1967. *Conjoint family therapy.* Palo Alto, CA: Science and Behavior.

Satir, V. 1983. *Conjoint family therapy.* Palo Alto, CA: Science and Behavior.

Schaffer, J.B.P., & Galinsky, M.D. 1974. *Models of group therapy and sensitivity training.* Englewood Cliffs, NJ: Prentice-Hall.

Scharf, R. 1970. Relative importance of interest and ability in vocational decision making. *Journal of Counseling Psychology, 17,* 258–262.

Schoenfeld, L.S., & Lehmann, L.S. 1981. Management of the aggressive patient. In C.E. Walker (Ed.), *Clinical practice of psychology.* New York: Pergamon Press.

Seiler, G., & Messina, J. 1979. Toward professional identity: The dimensions of mental health counseling in perspective. *AMHCA Journal, 1,* 3–8.

Seligman, L. 1980. *Assessment in developmental career counseling.* Cranston, RI: The Carroll Press.

Seligman, L. 1981a. An application of Satir's model to family counseling. *The School Counselor, 29,* 133–139.

Seligman, L. 1981b. Multimodal behavior therapy: Case study of a high school student. *The School Counselor, 28,* 249–256.

Seligman, L. 1983. An introduction to the new *DSM-III. Personnel and Guidance Journal, 61,* 601–605.

Seligman, L., & Whiteley, N. 1983. AMHCA and VMHCA members in private practice in Virginia. *AMHCA Journal, 5,* 179–183.

Sheehy, G. 1974. *Passages*. New York: E.P. Dutton & Co.

Shertzer, B., & Linden, J.D. 1979. *Fundamentals of individual appraisal*. Boston: Houghton Mifflin.

Shertzer, B., & Stone, S.C. 1980. *Fundamentals of counseling*. Boston: Houghton Mifflin.

Silverman, H.M., & Simon, G.I. 1979. *The pill book*. New York: Bantam Books.

Spitzer, R., Endicott, J., & Robins, E. 1975. Clinical criteria for psychiatric diagnosis and *DSM III*. *American Journal of Psychiatry, 132*, 1187–1199.

Spitzer, R.L., Skodol, A.E., Gibbon, M., & Williams, J.B.W. 1981. *DSM-III case book*. Washington, D.C.: American Psychiatric Association.

Spock, B. 1964. *Baby and child care*. New York: Pocket Books.

Stone, S.C., & Shertzer, B. 1971. *Minority groups and guidance*. Boston: Houghton Mifflin.

Sundberg, N.D. 1977. *Assessment of persons*. Englewood Cliffs, NJ: Prentice-Hall.

Super, D.E. 1957. *The psychology of careers*. New York: Harper & Row.

Super, D.E., & Bohn, M.J. 1970. *Occupational psychology*. Belmont, CA: Wadsworth.

Thomas, L.E., Morrill, W.H., & Miller, C.D. 1970. Educational interests and achievement. *Vocational Guidance Quarterly, 18*, 199–202.

Turkington, C. 1983. Independent practice today: Wooden desks. *APA Monitor, 14*(10), 21.

Walker, C.E. 1981. *Clinical practice of psychology*. New York: Pergamon Press.

Wantz, R.A., & Scherman, A. 1982. Trends in counselor preparation: Courses, program emphases, philosophical orientation, and experimental components. *Counselor Education and Supervision, 21*, 258–268.

Webb, L.J., DiClemente, C.C., Johnstone, E.E., Sanders, J.J., & Perley, R.A. 1981. *DSM-III training guide*. New York:Brunner/Mazel Publishers.

Weikel, W.J., Daniel, R.W., & Anderson, J. 1981. A survey of counselors in private practice. *AMHCA Journal, 3*, 88–94.

White, K.M., & Speisman, J.C. 1977. *Adolescence*. Monterey, CA: Brooks/Cole.

Whiteley, J.M. & Fretz, B.R. 1980. *The present and future of counseling psychology*. Monterey, CA: Brooks/Cole.

Wolman, B.B. (Ed.). 1976. *The therapist's handbook.* New York: Van Nostrand Reinhold Co.

Zax, M., & Specter, G.A. 1974. *An introduction to community psychology.* New York: John Wiley & Sons.

Zytowski, D.G. 1970. *The influence of psychological factors upon vocational development.* Boston: Houghton Mifflin.

INDEX

Ability tests, 74–77
Accountability, 1, 27, 30, 272, 314
Achievement, 76
  tests, 74–76
Adaptive functioning, 35
Adjunct services
  categories of, 227–230
  integration of, 218–219
  need for, 217
  utilization of, 219–227
Adjustment disorders, 33, 55, 64, 310
Adler, Alfred, 204, 263
Adlerian counseling, 39, 204–205, 263–264
Affective counseling, 185
Affective disorders, 46–48
Agencies, specific focus, 20
Agoraphobia, 48–49
American Association for Counseling and Development, 5, 7–8, 28, *see also* American Personnel and Guidance Association
American Mental Health Counselors Association, 5, 7, 10, 21, 26, 28
American Personnel and Guidance Association, 2, 5, *see also* American Association for Counseling and Development
American School Counselors Association, 5
Amnesia, 51
Amphetamines, 235
Anorexia nervosa, 40
Anxiety disorders, 48–50, 65
  of childhood or adolescence, 38
Anxiety neurosis, 49
Anxiety states, 48–50
Anxiolytics, 233

BIOGRAPHICAL SKETCH
OF AUTHOR

Linda Seligman is Associate Chairperson of the Department of Education and Associate Professor of Counseling and Development at George Mason University, Fairfax, Virginia. Her teaching specialization is mental health counseling and she has taught courses in diagnosis and treatment planning, couples and family counseling, career counseling, techniques and theories of counseling, group counseling, agency counseling, and supervision.

Dr. Seligman is an active researcher. She has published more than 30 articles in the leading journals in her field and has written one other textbook, *Assessment in Developmental Career Counseling*. She has served as a consulting psychologist for many organizations including the Salvation Army, the Department of Health and Human Services, and the Association for the Quality of Work Life. Her background includes counseling and psychotherapy in agencies serving groups as diverse as college students, veterans, foster children, and substance abusers. She is a licensed psychologist as well as a licensed professional counselor and maintains a private practice.

Dr. Seligman is a member of the American Association for Counseling and Development and the American Psychological Association. She is the editor (1984–87) of the *AMHCA Journal* and has been president of the Virginia Mental Health Counselors Association. She received her Ph.D. degree in Counseling Psychology from Columbia University.